ONE PILOT'S LOG

The Career of E.L. "Slonnie" Sloniger

Designed by Carolyn Weary Brandt
Edited by Ross A. Howell, Jr. and Jamie L. Bronner

Library of Congress Cataloging-in-Publication Data

Sloniger, Jerry
      One pilot's log : the career of E.L. "Slonnie" Sloniger / by
Jerrold E. Sloniger. -- 1st ed.
      p. cm.
      Includes index.
      ISBN: 1-57427-048-6

      1. Sloniger, Eyer L. 2. Air pilots--Biography. 3.
Aeronautics, Commercial--History. I. Title.

TL540.S56S56 1997   387.7'4044'092
                            QBI97-40648

Printed in Hong Kong
Published by Howell Press, Inc.,
1147 River Road, Suite 2,
Charlottesville, Virginia 22901
telephone (804) 977-4006
First Printing

ONE PILOT'S LOG

The Career of E.L. "Slonnie" Sloniger

By Jerrold E. Sloniger

HOWELL PRESS

This one's for you, Captain.

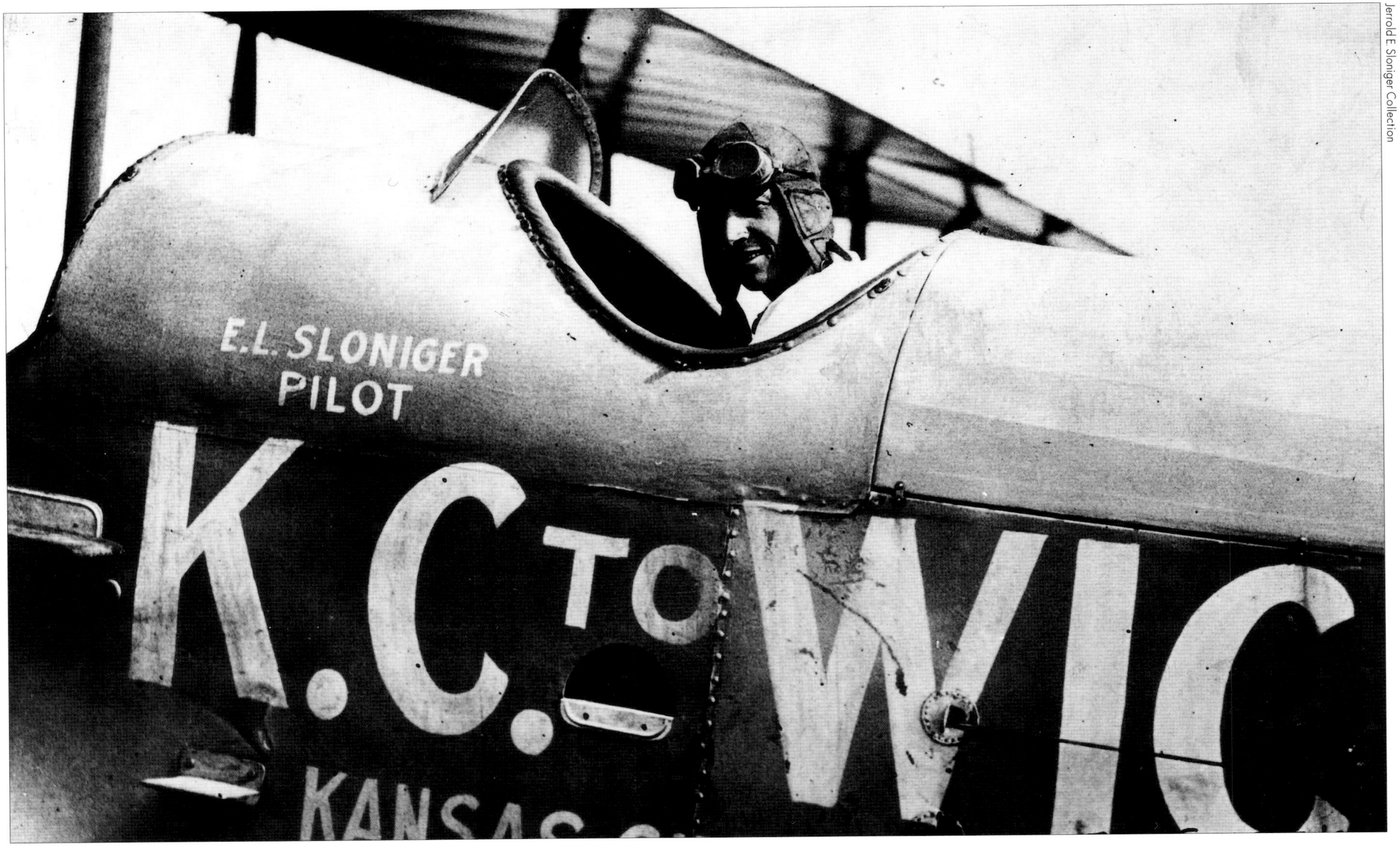

Jerrold E. Sloniger Collection

Acknowledgments

   I have been aided and urged on by far more people who knew and admired my father than I could possibly mention here. Many of them are named in the text. To them, and so many more, my deep appreciation. People who flew in the propeller days wanted the tale told. A considerable list of books and magazines was consulted along the way as well, again too many to list, but if there is a single source no serious aviation historian can be without, it would be the quarterly Journal of the American Aviation Historical Society. *For more than four decades they have been dedicated to an absolute passion for accuracy. Any mistakes came from my misreading.*

Jerrold E. Sloniger
Sinsheim, Germany
July 1997

Jerrold E Sloniger Collection

(Previous page) Slonnie flying the Kansas City to Wichita passenger run for Kansas City Airways in his personalized plane. **(Left)** Slonnie prepares to fly the U.S. Mail run for Robertson Aircraft Corp.

CONTENTS

Chapter 1

Looking Back, 1960

"A man who's working to fly is not a good pilot."

A collection of oblong ledgers called log-books rules the lives of all those men who earn a living in commercial flying. Every pilot's real worth lies buried among the everyday figures in those log pages. Accumulated hours can't guarantee a hot pilot, but few men survive to log 20,000 hours on luck alone. A professional pilot who lives to see fifty must have learned a few flying tricks, even though his motor skills might have slowed along the way.

In February 1960, a quiet man still known as "Slonnie" throughout the airline world, although he hadn't taken the left seat in a cockpit for more than five years, took exception to certain old-time pilots. Too many of them were resisting graceful retirement by age sixty, as suggested by the outspoken new head of the Federal Aviation Administration.

Slonnie had seen more aviation than all but a handful of his contemporaries. He'd flown Spad fighters over France in World War I, cargo across a trackless North Atlantic a war later. He'd flown in Mexico and China before aviation charts were made and captured cups as a stunt pilot. He tested and raced wood and canvas, open-cockpit biplanes but seldom mentioned the fact during a

quarter-century devoted to carrying airline customers. The only comment approaching a boast he ever made about all this flying was that he had never scratched a single passenger. From retirement, Slonnie became so convinced Elwood "Pete" Quesada of the FAA was right about pilot efficiency—what passengers call safety—he wrote one of his exceedingly rare letters, recalling the first time the two had met, more than thirty years earlier.

Slonnie had been an open-cockpit airmail pilot then, thirty-two years old and sharing a St. Louis apartment with a few friends who also transported letters in aging biplanes powered by dubious engines. One of these men had a flying buddy who remained in the Air Service and now found himself assigned to an Army crew attempting a new world record for time aloft. Hearing that Slonnie had already played that game, this young officer visited St. Louis for pointers.

By 1960 the survivors of that pilots' apartment were retired from active flying and the young officer had earned general's stars before taking over the FAA. Slonnie wrote, in part:

"Dear General Quesada, I want to congratulate you on your ideas and decision on pilot qualifications. In my last tenure as chief pilot I realized older pilots were not doing as well on their check rides as ones ten years junior to them. But I

was never able to convince the individual of that. At that time I promised myself to be honest and when my flying skill was on the wane I would give it up."

He did, quitting while his flying skills could still awe younger captains, even if they didn't meet his personal standards. Airline captains of the propeller era burned prodigious energy in total concentration. "Never let the airplane catch up with you," was the basic tenet for remaining alive in an age when a single hour of flying supposedly consumed the same energy another man might expend in ten hours with pick and shovel. Hence the rule that neither grizzled captains nor eager young copilots should fly more than eighty-five hours a month over regular airline routes.

When such men achieved the sleeve stripes of a captain and moved into the airplane's left seat, it was assumed (on paper) that their abilities became precisely equal to those of every other man with an active commercial license and captain's rating. The date they joined a given airline was the only seniority which mattered. Switch to a rival uniform, however, and you returned to the tail end of the copilots' queue.

Airline management, government, even honest pilots, realized this was no more than an arbitrary convenience for allotting pay and preference on choice routes. The most exalted seniority number couldn't expand a man's flying skills, or give him another chance when that runway failed to appear over the airplane's nose at the end of a blind approach.

In the last months of 1954 California Eastern was a small airline, one of many charter operations put together from equal portions of optimism, used airplanes, and flying men who had sidestepped or chosen to ignore the rigid, date-of-hiring seniority which dominated regular airline thought.

Called "nonscheds" because they weren't allowed to publish formal timetables, these airlines were born into the fly-anywhere boom of the late-forties, hauling medicines or livestock, military kids or Christmas fruitcakes. Most used the surplus Douglas DC-4 which sold so cheap that a couple of guys with wartime experience and mustering-out pay could buy one and become another "airline." These lines survived on their dexterity in sending every airplane out as full and often as possible, while scheduling pilots for every legal minute they might fly. California Eastern captains piled up logged hours faster than heroes on big-name airlines. They were tacitly assumed to be younger and allowed to fly up to 100 hours a month under certain circumstances.

"Putting three rated captains on board," Slonnie explained, "let them fly right through the clock. Whoever was captain that leg took over, another flew the right seat, and the guy off duty had the bunk. But that's a lot of hooey. I could always go to sleep almost anyplace but when one motor even sputters in the air you sit right straight up. Nobody's really sleeping in that bunk. Some stints were a milk run, sure. But maybe you had the left

National Air and Space Museum, Smithsonian Institution

Before he went on to become an Air Force general and later, head of the Federal Aviation Administration, Elwood "Pete" Quesada and a U.S. Army aircrew set an endurance record for time aloft in a Fokker Trimotor called *Question Mark*.

seat like I did that last trip, going into Chicago through a stinko overcast with loads of traffic around, ice on the props, and you're trying to hang onto a fuzzy beam.

"From California to Omaha, on to Puerto Rico and back to Oakland, we were gone 106 hours, 27 minutes, with more than 60 hours of that in the air. That left maybe 45 hours on the ground in four days and it doesn't mean we went to bed. By the time you got papers cleaned up and the ship serviced there was only enough time to sit around, maybe have something to eat, and take off again. We only saw a hotel one night.

"I'd never flown like that in all my life."

When this veteran of thirty-eight years in flying finally saw his home field again and climbed into the family car, his wife was shocked. She said, "He looked like the wrath of God. He'd gone out too soon after a little operation anyway, but when I asked if he didn't feel good he just said 'No,' and wouldn't talk all the way home. In the house I asked again. 'What is the trouble?' Slonnie just looked at me.

"'Well,' he told me, 'I have made my last trip.'

"He wasn't a man who would express himself fluently but when I asked if the company had said anything, he answered simply: 'No, but I've always told you that a man who's working to fly is not a good pilot. And it's become work for me.'

"He never touched the controls again."

Eyer L. Sloniger closed his fifteenth and last logbook on nearly four decades as a professional pilot, the only job he ever held or wanted. Casual figures scribbled in those ruled pages added up to 24,375 hours in the air, a total matched by a scant

handful among the thousands of pros sharing his trade in pre-jet days. Those special few had learned to fly when pilots were called plain damn fools more often than aviators, but the survivors among them flew nearly every month of their working lives and loved it.

Slonnie only quit when he could no longer fly to his own, single-minded satisfaction, retiring from a nonsched operation, although he had also held the most coveted seniority number in commercial aviation for almost two decades—Number One on the largest U.S. airline of its day.

Number One is a legend around aviation, but no pilot since Wilbur Wright started from such a lofty perch. For a boy named Eyir—he could never recall precisely when the spelling became Eyer, since pilots all called him Slonnie anyway—flying became both profession and passion, almost by chance. America was finally facing up to war in 1917 and a young man born on a frontier homestead considered it merely natural to swap premed courses for a uniform. Provided he could serve his country without walking. Or brushing horses. Eyir remembered all too many such chores from his sod-house days in western Nebraska.

Chapter 2

Nebraska Homestead

"Some day I'll see a man fly."

This was Frontier County, Nebraska, around 1900. Eyir normally recalled his birthplace in purely physical terms. Most open-cockpit veterans tended to think about weather or terrain features first. "It got hot in the summer and still does," he said. "That's mostly open prairie land in western Nebraska but we had a nice little lake about two miles from the house. In winter Dad and the hired man put runners on an old farm wagon and pulled it down where they could hand-saw ice out in big cakes."

Seven of the nine Sloniger children were born on homesteads the family settled near Moorefield, a village of barely 200 farm people along a railroad branch called the Highline, and not far south of that pioneer thoroughfare, the Platte river valley. Eyir was the middle child, born on July 28, 1896, in a sod house on the third claim owned by Commodore Perry Sloniger, who was already a land speculator. Those were two given names, not military rank. Eyir said, "We always heard somebody had married into the navy family but I was too young to pay much attention to which hero."

Grandfather Oliver Sloniger had farmed in western Illinois and ran a hotel there around 1870, but he was tempted by railroad handbills promising low land prices and interest, even fare refunded to buyers—for anybody taking up a claim along the Nebraska right-of-way and shipping their produce back east.

Oliver missed the initial, mostly Prussian, wave which took up free claims in York County but he could still buy bargain-priced railroad land in what would become Lushton township. Catherine Sloniger followed with their youngest children. According to the 1885 census, Oliver was already tilling land along the west fork of the Blue River valued at better than $4,400, including 100 swine.

Son C.P. saw more opportunity in moving out west. James Urmson and his Welsh-born wife Cecelia had stopped on Oliver's land to rest their stock. Oliver mentioned this jolly old Englishman stopping down by the river and C.P. said, "That's my future father-in-law. I saw a brown-eyed beauty with them today."

The Urmsons and their charmer named Margaret Elizabeth left for Frontier County seven years later. C.P. chose that year to take his patrimony of a team and wagon and go looking for work in that same southwestern corner of Nebraska. The stage company promptly hired him for its Platte River run.

"Dad must have been a pretty fair bronc rider too," Eyir said, "since he got an offer to join

Commodore Perry (C.P.) Sloniger, Eyir's father, as a baby.

The Sloniger family. The date of this photograph is unknown, although it was likely taken at the end of the family's time in Crete, Nebraska; in Norman, Oklahoma; or once the family arrived in Lincoln, Nebraska. From left to right, standing: Inez, Clair, Loren, Zazel; seated: Eyir, Margaret Elizabeth, Della, Urmson, C.P., Paul; and in front: Perry.

the Buffalo Bill show." C.P., about to file his first land claim, turned the showman down. In May 1885, he drove Margaret Elizabeth Urmson down the main road to Stockville, their county seat, to be married. The bridegroom was already listed twice by the census, as owner of different quarter-sections, with assets of better than $2,000 and forty-five acres improved, out of 320. His wife's sister remembered the first sod house he built for all its leaks. Loren, first of their nine children, was born there but before daughter Zazel arrived, in 1889, C.P. had a bigger soddy on a new claim.

In 1891 daughter Inez was born, grand-mother Catherine died, and Oliver moved west for a short while. C.P. had purchased the original Urmson homestead, a tree claim, but didn't depend on its cherry, peach, and plum trees, planted alongside native cottonwood and catalpa, for a living. He already cut a good acreage of grain and was almost always the first to own and rent out any new piece of farm machinery.

Four more sons were born in this house over the next ten years. Eyir recalled, "It had a good turf of prairie grass and sat about a mile and a half south and west of Moorefield, right by the road. They would skim that sod out with a special plowshare and stack the blocks outside a wooden framework. Roots held it all together so all you had to do was put a tin roof over everything and maybe frame in a kitchen and pantry on the back. The window niche was nearly two feet deep with board flooring, a wonderful place to sit."

A school chum of Loren's described this Sloniger home as the best sod house he ever saw. Zazel said, "Mama took the smaller room and the baby slept with her. The larger was our living room

The six Sloniger boys in Lincoln, Nebraska. Left to right: Perry, Urmson, Paul, Eyir, Clair, and Loren. The young boy in front is Loren's son, George Esmond.

where Loren and the hired man slept. Very soon a third chamber, big as the original house, was added on the east end for Grandpa Sloniger but he only stayed a year." Once he returned to Lushton, Zazel and Inez shared a double bed there, alongside the outsize family closet. Clair, first of four sons in a row, moved in next, then Eyir, Oliver Paul, and Urmson, in 1901.

By 1900 Moorefield already had its hotel, shoemaker, billiard hall (haircuts on the side), and blacksmith, whose wife sold millinery. All these doings were covered by their own *Frontier County Post.* Eighteen months after Eyir's birth this paper reported that C.P. Sloniger had just opened the town's second implement business.

Printed cardboard squares read:
C. P. SLONIGER, LANDS BOUGHT AND SOLD, TAXES PAID FOR NONRESIDENTS, AND A GENERAL REAL ESTATE BUSINESS TRANSACTED.

Already forty when Eyir was born and signing his name C. Perry, he was never much of a talker around home. Mama saw to discipline. These two, with hardly a dozen years of schooling between them, made sure every one of their nine children received a proper education. By the time Eyir was old enough for first grade the local school boasted two rooms. He said, "Dad bought a house in town then, kitty-corner to the school. Mother would move all us kids there in September and stay until spring. Of course, classes never got really big. When Loren graduated he only had one classmate."

Zazel also remembered, "We made our own entertainment. Square dances and waltzes mostly. Mama and Papa were very smooth dancers and could Mama ever tap." C.P. even bought an organ

Jerrold E Sloniger Collection

Pub. by J. J. Green.
Photo by A. S. Hovey.

MAIN STREET, MOOREFIELD. NEB.

Moorefield, Nebraska, the nearest town to Slonnie's birthplace. It is shown here in the era of C.P.'s homestead.

for the sod house. "Papa had a fine baritone voice," Zazel continued. "He played bass viol and took turns calling dances."

Eyir remembered dance nights for special food. "Mother would take liver and kidneys, along with chicken or pork, and make great big pies with loads of gravy. Not much game though. Dad was just too damn busy to go out shooting." After supper Eyir would crawl to the back of the deep window cutout and hope the family had forgotten him by bedtime. "One night," he remembered, "I was watching the music-making when Dad spoke up kind of suddenly, between dances. He said, 'Some day I'll see a man fly.' I don't know why he said that and they all kidded him, but I knew he was sure."

This happened more than a year before Orville and Wilbur did fly. If the Wrights' first flight was reported to Frontier County it was probably disbelieved. A magazine named *Gleanings In Bee Culture* was about the only journal to report that 1903 event with understanding. The majority accepted the *New York Times* standpoint when Samuel P. Langley, Secretary of the Smithsonian Institution, failed on two flight attempts just prior to the Wrights. That staid daily suggested the professor should give up flying as both a waste of time and peril to his scientific standing.

Yet the word "aviation" was coined as early as 1866 and this idea of flight had captured more turn-of-the-century print than early automobiles. In 1809 an Englishman named Sir George Cayley launched his coachman on a successful glide. The shaken hostler quit after one try, saying man was born to drive horses. By 1843 William Samuel Henson could find ample British backing

The Sloniger house in Crete, Nebraska, where the family moved from Moorefield so that the eldest children could attend Doane College.

for his proposed aerial steam carriage for the India run.

Otto Lilienthal, whose work the Wrights studied carefully, made more than 2,000 hops before a batwing glider killed him in 1896, while Octave Chanute, a leading railroad and bridge engineer, had flown "a conventional biplane glider" at Indiana Dunes, along Lake Michigan. By 1899 the Wrights could order a packet of Smithsonian monographs explaining how Langley was spending fifty thousand from the government till on man-carrying machinery. These Ohio brothers recognized three basic but vital points. Their propellers owed nothing to nautical screws. Wing warping provided lateral control—the key factor. And they fitted a movable vertical rudder. Others might leave the ground. The Wrights could maneuver.

C.P. was chiefly interested in seeing a flight personally but it would be 1910 before an airplane took its place alongside prize hogs and horse races at the Nebraska State Fair. Eyir had finished two years of school in Moorefield when the family moved to Crete so Loren could attend Doane College. Zazel would graduate from Doane as well. A teacher into her eighties, she was always surprised Eyir was the only one who failed to graduate from a college.

After losing a fight to become the new county seat, Crete had just two blocks with paving when the Slonigers arrived. Eyir said, "Dad bought the furniture store. Then he and Loren went up to Omaha for mortuary school, since they sold coffins, too. Then he went back into real estate and sold the furniture business." By the thirties Zazel would

Eyir promoting the Doane College Senior Class Play for one of his older siblings. His
brother, Loren, and his sister, Zazel, both graduated from Doane.

call him land-poor. C.P. soon bought a downtown house with five bedrooms and a second-story bath with running water.

Eyir's lifelong interest in books stemmed from a family living across the vacant lot. He recalled, "A big, pompous fellow with a judge's black hat, cutaway coat, and flowing moustache. And a wonderful library. I could sit in his big leather chair and read a history book all afternoon. One day he said if I'd come and live at his house I'd get a wagon and a team of goats. I went home and had a bag all packed when Mother caught me."

He did find a middle initial in the Hastings library. Everybody in Crete was intrigued by the unusual family names but only Oliver Paul and Commodore Perry had more than one. Eyir had arrived on his Grandmother Urmson's birthday so she named him. He added an "L." in Crete, although he could never remember why and used only the initial. Zazel insisted, "He added L. for Locksley." Would it be stretching coincidence to suggest poet Alfred Tennyson's *Locksley Hall?*
"For I dipt into the future, far as human eye could
        see,
Saw the vision of the world and all the wonder that
        would be;
Saw the heavens filled with commerce, argosies of
        magic sails,
Pilots of the purple twilight, dipping down with
        costly bales."
Eyir himself recalled no boyhood fascination with airplanes. The *London Times* had pronounced flight impossible after all, so the *Daily Mail* posted 10,000 pounds sterling for an air trip from London to Manchester, doubtless feeling the money was safe. Actually, the Wrights' Flyer III was already a practical, powered airplane, covered by patents.

Once America's president became interested in aviation, his generals authorized an aeronautical division of one officer and two enlisted men—one of whom promptly went AWOL. The Army advertised for public bids on an "aeroplane" and the Wrights won that contract easily, at $25,000 per plane. By 1908 an air meet in New York could draw 20,000 spectators.

The Wrights regularly stayed aloft an hour or more and Wilbur only missed the first 100-mile trip by a hair in 1908. On another occasion he gave rides to thirty-five people within a single day. A passenger with Orville became the world's first heavier-than-air fatality. Neither was an outstanding pilot although Orville might well have become one. He took the controls the only time both went up together.

A new breed of daredevil flyers had begun to appear, so Europeans founded the Fédération Aéronautique International to curb their élan. This august body then refused to recognize all Wright records set before the FAI existed. Bleriot underlined the new age that July by fluttering across twenty-two miles of English Channel, a feat equaling Charles Lindbergh's, given his equipment.

English pioneer Claude Grahame-White opened his book on learning to fly by explaining at length how to build your own airplane first. A major competition within sight of Reims Cathedral, sponsored by the champagne industry, confirmed 1909 as the year airplanes arrived in Europe. Glenn Curtiss, the Wrights' chief U.S. rival, won the premiere speed prize, while Eugène Lefevre became the first man fined for reckless

flying. New York even had an airplane sales agency. Curtiss achieved the first water takeoff and saw five of his planes in the air at once off Sheepshead Bay, New York.

Representative Sheppard of Texas sponsored a House bill to investigate the practicality and cost of flying mail by airplane or airship. It died in committee. In October 1910, Teddy Roosevelt took a ride with Arch Hoxsey. A popular aviation book of 1910 warned its readers: while flight may be successful, the landing may be disastrous.

C.P. barely missed his first chance to finally see a man fly by leaving Crete in July 1910. Inez had just finished high school so the family moved to Norman, Oklahoma, for its larger university. Somehow most of the earliest flying exhibitions missed their new state. The family settled in a house so citified it didn't even have a vegetable garden. Eyir started both high school and his swift rise through Boy Scout ranks to Eagle in Oklahoma.

And C.P. finally saw a man fly. It was Arch Hoxsey, flying's clean-cut golden guy in a pince-nez, who had never seen an airplane himself until the previous January. By September 1910 he was the pride of the Wright team when C.P. took fourteen-year-old Eyir to the Nebraska fair. He remembered, "His motor cut out and Hoxsey landed on the cow barns." Eyir's first glimpse of aviation had been of one of flying's true glamour men but he saw no airplanes at all in 1911, the busiest year in early American exhibition flying.

Aviation was growing up. An Italian dropped the first aerial bomb—on Turkey—and would-be pioneers had to seek out lands like Madagascar or Korea to record a first flight. Harriet

Quimby, Broadway critic for *Leslie's Weekly*, scandalized ankle-skirted America by flying across the English Channel, before falling to her death in Boston Harbor. Pantaloon costumes garnered more headlines than her daring.

America's military still owned fewer airplanes than Japan's even dozen while an ad in *Aero Market* offered plans which would turn your bicycle into an airplane for only six bucks. Small fairs paid from two to five thousand dollars for a two-day air show. The Wrights banked a million during 1911-1912, paying pilots two dollars per minute.

Connecticut filed the nation's first air legislation, seeking to keep unlicensed pilots within sight of their home fields. When Earl Ovington flew our first official airmail on Long Island, New York, the event passed almost unnoticed. A week earlier, on September 17, 1911, two thousand had turned out to see a lanky, cigar-chomping athlete named Calbraith Perry Rodgers christen his 35 HP Wright EX the *Vin Fiz*, in honor of his sponsor's soft drink, before leaving Long Island in pursuit of the $50,000 prize offered by William Randolph Hearst for the first crossing of America by air within any thirty consecutive days.

The Wrights insisted no airplane was ready for such a test but sent their ace mechanic along anyway, saying, "Cal will need him." He did. Rodgers said, "Wrecks are part of the game and are to be expected, but of course are unwelcome." Averaging some 52 MPH when he did fly, Rodgers was the first to cross America by air. But he took forty-nine days and received a gold medal from the Aero Club in lieu of Hearst's money.

Newspapers predicted that if they flew much more there wouldn't be any pilots left, and then Wilbur Wright died. In bed. Lincoln Beachey ruled the American exhibition circuit, flying more shows than any other man, over twenty-three states, D.C., Cuba, and Puerto Rico, while Frank Champion emerged as his busiest rival. When the latter touched down near Norman in 1912, C.P. took Eyir again, and Paul.

Only five years short of his own cockpit debut, Eyir recalled he still had no sense of mission. "Paul and I went because we were the only boys around the house. When Champion didn't fly right off I bought two roller coaster tickets and still saw the flight. It didn't impress me any more than the horse races."

Visionaries already predicted metal commercial airplanes with at least two engines. When one gave trouble it would be overhauled in flight. Avro in England enclosed the passengers, years before most pilots would consent to sit inside. Six to ten thousand dollars would buy any of several airplanes supposedly enjoying production status. Their pilots could even control engine revolutions now, an advance far more important than raw power increases. The world witnessed its first fatal, two-plane crash and Chicago's Gordon Bennett event drew teams from Britain, France, Belgium, Holland, and Switzerland—but no U.S. entry, although an American team had won the nations versus nations challenge, sponsored by the New York publisher, a year earlier.

Lincoln Beachey took his tailored pin-stripe suit, high collar, and two-carat diamond stickpin onto the vaudeville stage, but his glamour failed to carry over. Then Beachey heard, in September 1913, that a Frenchman was being acclaimed for the world's first loop (two weeks after P. N. Nesterov actually did one, in fact, but the Russian merely caught hell for endangering the Czar's property).

Beachey had never looped an airplane because the stunt hadn't occurred to him but now performed some three dozen before the year ended. And 1914 became his busiest season ever. He flew an estimated 1,000 loops before 17 million people in 126 cities. Cash in advance of course: $500 for the first loop of any day, $200 apiece thereafter. When the master appeared at Nebraska's state fair, eighteen-year-old Eyir was amused by the carny spiel, which he still loved to imitate years later: "Lincoln Beachey—he loops the loop, something birds can't do and God made the birds!"

The Slonigers had moved to Lincoln because it too had a major university and they preferred Nebraska. America already boasted its first passenger airline, launched on the first day of 1914, between St. Petersburg and Tampa, Florida. Igor Sikorsky had broken the multiengine barrier with Grand and Ilia, MIT kept a four-foot wind tunnel busy, and the American continent had been spanned nonstop by air—across the Isthmus of Panama. Americans flew for both sides in a Mexican war, exchanging pistol shots in the first air-to-air duel, and the *London Daily Mail* posted $50,000 for any heavier-than-air Atlantic crossing within seventy-two hours. It would be five more years before that check was banked.

Military flying was clearly viable by now, although U.S. Army leaders still considered airplanes noisy contraptions which scared their horses, while admirals thought them no better than submarines—dirty duty for the lowest type of sailor.

When Congress appropriated a million dollars for 1914 aviation the Secretary of War cut that to $400,000. Germany budgeted $45 million.

Like many states, Nebraska was complacently vague about war, in part because its largest single ethnic group was German. Their National Guard did assemble some sixty would-be pilots in Lincoln during June 1916, fed them a while, and then sent them home. About the time Vincent Astor bought a radical, tailless, Burgess-Dunne airplane, C.P. brought home the Sloniger family's first automobile, a Chandler six with white wire wheels.

Eyir finished high school in 1916 and weighed the career merits of medicine versus geology. This son of a stagecoach driver, born on a pioneer homestead, was very close to opening his first aviation logbook as his freshman year at the University of Nebraska began, but he still felt no compulsion to fly.

September 1916   Flying hours: 0

Chapter 3

Pursuit Pilot

"I just didn't want to walk."

In 1902 C. P. Sloniger expected a man would fly and he intended to see it, but nobody in the family recalls any predictions that one of his own sons might try. Actually, Eyir wasn't even the first Sloniger to consider aviation. In 1916 he was slightly young by Air Service standards. With all of $13 million to spend, the military sought college-educated men of at least twenty-one years of age. Then Pancho Villa raided New Mexico and brother Clair, two years older than Eyir, went south with the Nebraska Guard, hoping to move into its aviation arm. The United States eventually put fifteen air squadrons on the border but Clair lost an eye in a camp accident before he could volunteer for one of them.

Eyir reached age twenty-one next, about the time his state voted dry and only months before America passed a draft bill. Strong German sentiment had been holding enlistments down. He was in college by then, "And not due to be drafted, but I just didn't want to walk. And horses need brushing all the time. So I went up to Fort Omaha and applied for heavier-than-air."

After December 15, 1917, applicants wouldn't be able to name their branch. Nebraska's

induction center had been a balloon school since 1908 and American soldiers had been lifted aloft by gasbags since the Civil War, so the Guard naturally tried to stamp his application "balloon." After all, the country faced war with fewer than 150 air-planes, none of those combat types, ranking only fourteenth among aviation nations. China, by comparison, was buying Christofferson planes from the U.S. in lots of twenty-five. Most Americans still considered flight a foolhardy adventure at best. It wasn't until war finally hit home that the Air Service became the most glamorous branch since Jeb Stuart's raiders.

A recruiting sergeant told Eyir heavier-than-air wouldn't be available for six months. "A couple of friends took balloon but I waited and two weeks later got airplanes. Except that they had a 120-pound minimum for pilots and I only weighed 118. Lots of bananas and milk before the physical took care of that. And it got me out of university. I didn't believe then that education mattered for a pilot." The army apparently felt Eyir had enough college by 1917.

Eyir left for ground school in Berkeley, California, just as his country finally geared up to build 20,000 training planes with some of the $640 million voted for aviation at long last, the largest single American appropriation to that date. Eyir's "Pilot Book" opened on eight weeks of airplane,

Eyir at ground school in Berkeley, California.

engine, and—inevitably—military studies. The family got regular letters from Berkeley: "They are leaving here by the carload. Don't know how long I'll last so you can expect me home any day now." This emphasis on study reversed an earlier army feeling that men who knew too much about mechanics would only be nervous pilots.

"Many were washed out," Eyir admitted, "and there was a hell of a lot of drill, but I had fun and made decent marks." He graduated on February 16, 1918, with a modest 74 average—only engines and aerial observation edged over 80. Gunnery wasn't so bad, but drill was not his strong subject. "I had to list my ROTC time but we'd never shown up much at Nebraska, since a fraternity brother had picked up the roll books and changed absences to presents. When I was called out to lead the platoon in Berkeley, smart military chums in line behind me had to coach pretty hard."

Getting to Kelly Field, Texas, and into an airplane was all that mattered. Eager to be pilots, they ignored stories of airplanes busting up daily there. Cadets, drawing $100 a month, usually spent their Sundays at nearby Stinson Field, a private operation where Eddie Stinson and his two sisters were the real flying pros. Kelly Field might put a 100-airplane formation up for Treasury Secretary William McAdoo but it lacked bed space for students already assigned there. Hopeful cadets waited in horse-barn billets, praying for flight-training slots.

"Then an order came down for one squadron," Eyir recalled, "and the best-drilled would go. Our bunch had an old spit-and-polish infantry man who worked us hard so we got the ticket." On March 10, 1918, the drill champs

reported to Kelly Field, a sprawl only eleven months old but already the largest aviation establishment in the world. A week later Eyir finally logged his first flight—fifty minutes of dual instruction at 4,200 feet. The plane was a Curtiss JN-4D. The service had ordered trainers from at least a dozen firms, favoring car manufacturers, until Washington realized that a two-seater flying machine, made from 500 feet of prime timber and endless wire, was not quite twin to an automobile. Detroit might out-lobby trained aeronautical-engineering upstarts like Donald Douglas or Grover Loening but car people didn't always deliver airplanes with tail skids attached.

That left Glenn Curtiss to hire 20,000 new workers and build the bulk of military trainers. Eventually, seven companies turned out his JN designs, all powered by Curtiss's own, relatively reliable, V8 engine, the OX-5. Its 90 HP pushed a JN, affectionately called "Jenny," along at 80 MPH. The Jenny needed ten minutes to climb 3,000 feet, but the plane was light and compact and could even lift a pair of pilots.

Eyir logged all his early hours in Jennies, as America struggled to deliver those 4,500 pilots promised to France. Mostly he flew the 4D model but a few hours came in the JN-4B. "The only difference," he recalled, "was a Dep system in the B which gave you a steering wheel to turn instead of a control stick. Until somebody decided that was too complicated for us." Ground-bound experts had declared, in 1913, that no average man could ever learn to fly. Those Wrights? They possessed abnormal quickness. The Army countered that flying only took half the skill and nerve required to ride a dispatch motorcycle down a bumpy road at

50 MPH and anyway, airmen only had to remember that they couldn't afford mistakes. The truth lay somewhere in between.

Eyir managed a mere nine and one-quarter hours of air time in his first ten days but he was already logging practice landings by the third day. Kelly students were learning to run from men who were often no more than shaky walkers themselves. "Beginners had maybe two real civilian instructors," Eyir explained, "since Eddie Stinson only taught what our base newspaper called stunt flying. The rest of our instructors were only the better learners from some earlier student batch. When I got there a Nebraska Kappa Sig was teaching, so we moved my little tab over on his hook and I reported to him for my first ride. He went out over San Antonio and fell off the top of his loop, probably the second one he'd ever made. Dust was coming off the floor. Inside a proper loop you sat heavy like somebody was pressing on your shoulders. Anybody could tell by feel when it was right. If you lost speed, just tighten the loop."

Eyir recorded his first solo hop on March 28, 1918, without topping 200 feet on the one flight every pilot is supposed to recall for all ages. Writing home, he skipped that news but thanked his father for Lincoln, Nebraska, newspapers. Following a cross-country exercise in April he enclosed a sketch map with checkpoints marked as "lake" or "asylum" and added, "I drove down in the back seat and another kid is driving it back, with a good wind on our tail. The air is fairly smooth but you can see the vibrations of the engine in my writing. We are in a cloud and the ground is out of sight, in fact the wing tips are too. But the fellow behind is a good driver." Three days later he completed this note, "From about 2,500 feet in the air" (his log said 1,500), commenting, "I said the kid driving was good but about five minutes afterwards we went into a cloud and came out headed the other way."

He didn't tell his family that spins were the common result of clouds over Kelly and cadets were sternly warned that only the most proficient or fortunate would live to describe a spin. Instructors kept a fire extinguisher handy to detach any student who froze at the controls of a spinning airplane. Eyir said, "When I first got there we had a big hangar sign: In case you fall into a spin, neutralize the controls and when it stops, give it the gun and pull the nose up. Then I discovered you could stop a spin much faster by using opposite rudder. Of course you had to get that rudder off immediately when it stopped spinning or it would whip the other way."

Eyir's natural feeling for flight surfaced early. Despite—or because of—such private experiments, the student earned his wings after 68 hours, 57 minutes of primary time and received the log note, "recommended for pursuit school." That indicated the Army's idea of a hot natural pilot. Naturals might also be shunted into instructors' training. Eyir wrote home, "I will have to go to instructors' school for 20 days and I'm getting kind of homesick. The end of the course was so close and then it was pushed back. Can you imagine me as an instructor?"

His real goal was West Point, Mississippi, and pursuit school. After logging only 1:50 hours at the school for instructors, he reported to Payne Field, West Point, in late July. Now a 2nd Lieutenant, Aviation Section, Signal Reserve Corps, he

discovered advanced maneuvers were still performed in a Jenny 4D, unless you got one of the lighter, Toronto-built, Canadian Curtiss airplanes. Dubbed a "Canuck," this model was preferred by many acrobatic neophytes, although it had a bad reputation with the cautious. Eyir said, "On cross-country flights they sent you off fifteen minutes apart so you couldn't follow the guy ahead and that gave me time to practice spins and loops. One day I wasted so much time this big guy named Tipton caught up and zoomed past in a big climb. I stuck the nose down to get up some speed and pulled up and over into a loop. When we got back Tip grabbed hold of me like a terrier with a rat and shook hell out of me, yelling that I shouldn't ever loop another Canuck, the wings would come off. Hell, I'd been looping them for weeks. "The wings didn't come off today, did they? He told me, 'No, but they will.'

"I loved acrobatics and never understood why so many guys were scared to death of them. By the time I got to acrobatic school I was pretty practiced. Of course I'd been cheating on lots of things. It's a bunch of hooey that you can fly by the seat of your pants. So I put a heavy nut on a piece of string and suspended that from the cowling over my instrument panel. Tried it out in clear weather and it didn't take long to figure out a reading for any kind of wing tilt in the clouds."

Eyir even invited his parents down to see how he flew. "Dad and Mother came and couldn't get on the base but I made a short cross-country flight and told them where to look. That was the first time they saw me fly." For log purposes this flight shortly before his twenty-second birthday was called "practice stunts." Next on the list was

formation flying. "That's just practice too. When you first went up in a three-plane flight you probably stayed 100 feet from the other two, then you began to tighten it up. We had maybe five hours of formation and by the time we got through you'd pull right up and read the guy's instruments for him." Flying both the army way and with his own embellishments, Eyir added 131-plus hours to his log, for a total of 200. His natural knack caught the official eye and they offered instructing again.

"We had a colonel who was never much of a favorite with pilots and he promised if I would teach a while I'd be on the first bunch to sail. Then I hit sick bay with a throat infection and a friend told me sixty pilots were posted for Hoboken, New Jersey, the departure port, but my name wasn't on the list. I talked myself out of the hospital, but this colonel gave me that old line about doing more for my country in Mississippi. He had promised France though and I wanted to go. He got nasty and I had to say, 'Look, you can't draft me for another year. I'll walk out.' Then I jumped on that train and went via Lincoln for about a week. Guess I was halfway AWOL.

"In New York I spotted a guy who'd been with me in ground school and he was a little late for Hoboken, too, but we checked into the McAlpine Hotel anyway. It was the aviation place then, with a hell of a good room for two-fifty. I discovered the officer checking us in was another Lincoln boy and he could fix things—when did we want to sail? We'd never been to New York in our lives so he gave us a few days and no AWOL on the books. About this time I got Spanish flu and felt like hell for four days but we'd been to the Belmont races at least." On October 3, Eyir wrote his family,

"Almost over the flu." On the eighth, "Got sailing orders, loading at 1100 tomorrow. I'll be on the pond when you get this, headed for over there."

"That same boy from Lincoln put us on the *Plattsburgh* because officers would get a state-room," he said. "It was an Atlantic coaster, really, but our gunners had won some sort of medal so we were supposed to take care of two other ships in the same convoy, the *Harrisburg* and *Maori*. They were stacked with troops. The *Plattsburgh* was an old boat, but the only excitement was flu and a sub scare. Flu broke out on the other two ships first and we'd watch them go down the chute in canvas bags every morning. About two days out of France a sub was spotted around ten at night. We saw one torpedo go behind us and in front of the *Harrisburg* and our ship almost jumped out of the water getting away. Some guys wondered why we didn't stay to protect those other ships, but nobody asked out loud. Next morning we had to wait for them."

Eyir wrote home, "We land tomorrow and I'm sure glad I am an officer after seeing the food and quarters for the troops. I censor their mail and you hit some rich stuff." The *Plattsburgh* anchored off Brest, France, and Eyir dutifully mailed his Red Cross postcard, filling in name, rank, and Air Service over the stock legend, "The ship on which I sailed has arrived safely overseas." He also paid for a brief Postal Telegraph cable, "Safe, well," and signed it "Eyer," the first time he used that second "e." This might have been a cable-clerk's mistake but it became his own spelling from then on, although Eyer himself couldn't remember why.

"After Brest came a holding camp where twenty or thirty guys had already been waiting six weeks so I figured I'd be around the rest of my life,"

Eyer remembered. "But my name went up after a couple of days. I was right there and ready at nine the next morning." As he wrote home, "Pursuit pilots are sent out pretty rapidly," adding, "I'm still trying to dope out the money and trying to talk French." And he reminded the home front that a single, three-pound Christmas box was allowed.

At the first stop of their train ride to Issoudin, an advanced training field, Eyer discovered, "They were sending three new Fiat touring cars to Issoudin so we switched to those, with a driver in each one. There was a big break between commissioned and enlisted men then, but flyers had no background in saluting and that stuff. The first night my driver took me to a hotel and I told him to come on in for a brandy. After a couple we hit all the other bistros in town and I got pretty clubby with that sergeant. Turned out he was the man who signed cars out from Issoudin motor pool so we could always get one to head into town, even when gas was supposed to be scarce."

Plane News, the Issoudin base newspaper, insisted Honoré de Balzac's home was the chief and only attraction in town. It also admitted that pursuit pilots were inclined to be temperamental and hard to handle, compared to other "airnats" on base, who had reportedly picked that name for themselves by a margin of thousands of votes. Eyer didn't mention Balzac but told his family, "We are out on that field by five to six every morning, ready to go up," adding, "we go to town for dinner and have found a house where this French lady serves steaks and french fries. Our army menu is not the hottest. Canned bacon or local meat, and that's mostly lamb." He would admit later, "We thought we were doing all right with that lady, until we

found out it was *cheval*, meaning horse. Tasted about the same as beef." Otherwise, supper meant the Red Cross, which cost a little more. But they served in a hut which *Plane News* praised regularly, mainly for the influence of its good Christian women. None of the young lieutenants dared complain too loudly about official cooking since the first who tried was promptly made mess officer.

Some of the men simply "got lost" on cross-country flights and landed near one of those fine Loire chateaux north of Issoudin for a week-end. Many pilots carried cases of Ivory soap or boxes of sugar against just such reputedly forced landings. By this time Issoudin, officially named the 3rd Aviation Instruction Center but more commonly called the worst mud hole in France, claimed to be the largest flying school in the world. Barely a year old, the complex had already spawned an Issoudin mud guard to shield fragile and expensive propellers from muck the wheels threw up. The base included ten flying fields which Eyer identified in his—apparently uncensored—letters.

Future aces lived in typical army barracks with double or triple bunks, two stoves, and wooden floors, plus a common room for blackjack, red dog, or craps. Eyer was posted to Field Two which he rated, "Better than either of the other main camps. And our ships are wonderful." By November 6 he could send a sketch of the Alps from the air and add, "Raining again and that could keep me here all winter, to complete the course. We got paid."

New arrivals got an immediate flight check and were invariably told how poorly they handled an airplane, then shuttled from gunnery to tactics, to more flying. Field Six was typical: a corrugated tool shed and an American Indian soldier with a flag on a stick to control takeoff and landing practice. Combat training was flown in anything the Allies could spare. Official reports called this the stiffest course in the armies, a finishing school for pilots, who quickly noted a cemetery right across the main field from their flight line.

Plane News preferred to dwell on the 50-hour life of a rotary engine when treated gently or huff over the fact that officers sported too many classy outfits. Eyer remembered they usually wore, "The regular, high-neck tunic with a leather coat, plus helmet and goggles. Fancy silk scarves just pulled at your neck and flapped." He couldn't recall the bulletin warning aviators not to wear spurs when flying, a rule the editors of *Plane News* considered at least as important as not taking a machine into the air unless the pilots were satisfied it would fly.

With an armistice clearly looming, Eyer's prime concern was managing to complete pursuit training. His routine went, "Fly either morning or afternoon and spend the other half-day in classes of some sort. But no more drill." The Americans still took engine instruction, whereas the French, considered elite flyers, would always have mechanics handy. American instructors urged their men to study those new and most curious French rotary engines. This engine type had its crankshaft bolted to the firewall while all seven (or nine) cylinders spun with the propeller to achieve cooling—plus considerable torque reaction. Many pilots recalled rotaries as confusing, annoying, and frustrating until you got the hang of them, since there was no proper throttle. Others insisted they would never let a pilot down if treated gently.

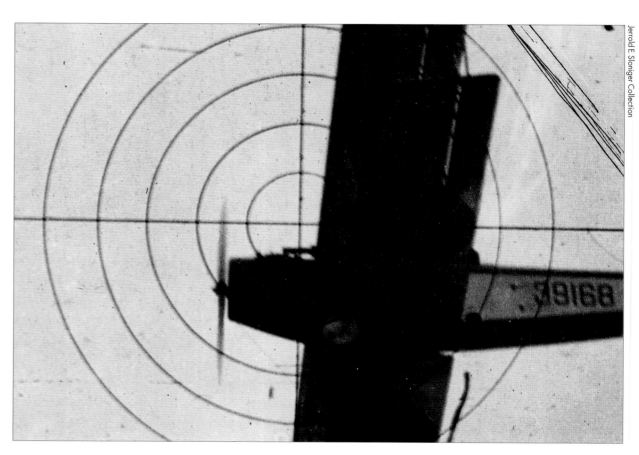

Jerrold E Sloniger Collection

An early aerial photograph illustrating how pilots used gun cameras for combat training in WWI. This is one of Eyer's shots.

Reflecting this wariness, French instructors thought their American counterparts were crazy to go aloft with a student. Gallic cadets learned on machines called "penguins," whose flight habits imitated their namesakes. The French only flew these at dawn or just before dusk, when the air was calmest, and were taught to pick an apple tree if the engine failed, since those had more small branches to cushion the fall.

Eyer had to try a penguin, of course. "One Sunday when we didn't fly anyway, an Iowa kid and I spotted a row of these clipped-wing jalopies with two- or three-cylinder motors so they could hop maybe six feet off the ground. We talked a French sergeant into cranking up a couple and started off. You cut the motor before you ran out of field, but you know, landing from six feet is just as hard as doing it from 6,000, except that if you stalled from six nobody got hurt much. Pretty soon we got into a race. See who would cut the engine first. They didn't have brakes either, so we had a hell of a lot of fun."

Army training, especially on cloudy days, was more serious. "How we got above a cloud ceiling with no instruments, I'll never know. You went up by feel. If it shivered you were stalling, if the wires started to sing—up nose. After training up there in the sun, throttle back and drop down through. Keep those wires at the right hum, break out, find yourself and go home."

Plane News called these single-seater pilots "loners," even as its editors were insisting the base was striving to train thousands of good, average pilots, not put aces at the front. Their flight surgeon did admit it was apparent flyers were unlike other soldiers. He found them intricate, highly sensitized pieces of mechanism, in part because flight placed high demands on the nervous system but relatively little on the muscles. Pilots, he decided, should avoid all fatigues, including alcohol, tobacco, cards, or love.

Eyer, already a journeyman smoker, agreed in part. "France is all right but it was made for Frenchmen," he wrote to Lincoln. "Up to date I haven't seen one beautiful woman and the red wine...well, I drink coffee when we can't get good water. It's the coldest damn place too. Think I'll stay in Lincoln for a while now. I have seen and learned things I wouldn't believe before. This land is about 100 years behind and making no visible efforts to catch up."

None of that, not even cold severe enough to catch the attention of a boy from the blizzard-swept Nebraska plains, mattered when he could fly pursuits. "Away back in ground school," he wrote, "I had the ambition to fly one of the little fighting scouts. Well, I realized that. From now on that's my work. The plane at least. It doesn't look like too much real work in store for us here." In fact, he never saw a German plane in anger and credited that for getting home alive. Two weeks was the average life expectancy for a fighter pilot in combat. The closest this new pursuit pilot came to the fighting was the odd training patrol over America's small sector of the front, with bombs to drop by guess and live ammunition to use up on the way home. "It was tracer every fourth round so you could aim the plane like a water hose. Guns jammed once in a while, sure, but not too often. They raised a lot of sheep in France and we'd see these big herds on the way home. Tip the nose down and spray them. The French got pretty mad

Eyer poses in uniform in France, eternal cigarette in hand.

and we got a hell of a dressing down."

Their own equipment was so finicky even *Plane News* had to admit forced landings thirty or forty miles from home base were hardly rare. Their recovery team was credited with bringing in eighty-three wrecks that November. "Slonnie," as a few friends were starting to call him, did his part for the statistics, after twenty-eight trouble-free hours behind a rotary.

"We were practicing out of Issoudin and I was flying number two, just sitting there quietly, when a jug blew clear off. When that cylinder left it cut the casserole engine cowl in two, so half hooked on my left wing strut, the rest on the right side. I just pulled off and around, looking for a good open space, and here was this big flying field with circle and cross right underneath me. Duck soup. From four thousand this was going to be a cinch. It was Chateroux, a French primary school, and a boy on solo in an old Caudron pusher job was coming in to land, so I volplaned down and pulled off to the left to let him have the middle." The volplane glide is a rapid, descending swoop with great flair, an air show trick, but very useful with your engine dead. "I landed first, dead stick, but I'd kept my speed up in the dive. Guess the Caudron pilot was startled by the faster ship because he dug a wing in and ground looped.

"He was the guy who'd gotten excited and clobbered his landing after I was already sitting on the ground but he ran over to give me hell. Once he calmed down I called for a car and a mechanic with a new engine. Found about a hundred American cadets there, sent over because there were no airplanes to train them in the States, and still waiting. We'd been through ground school, flying school, and had wings, while they got maybe two or three hours of flying a month, in French castoffs—not even rotaries."

Brandy and milk was the favored solution to flying behind a French rotary engine which sent its total-loss castor oil mist straight into your face. Eyer said, "We flew mostly Nieuports with a 110 HP Le Rhone or 160 HP, single-valve Gnome motor—and both were sure rotaries about throwing castor oil. The 28 was the best of the Nieuports, very maneuverable with that big, monosoupap Gnome, a fighting airplane if you didn't dive it too hard and peel the wings off." Others who flew them were less enthusiastic, despite the racehorse lines. Some insisted you could hardly bank one to the right against all that torque reaction and after any long flight pilots leaned left all day. They would crash for sure too, if your finger slipped off the button during a landing. That button atop the control stick ruled all rotary life.

Eyer explained, "To land you pressed down to shut the engine off for a while, because it wouldn't idle below about 950 RPM and the plane would keep flying at those revs. Just before it died completely during a final approach you blipped it alive to finish up. Then taxied in on the blips. Your left hand was even busier in a Le Rhone-powered plane, with those manettes, little levers to handle mixture, arranged in a quadrant with no friction lock. You hooked your first finger around one lever and middle finger around the other and kind of wiggled them to get the motor running nicely. To tell the truth, no rotary really idled very well at any time." The larger Gnome, with a single fuel-air control lever, was slightly easier to fly. This one-valve, or monosoupap, engine was even rated

dependable, meaning a sixteen-hour life expectancy under full load.

The Lincoln pilot recalled one problem though. "Only bad feature, really. It would burn on you with no trouble at all. Instead of cutting out the whole engine to land you cut either three or six cylinders, depending on your glide angle. But gas was still spurting out of those and dropping into the bottom of that casserole cowl. Maybe a cupful as you slowed down and when the hot cylinders got down there, bingo. I was taking a monosoupap Nieuport off once, when the mechanics came running after me, throwing rocks and waving their arms. Stuck my head around the windshield and it looked like the whole ship was on fire. So I cut right back and slid out along the fuselage towards the tail before I tumbled out. That ship rolled another fifty feet and really went up. It was the first of only three fires I ever had, and I never liked any of them much."

Officially the Gnome-powered Nieuport was disparaged because biplanes wasted fuel, so French designers turned out a single-wing Morane for more speed. Eyer said, "That was brand-new and a good airplane to fly too, except that it didn't have any altitude. Very nice under six thousand but up high, just dip a wing and she'd stall and whip off into a spin on you. Still, it was one of the most maneuverable little jobs I ever flew. Remind you a little of the Fokker for tight turns, but not enough wing." This was high praise since Fokker's D VII single-seater was so superior it became the only machine banned by name in the Treaty of Versailles.

In truth, WW I was a trench war with aviation the least-effective branch. General John

Pershing had reason to be more concerned about fodder for his (unused) horses, since all the airplanes shot down by both sides had more bearing on headlines than the war's outcome. Aces were good copy but far less vital in the long run than the impetus combat gave to new plane design. Most pilots saw very little future in army aviation as a career. Hollywood's fascination with air heroes only peaked a decade later. Eyer wrote his brother Clair, "I missed the front by four days but I've seen enough of the Army."

Then it was more training, "Mostly to keep us busy," as he wrote home. "I'm flying again but not very hard and they are starting to send some home. Think I'll go soon. Hope so. Winter has set in. Trying to get leave and look this country over a little bit."

"In between," he said, "we were just sitting around when a bulletin went up for ferry pilots to Colombey. A pal had gone the trip before and come back with this story about some chateau with beautiful daughters so I followed him the next day. He'd fly one way, shake his head, look at the map, and fly someplace else. Finally I pulled alongside and motioned that my gas was about out. That's when we spotted a big army camp with a parade ground. So we landed. The colonel chewed us apart for desecrating his parade ground but after giving us plenty of hell, he gave us some gas, too. Colombey came out later as the place where they rolled all those brand-new airplanes tight together and burned them at the end of the war."

Not that Slonnie cared at the time. His leave had come through. "We got a week, but only twenty-four hours of that in Paris, so we went to the Follies and took a box with Rube Yokum,

another ground school chum, sitting up front. This little girl sang: 'Yankee Doodle parle vous Francais in zee propaire way?' Yokum, who had a hell of a good tenor, joined right in, holding out his arms to her. It brought down the house. Finally he had to step out of the box and take a bow."

Completing his week's leave on the Riviera, Eyer wrote home, "Nice and Cannes are more American than Paris and I saw Corsica." He didn't mention a side trip to the Monte Carlo Casino but always treasured an inlaid ivory chip. He mentioned a return to Nebraska University in almost every letter but most were so full of flying that schooling didn't seem his likely choice.

The army eventually sent him to Angers, noted chiefly for brick barracks with cement floors but little heat, as first stop on the way home. "One morning," Eyer said, "the fire wasn't going so I yelled for the private and gave him hell. He said, 'Aren't you from Lincoln? I was in your Sunday school class.' And that was the only boy I bawled out in my whole army career. The next bunk was a Lt. John Kearney, an old infantry man who looked about fifty-seven and told me: 'Hell son, I crawled all over your state on my belly, hunting Indians.' When I asked if he was any relation to General Phil Kearney he said, 'Distantly son, distantly. He's my father.' He spoke French so we went to town for a good meal and plenty of wine and when I came back from the boy's room everybody in that restaurant cheered. John finally admitted he'd told them I was his son, the great ace, and the French thought it was very romantic, the famous son and his daddy managing to get together."

Plane News advised them all to eat, drink, and be merry for tomorrow the States would be dry,

Eyer thought he looked "snappy" in his WWI uniform.

adding that aviators should go home and keep the trust. The pool of skilled pilots couldn't be promised flying work, but flying officers might take their helmets and goggles home anyway—unless a later order forbade it.

Slonnie sailed on the *France*, "going home in style," while the Issoudin paper wondered, who might be first to fly the Atlantic? Americans, they felt, only needed to scale up current airplanes. The British were already building to beat them. Why let that happen when America was better equipped? The paper went on to talk of connecting the two coasts of America by air. That ignored their own, earlier coverage of the Army's first, inept attempts to fly local mail. Crews had worked all night, early in 1918, to get at least one plane fit for a Congressional mail send-off from Washington after years of scraping to find $100,000 for this first try. English pilots were already flying regular London-Paris passenger runs on what would soon become the world's first permanent, civilian airline route. The Post Office felt airmail should pay its own way at only twenty-four cents a letter but loads dropped sharply within four days of that novel first flight. Pilots were soon carrying train-paid mail to have any load at all. The rate was cut to eight cents, with a new stamp, and by early August 1918, the postal service had inherited all airmail. The Army promptly gave commendations to its six mailmen, who had accumulated sixteen forced landings in 421 hours of flying. One was forced down five times in thirty-nine trips. Although none of the six were lost, two lives had been claimed during tests of the first Liberty engine for use on this mail run.

Slonnie was sunning on the Riviera about the time his country announced its first official aerial weather forecast: snow and gusty winds aloft between New York and Cleveland. Neither that nor his leave were more important than a discharge, only a few days after his commission papers finally caught up with him. "A bunch of us got off in Hoboken and went through the old rigamarole. Just chatting, with our logbooks pitched on the desk, when the guy there yelled my name. It was a boy I'd gone to school with back in Norman. He'd just finished flying school and was going to stay in and send his kid brother to school. But he bought it about a year later. I had a personal chum check me

out at least and went on home." His youngest brother remembered that Eyer took a streetcar up Tenth Street in Lincoln and came into their house through the back yard. He and their father were in collusion about that and almost scared Maggie to death.

"I got back in time for half a semester at the University," Eyer said. "Only took ten hours and half were French. The teacher would speak to us in French and I would always answer until finally he wouldn't call on me any more. When the first class was over he told me to stay and asked where I had learned it. Actually, our airplane mechanics had been French apaches who wouldn't fight in the war and that's where I got my French. You can imagine how that fit in at the University of Nebraska. I stayed in school until spring vacation and then told Dad I could raise enough money down at the Kappa Sig fraternity house to buy an airplane. He wanted to know if I could make any money with it. That part was easy. Twenty-five bucks for fifteen-minute rides and pay for the plane in three months. So he offered to loan me the money instead, and I could go get my first airplane."

March 1919   Flying hours: 230:29

Chapter 4

Barnstorming

"You made more money in six weeks than I make all year."

An airplane of your own, guaranteed to pay for itself? That was only possible for Kelly Field graduates who decided on the barnstorming life early.

The armistice released some 25,000 pilots to peaceful pursuits, with scant argument from all those military-trained flyers who wanted out of their country's infant air arm just as soon as possible. The few who remained Air Service officers were sure to be ill-paid and scarcely appreciated, if not openly scorned, even by their recent comrades. Most American pilots had qualified for aerial combat too late for the ace era. The few famous ones probably learned from the French and flew out their wars in foreign squadrons. Whatever their training, flying as a career appealed to less than a handful right after the war. And their families generally agreed. Very few fathers staked their sons to an airplane in the spring of 1919.

Slonnie recalled, "There were about ten Lincoln boys who went air. When we got back, a few decided to promote a plane from some local guy, but most cracked up and got out of the business before their ships were paid for. Including mine, we had five working airplanes originally. The first belonged to three guys named Harding, Zook, and Bahl, but their Hall-Scott engine set it on fire about the fourth day. Bob Copsey, my first army instructor, promoted a plane and so did O'Shea of the Ford-dealer family and one named Wilmoth. Those last two lost their airplanes within a couple of weeks. Then Harding and Zook put Bahl back in business with a Jenny. He could fly all day, Copsey was part-time, on weekends, and I went out afternoons, after school. All three of us did all right to start with." It took a pretty determined optimist to bet on a commercial future for U.S. aviation that spring, with thousands of veterans jobless, whether they boasted flying skills or not. A second Jenny age of training planes turned into barnstormers only came about because that already-obsolete two-seater was so widely available. On the other hand, all those cheap Jennies meant nobody could sell new airplane designs for another decade, until stiffer safety regulations appeared. Fence wire was the favorite Jenny repair medium and business sense among barnstormers seldom went further than to promise there would be no charge for your ride if the wings came off. American cow-pasture flying was a far cry from the Italian who wanted planes decorated and signed by futurist artists so he could stage grand aerial ballets where a loop indicated happiness, a spin impatience, and rotary engines added the feminine note. An English group beat the Americans in founding the world's first international airline, but only because their government put up 300,000 pounds sterling. The first private airline ticket, from Manchester to Blackpool, still cost more than the train ride. Surplus airplanes were too expensive in Britain for barnstorming to prosper.

America's Middle West, however, seemed predestined for gypsy airplanes. Many roads out of Lincoln were still rough, humped, and deep in dust, ground to talcum by iron-wheeled carts. When ruts gouged too deep they were abandoned for a parallel set. The first flying experience for Great Plains Americans was probably fifteen minutes amid the oil smells of a Jenny. Once they had taken that trip over the family farm, some even identified a bit with aviation heroes. The first of these, in 1919, was Lt. Commander Albert C. Read, island-hopping across the Atlantic in the Navy's NC-4 seaplane. His flight pioneered the joint effort, where surface ship backup and planning replaced blind hope. Even so, Read's was the only one of a three-plane fleet to complete the trip. That same May French-born, New York restauranteur Raymond Orteig wagered $25,000 against a nonstop flight from New York to Paris, although the tall, blond pilot who would win it in 1927, to effectively end the barnstorming era, hadn't even taken his first flying lesson yet. Two Englishmen

National Air and Space Museum, Smithsonian Institution

A Curtiss JN-4 "Canuck," the Canadian-built version of the U.S.-made Curtiss "Jenny." Slonnie chose the Canuck because it was great for flying stunts. "It was maybe 150 pounds lighter than the Jenny and that much more maneuverable."

made the first true, nonstop Atlantic crossing, from Newfoundland to Ireland, only a month after Orteig's announcement. John William Alcock and Arthur Whitten Brown, flying an ice-plagued, open-cockpit bomber from British surplus, won a prewar *London Daily Mail* prize but somehow failed to capture American attention.

Slonnie was typical, too involved with his own plane of far less endurance to even notice their feat. "I told Dad I could make 100 bucks a day if I only carried four passengers and tied it down to attend classes. You'd come in over some town, give them the loop and roll, and find a field. Time you landed that old Canuck there would be crowds of cars pouring out of town." Many barnstormers wouldn't loop any airplane but Slonnie picked the Curtiss "Canuck" precisely because it flew stunts better. "It was maybe 150 pounds lighter than the Jenny and that much more maneuverable. Little better performance, handled small fields better, and a little faster. The reputation for coming apart was the bunk. I had wing pins in there as thick as my finger. You couldn't shear one. I never knew anybody who had a Canuck come apart."

Their structure was common for the era: Sitka spruce spars and undercarriage with linen—later airplane cotton—covering, pulled taut by two coats of dope. Although Slonnie paid $2,500 for his hotter Canadian special, U.S. Jennies dropped to $400 used and $600 in the factory crate within a few months. All depended on an OX-5 power plant, called the disposable engine because it was too cheap on the surplus market to be worth much repair. Curtiss's water-cooled, 90 HP V8 thumped away at 1,400 RPM in so many planes it spawned a formal club of men who had once flown behind an

OX-5. Further Canuck advantages included an aluminum spreader bar for the landing gear and laces between cowl and fuselage. Nose repairs could be made without ripping fabric off the body. But its most important feature was ailerons in both top and bottom wings, twice the Jenny's supply, for pilots who liked snappier handling.

Slonnie had all this in mind when he boarded a Toronto train rather than buy a cheaper Jenny close to home. During spring vacation, 1919, he brought his money along for a close look at rows of Canucks, owned by a man named Ericson, who had cornered the surplus Canadian JN market. Slonnie said, "They must have had four or five hundred. You went down the line, pressing the leading edge of each wing. If it crackled that dope was kind of on its way out. The big thing was to step up on a wheel and wiggle rocker arms sideways where they stuck out, up on top of the engine. If they were a little bit on the loose side, that engine was going to need work pretty soon. Then check the prop. They had maybe a dozen kinds and what we called a 'toothpick' would turn a little faster than a great big sickle job.

"The Ericson people left us alone but they had logbooks for every airplane. I picked half a dozen possibles and went inside to take a peek at each log. When you found one you liked, they cranked it up. There were no pilot licenses then except the FAI (Fédération Aéronautique Internationale) book for Frenchmen. If you could get the airplane up and bring it back you were a pilot. By the same token, I didn't have a driver's license either. I found a Canuck I liked, landed again, and went up to pay. They filled you up with gas and gave you a pat on the back. Give it the gun

and you were on your way home. A Canuck burned about eight gallons an hour, cruising around 75 MPH, so you flew maybe 100 miles and began watching for a good open pasture, well before the tank ran dry. I had some spare tins and the carburetor was down at the bottom so you didn't have to shut down to refuel. Just chock the wheels, tie the throttle lever back, and get out with the funnel, gas, and a chamois to strain it.

"Got away from Toronto about nine that first morning and took all the rest of spring vacation getting home. Before I could gas people would come out and ask if I was taking people up. Hell, yes. Twenty-five bucks and they always said okay. Be six more months before I had to drop it to a dollar a minute back home. About when I got those first people back somebody else wanted a ride. Hop maybe a dozen but I wasn't getting any closer to school, so I started throwing business away. I never should have thought about the university. Could have taken four, maybe five hundred dollars out of every town and used up three months, just flying back to Nebraska. Even the gas was free. Some filling station man would always be out there so I'd ask him to fill my cans. How much do I owe you? The answer was always: Nothing. You use my gasoline and everybody out here knows me. So I'd say well, it's the best gas made and stick twenty free gallons up front. Two cans on the floor and two on the seat with the belt around them. Dad had given me a check for $3,000 but I never touched the extra five hundred and never slept under a wing all the time I was barnstorming. I could always afford a two-buck hotel and got home with all Dad's money and another $500 in my own pocket."

When he arrived younger brother Urmson was naturally fascinated. He said, "Eyer had a friend who flew and purchased an airplane but it burned, so I always claimed ours was the first one around town. Our place on D Street had a barn at the back which Dad had converted for two cars. When the plane came we moved the Ford roadster over with our Buick tourer, to fit that fuselage on the right. Later Eyer cut a larger door to the haymow and the wings went up there. We used the Buick to tow his plane out to a cow pasture we called the airfield. Wheel the fuselage out and set its tail skid on the folded car top. I'd hold it there while he drove. Then go back and get the wings, two at a time. Then we had to take pitchforks and go along getting dry cow droppings out of the way for takeoffs."

Slonnie remembered his airport as, "Just a field south of town because it was mostly south wind in the summer and you could land or take off away from the houses. I think maybe aviation grew fastest in the Middle West on account of all that flat country. Take New York. You didn't have big wheat fields under you all the time. We could always land in alfalfa too but I tried a flax field once and that is a very tough plant. Didn't nose over but it slowed me down awfully quick and I had to take off along the same swath. Sometimes we had pretty muddy fields but the Canuck would take that all right. About all you had to remember for short-field landings was not to go into one you couldn't get out of. We still had to pull the tail around pretty often in small fields, back it right up against the fence. The motor was way up front so it only took sixty or seventy pounds of lift to get the tail around. I must have lifted a million of them."

Ground maneuvers only became tricky with a crowd. Then Slonnie had help like Urmson, who stayed close in hopes he might be allowed to fly himself. He rode with his older brother quite a bit but mostly there were passengers, so Urmson would fasten them in, pull the chocks away, maybe hold a wing to turn the plane in a tighter circle, and keep people back. Slonnie always said Urmson was too young to fly, even though he was nineteen by then. Barnstormers took aviation into back corners of America, where spotting hidden ditches and stumps in tall grass was an everyday necessity. An unlikely percentage of this vagabond flying generation came from farms, bringing their keen weather sense along. Beyond that, many of the '19 crowd might be some sort of dreamer with a tinge of showman, but all were good repairmen, able to fix an engine or sew a gashed wing panel with equal ease.

Survival in the air depended largely on a sharp sense for location. Section lines generally followed the compass and shinier railroad tracks indicated well-traveled lines to a major town, but only a farm-born pilot would watch where the cow rumps pointed as a wind indicator. Few noticed or cared that an Easterner was already experimenting with directional radio beams by the spring of 1919. All would have enjoyed the joke though, when this inventor directed his test pilot precisely 180 degrees off course. Mail pilots, the pony express of their age, continued to navigate like the barnstormers they were, sideslipping into miserably short pastures as seldom as possible because lopsided cooling warped the valves on one bank of your V8. By the early twenties there would be mail flights into Omaha, an easy Canuck hop northeast of Lincoln, while international mail had made a tentative appearance in North America as early as the summer of 1919, accompanying the Toronto-New York air race.

Slonnie said, "We knew nothing about aerial navigation then and didn't even have a compass that worked, but you knew the general direction to Omaha, say, and got straightened around on a direct railroad. Then just watch the shadow of a strut on your lower wing. That moved with the sun so you figured in the time of year too. Maybe cut across until you hit some other tracks, then go down and read the name off a train station and check your map. Just guesswork at night. Later, when we started flying more after dark, I discovered I could spread my fingers and point the middle one at a certain star, then take the course off my index finger. Besides, maybe ninety percent of all the chicken houses in western Nebraska had their doors on the south side, if you needed a general heading. Most of that first spring I hopped passengers out of Lincoln. Or maybe headed out a little further on weekends. I had morning classes but before school let out in June, there were other ships in Lincoln and unless somebody knew you personally, he might ride with the other guy. One Friday I told this fraternity brother who helped sometimes, let's go out to York, maybe fifty-sixty miles west. I didn't want to sit around Lincoln an hour between rides.

"We had nothing but a tool kit and the clothes we wore but headed for York and landed about three. God, I worked right up to dark, plus all day Saturday and Sunday. Fill up and haul some more. We'd picked a good field and made a deal with the farmer. Twenty-five dollars or give his family a ride. Then we jumped on to Aurora, maybe fifty miles away. But we couldn't do a thing there. Some towns were boomers, others would plod along. Usually there was a big enough element wanting to ride, especially if you were first into their town. Farmers were making a fair living about then and we got the early cream. Maybe that's why I seldom got turndowns, even for acrobatic rides that cost extra. Before airplanes got more common, about one in ten wanted that. You had to take them a little higher because the old Canuck lost maybe 300 feet looping. Did a whale of a business. My friend got five percent and made fifty bucks a week. A mechanic I hired another trip was happy to make twenty-five. And we had a lot of fun. When competition showed up we dropped it to fifteen dollars and I thought we'd go broke but we still carried three passengers an hour, easy.

"We'd left Lincoln that first time without even a toothbrush and were out six weeks, buying new clothes and wadding up the dirty ones to ship home. Couldn't wait for laundry. Ended up with more shirts, shorts, and handkerchiefs that fall than I would ever own in my life. Gas was still free. Some station would send its truck out. Line up alongside my ship and they'd print a picture in the local weekly. People figured it must be good gas if an airplane could use it. Actually, we could burn anything. After we got going I'd call ahead to somebody I knew fifty miles up the road and tell them I'd be over the next morning. Or a frat brother would call and ask me to come. That's when I got the idea of asking for a guarantee. Ten passengers and we'll visit your town. Even got Chamber of Commerce people calling because we always showed up.

"About the only thing you had to replace on the plane was shock cord, which held that axle to the landing gear frame. One side broke out in Kearney and I didn't have a piece left long enough for a fix. It took weeks to get more of the real stuff from Chicago. We found some clothesline but that only stretched a little bit so I had to temper my landings. Got to thinking that night and bought a Ford inner tube. Cut slices about an inch and a half, like fat rubber bands. It was better than shock cord, which cost a dollar a foot. The ship needed ten feet of that to a side but you could fill a whole side with a buck-ten tube. That got us into Gothenburg. A sleepy little town but this frat brother was sure he could get ten out. I arrived in midweek and went to his place for dinner. He told me he only got six rides but he'd pay for the other four. That was no dice but I'd take his wife for the first ride and see what happened. I hadn't given Gothenburg a show yet so I took her up for the loop and she was delighted. Everybody wanted to go then but they all said, not for a ride like that. We were only doing medium so I called another boy in North Platte and told him to put a story in the paper. I'd be in Thursday. They had a big field all ready, out east of town, because the Army was going to fly clear across the country and picked North Platte for one stop. That had been going on for weeks but their planes would get an hour out from the coast and lose an engine or something.

"My chum called back and said the paper wouldn't take a story. People had been yelling wolf too long. I told him to put in a paid ad. It was a big town and worth it. But the paper wouldn't even take an ad paid in advance. Okay, I'll be over town about noon anyway. When I showed up they streamed out by the thousands. Thought my one little ship was that whole Army squadron, finally making it. We'd been out weeks by then and North Platte was about 2,500 feet up so you needed a lot of level ground. After ten days the owner of our field said cars were ruining it. The weekend was coming up but I couldn't buy him over. Half a mile closer to town there were some cattle feed pens with fences. If passengers weren't too bulky we might make one last weekend. Then I told my pal, we've paid for the airplane, let's go home.

"With maybe twenty airplanes already working in Nebraska by then you tried to duck the local boys. We jumped to smaller towns going back. I don't know if that Canuck was the first plane they'd ever seen in some burgs but ninety percent of the time it was the first which actually landed in their town for sure. It was out west that this fellow came to the field about the time we were tying down for the night and told me all about his own airplane, the first one he'd ever seen. Mine was the second. Building it at home with an all-metal fuselage. Tube fuselage frames were just coming in around America, at least to read about, and he got the idea of taking gas pipe, with T-joints every so often. Couldn't have gotten that load off the ground with a jet engine."

Perry, the youngest Sloniger, remembered how his brother would return from these trips. "He'd fly low over the house and if it was towards dusk four or five neighbors would get in their cars and head for the field. Line up and turn their lights on for him. Eyer let Urmson and me wash the wings before he got the tent hangar. After that came we started giving people peeks inside for a nickel and Eyer blew up." Owning your own tent hangar was one sure mark of success in barnstorming. Enough were sold to suggest many pilot-owners lacked a supply of younger brothers to clean their airplanes.

Slonnie said, "There were plenty of ads for all kinds of stuff, in *Aerial Age,* but I never even hopped up the OX-5. Motors were cheap, sure, but you couldn't always get another one in a hurry, so you kept yours going. The only mechanics were what I'd learned in ground school but you could have taken one into any car garage, except that those boys would back off like it was a rattlesnake. Tell them it was just like a Buick but they were leery. It was an overhead-valve job so you stuck a feeler gauge in and turned the prop to see if you had proper clearances. Once an hour, give the rocker arms a squirt of oil. Next hop, keep your head down behind the windshield. "Low-compression motor too, so we bought any good spark plug from some hardware store. The plane came with an aluminum cover like a car hood but those slits sucked dust in so I left it off and threw a canvas over at night. The OX-5 was easy to start. Wind the propeller around to get a fuel charge in the cylinders, then turn the switch on and pull your prop through. Of course you put chocks under the wheels so it didn't jump out and cut you into slices as it went by." Slonnie clearly believed the Curtiss engine handbook which warned pilots not to develop that destructive disease, tinkeritis. When the motor is working all right, let it alone.

"That motor only cut out on me once, taking off from Lincoln. And the carb acted up another time, when a collar on the float valve lever came unsoldered. Couldn't run it up long enough on the ground to tell what was wrong and local mechanics fought shy so I took it down myself and found a good boy to resolder on the old marks. Never had trouble again. There was no ground help so you took care of an airplane because you were the one flying it. If it got a little wing-heavy after a rain, just punch a couple of holes in the bottom edge on that side and let out a gallon or so of water." Rain on weekends ruined many barnstormers, although Slonnie remembered flying pretty regularly. He had a frat house full of backers, of course.

Harry Minor, wiry heir to a vast ranch in the sand hills of western Nebraska, was his closest friend. He remembered a lot of time spent in that Canuck. Once, in York, the field was short, so Slonnie sent him over to a farmhouse to buy a bed sheet. The pilot would come in over a bunch of trees and put his wheels right on the mark every time. Pretty soon they had hundreds out. Take them up, dip a wing, and bring them back. They worked all day and took nearly a thousand dollars home that night. Slonnie and Harry took the Canuck up to the Minor ranch several times but it didn't really like the altitude. It took a long time getting up to 2,000 feet but they did give a few rides in Hyannis, the nearest town. Once they had the easy money they were supposed to show the crowd a spin. Harry asked his pilot if he thought he could get high enough to do one before dark. Slonnie laughed and gave it a try but they came out barely above a haystack. After landing Slonnie said, "I don't believe we will try that again out here."

On another trip from Lincoln, Harry had a bag tied to the wing. He looked up and the rope around it was burning. Before he could poke him

the pilot handed over the fire extinguisher he always carried. Slonnie added, "My exhaust stack had a crack by the top fuselage longeron and burned the wood almost through. We got going again, barely clearing the wires, and limped on into the ranch. Fortunately Harry's dad was building a new house and had some good carpenters so we found one old fellow who took a piece of oak about an inch square and spliced that in. I rerigged, pulled the wires up tight, and everything was fine again. Any time I got tired of Lincoln we'd go up to the Minors. One day the whole crew was going down to the south ranch so I took old Joe. Harry was slightly built but his father was about five by five. I couldn't even get my front belt around him. Just sort of wedged him in. By the time we got over the south ranch I had about 3,000 feet so I cut the motor and yelled at Joe to grab hold of that cowling right in front of him, I was going to loop. He'd have torn that cowling out of the ship before he came loose. I made it a good tight loop so he didn't even need to hold on, spun down, and landed. When I cut the motor back, which you do in a spin, I could hear old Joe yelling: 'Give'em hell, Ey-rah, give'em hell.' He always thought that was my name."

This was an age when sharp college students wore twenty-dollar shoes and listened to *Whispering* on the Victrola, while better frat houses had a Buick or Cole 8 parked out in front. But the Lincoln headlines went to a Kappa Sig who brought his date to the prom in his own airplane. Reporters claimed co-eds at Nebraska University dreamed of a flying date with Slonnie, once classes started again in the autumn of 1919. "I always intended to graduate," he said, "but fall was county fair time and people kept calling me. My price was

$400 for a twenty-minute show. Not very many would do acrobatics and it sure wasn't bad money. Three days a week and not bother with passengers. There were supposed to be three airplanes working regularly around Lincoln but some guy would come up and say: 'Look, I got this show date but I cracked up my ship.' I'd figure out the distances and call his fair. Give you twenty minutes for only $200 if I can do it at two in the afternoon. Mine were mostly at four. By then I had hired a mechanic from the local Chandler dealer. He'd been in the aviation section of the Signal Corps and wasn't afraid of an airplane motor. I paid expenses on top of his $25 a week and he liked roaming around better than sliding under automobiles. We'd fill the ship with gas and put on one show, then head right over for my four o'clock date. He rode up front for the first show and loved it. Crazy guy but one hell of a good mechanic. After the show at four we'd fill the tank again and go back for the early show next day."

Slonnie discovered pretty quickly that, "I was doing just a little more flying than attending class, since I was out someplace with that airplane Thursday and Friday of almost every week. By mid-semester I was down in practically all my hours and had to go before what we called 'the benzine board,' to see if I would be washed out of school. That was the Dean of Men, a hell of a nice guy, another dean, and my first French teacher, who had cried when I went 'over there.' White hair, black eyes, and the maddest gal you ever saw. The only person who said anything nasty to me was Miss Conklin: 'He's a loafer, won't come to class. Throw him out.' Whenever one of the men would ask a question, those black eyes would snap and she'd speak right up again: 'He won't study.' Finally they got through taking me over the coals and this other dean asked why I had missed so much. Fortunately I had this neat little pile of contracts with me: $400 and $200 each day for three days a week. He said: 'Look, you made more money in six weeks than I make all year. Why don't you quit school?' I tried to tell them I wanted to go ahead with an education. These fairs weren't going to last forever and I'd been lucky to have no trouble. Never missed a show date. Finally, they let me finish out the semester."

Slonnie knew all too well that "Nebraska winters were no fun to fly anyway. No antifreeze and a good speed would have frozen that old motor solid, so you put the plane away when the weather got shaky. Towards late fall you might drain the radiator at night. Then, if you got another sunny day, you could still fly. Heat a couple of five-gallon cans of water on the stove at home. Pour one in and drain it and pour in the other one and give that prop a swing. For winter storage I pulled the plugs and squirted a bunch of motor oil on top of the pistons. Turn the prop to smear it up inside. If you had picked a good tight motor there was no trouble. We ran mine through the spring, summer, and into late fall of '19 and when I took the ship in to re-cover, I had the engine overhauled too, because I thought I had another whole year ahead."

Curtiss's handbook on the OX-5 claimed that under normal conditions valves were practi-cally free from warping and pitting. Slonnie agreed. The book went on to say their engine should have a complete inspection after fifty hours of operation. Slonnie ran his six times that long. He was more concerned about the cloth. "I don't know how long it might have lasted, standing out in hot weather or

winter, but you could always tell by pressing between the little ribs behind the leading edge. A small aircraft factory was just getting started in Lincoln by that time, putting together Standards with Hall-Scott motors at first. They even found somebody with an idea for an original ship, a monocoque monoplane. I flew it. Nice little airplane. Anyway, they did repair work too and had a lot of surplus stuff, so I bought the cloth for my Canuck there. By that time we used cotton, not linen, so it had to be sewed with pretty wide seams.

"Harry Minor drove Dad's Buick to get the ship into town. Wings first, then the fuselage. I was in back, holding on to the tail skid with both hands. It was heavy and we had to keep the tail down or the nose would drag. Harry decided to drive all over campus row while this other guy in front stands up and puts on his law-student voice to tell everybody, 'This is the fuselage of the great German ace.' Meaning Heini Schuff, who's in back, hanging on with me. Harry was taking the corners hard and the undercarriage was swaying. I'm yelling my head off but he had a whirl. I could see my Canuck on its side with a longeron busted out. All I'd have left would be four wings. But I couldn't let go of the skid to get at the wheel.

"When we finally got home and started to recover, mother sewed the cloth into strips four feet wide. We'd start from the trailing edge of the wing, leaving plenty of room for stitching. Over the top to the leading edge and back down underneath. Hand-sew it to the leading edge and sew the ribs from top to bottom. I'd never done one but knew how it should work. Just a little common sense. Then put on the dope. Three coats of clear and a coat of varnish." Zazel helped brush dope on and still

recalled the job all too well, decades later. They had brought the wings into the front three rooms of their house and banana oil left quite an odor. Their mother was game for any such project, though.

And she loved to fly. There was always some trip, like out to Uncle George's farm, the original Sloniger spread in Nebraska. Slonnie had taken the front seat out to carry leaflets somewhere so he just turned a bucket upside-down for his mother to sit on and she hung on to the belt, up under her chin. On the other hand, Slonnie recalled, "Dad only went up a very few times, when I would stunt over Lincoln to get people out." Once the Sloniger Curtiss was re-covered, its pilot said, "I even painted my name across the bottom wing in big block letters. That was funny too. Not long after I got it flying again in the spring of '20, I ran into a fellow down at the hotel who was supposed to be a pilot. We were chatting and I asked what his name was. He said: 'Sloniger, you may have seen it on my plane.' I just said, 'Hell, that's my name and I didn't know there were two of us in this business.' I never forgot how embarassed he was."

Flying his Canuck a second spring, the true Sloniger discovered that even his name on the wing couldn't keep fees up any longer. "Not much business, so I was up at the Minor ranch again, loafing and greasing windmills. It's all rolling sand hills out there. I could land and taxi within twenty feet of a mill. Took two days that way instead of two weeks by horse. Barnstorming was getting kinda shot already. No hundred bucks a day stuff, and that's when I got my first offer to fly for somebody else. A Lincoln man named Hammond wired the ranch and offered $1,000 a month to go to Mexico. Actually, I hardly thought about it at first. But after I returned to Lincoln at the end of spring vacation I lost the Canuck in a windstorm. We'd tied down and locked the controls but that didn't work and I found my ship upside-down on the golf course. Sold the wreck and was short of money about the time Hammond offered again. Salary plus commissions. Took me a long time in commercial aviation to make as much as I could down in Mexico. At a guess, about eighty percent of the original guys cracked up their airplanes or dropped out within a year but I guess I was lucky. There was always somebody wanting a pilot. One job led to another. No trouble staying in flying and liking it made everything simple." The spring semester at Nebraska University opened in 1920 without Slonnie, who was on his way south to Tampico.

When the government required that pilots keep logbook records of their flying hours, half a dozen years later, Slonnie considered his year with the Canuck and figured he'd put 300 honest hours on that airplane. Like many early pilots, he would always be openly skeptical of sky-high, pre-log totals claimed by some of his contemporaries.

March 1920   Flying hours: 530:29

Chapter 5

El Piloto

"With an airplane then you were propositioned for everything."

The law of aviation averages alone would probably have sent Slonnie south of the border. Any Yankee pilot worth his cordovan boots and foam-rimmed goggles was likely to fly the Latin routes at some point. Mexico had relatively few people, thinly scattered across a random mix of abrupt mountains, empty deserts, and lush savannas. It was a land obviously waiting for air transport, even if the Mexicans didn't quite realize that fact in 1920.

Even wire-rigged biplanes offered a reasonable ride compared to Mexican rails or roads. They were certainly softer than a mule and hardly more temperamental. Flamboyant early aviation simply suited Mexican scenery. The first official U.S. airplanes to reach the country made a reconnaissance of Veracruz harbor in 1914. A year later Pancho Villa hired the entire J.S. Berger aerial exhibition team as his air force, along the Texas border, until his pilots discovered both sides were firing on them. Even Gen. John "Blackjack" Pershing, hardly an air power advocate, deployed America's First Aero Squadron along the Rio Grande during his 1916 expedition. Among Mexicans, Major Alberto Salinas was the first to

found an air wing, clear back in 1912, although most pilots found it more profitable to work directly under the local warlord. The next round of flyers and airplanes mostly came from north of the border but freelance fighting was getting scarcer by 1920. Alvaro Obregón was about to become president and he favored peace with the United States. This forced a good many native bandits to live off internal prey and that led, indirectly, to the success of the Eastern Mexican Aviation company—or Nebraska Aircraft as it was known around Lincoln, where the owners were two local men, Winship and Hammond. The latter hired Slonnie.

"Officially they had a mail contract from the Mexican government," Slonnie explained. "In those days most mail deals went by the pound, which looked okay since there was no telephone or telegraph which worked very regularly between the capital and Tampico, one of the largest oil fields anywhere. Turned out though, we could stick the mail in an inside coat pocket most days. We set it up to be one round trip every day but pretty soon it was twice a week. By the end I might go over to Mexico City once a month."

Perhaps 1920 was a bit early for scheduled Mexican airmail. Nations as diverse as Italy and China had already discussed something like that, at least, but even the U.S. would have to wait another year for halfway-consistent, countrywide service.

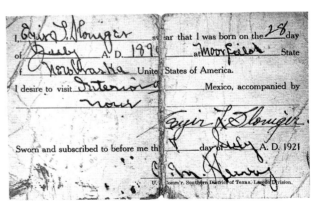

Slonnie's visa for entry into Mexico.

The Lincoln, Nebraska, crew prior to departure for Mexico. The two planes at center are dual-cockpit, Hisso-powered, Lincoln Standard Tourabouts. On the right is the LS Speedster. The plane on the left is probably the only LS Cruiser ever built, which was unreliable and never made it to Tampico. Slonnie is standing below the prop of the Cruiser, not wearing a tie.

Mexico was still four years shy of its first proper airline, which would be called *Compañia Mexicana de Aviación*. CMA survived to be one of the oldest lines in Latin America, boasting it had begun with Standard airplanes left in Tampico by roving barnstormers. They meant Lincoln-built Standards which Nebraska Aircraft flew down to fulfill that government mail contract.

The original Standard, a dual-cockpit, two-seat, wartime trainer like the Jenny or Canuck, was built by Charles Day, backed by Mitsui, the Japanese bankers. Slonnie said, "This outfit called Nebraska Aircraft bought a whole bunch of used airplanes from Standard, along with a big batch of Hispano Suiza motors, to start a Lincoln factory in 1919. So many ribs and spars they had to stick them out at the fairgrounds until they found a building on Main Street.

"A Hisso was the best engine we had then, when it ran. That Hall-Scott in the original Standards would catch fire with no trouble whatsoever so we all liked the Hisso better. Put a larger radiator in the nose and you had a pretty good deal. Except you couldn't see to taxi. You could buy surplus Hissos by the carload and they would take about a hundred hours before an overhaul. That's if you used the basic, 150 HP kind. Even it had a valve problem. No cylinder head cooling, so they burned valves like tissue paper. Catch a bad valve when you didn't want to tear down, you could take one spark plug out and punch a bunch of that pink tape we stuck over wing ribs down through the hole to fill up your combustion chamber. Then shove the valve down a ways, smear some grinding compound on it with a stick, pull it up again by the stem, and twist and twist. Get away with that for

maybe another week. "You always had to cool any Hisso off pretty carefully, but fortunately they weren't welded-jacket jobs, so you only needed a special crowfoot wrench to pull a cylinder. We carried very few spares down to Mexico but shipped a lot in later. And we never took tools on runs out of Tampico. Get a bad motor somewhere, they had to send stuff. We didn't even have a mechanic originally. Then Victor Hugo, who'd been overhauling stuff for Standard Oil, wanted a job. We had a motor just out and he did a great overhaul on it, scraping in bearings, new rings, all that. Spoke good Spanish too. When he wasn't handy we fended for ourselves.

"With a Hisso the Standard Tourabout was a good plane for Mexico. That was the original design with the front cockpit converted for two, to make the plane a three-seater. Except that a couple of fat people couldn't really get in. It's the kind of airplane I flew down there most of the time. But they had hired Vince Burnelli as factory superintendent in Lincoln and he took four top wing panels, which were longer than the bottom pair, to make what was called the Standard Cruiser. It carried four passengers up front, plus a pilot, but no Standard needed even the wing area it had to begin with. Four top panels made the Cruiser a sloppy job to fly. Plus the fact, Burnelli used a 220 HP Hisso, a geared-prop motor which could swing a bigger stick. But that meant winding it pretty high and any Hisso was already kind of fragile even at normal revs.

"Eastern Mexican was really just another part of Nebraska Aircraft with the same bosses. Winship and Hammond decided to go along to Mexico in the Cruiser, with Chris Pickup flying,

Tampico pilots (from left to right) Chris Pickup, Palmer, and Slonnie with their sparse luggage.

because it had that great big front cockpit. I got their trunk in my airplane. When Urmson took me out to the field with just one suitcase, here's a footlocker sticking clear up over the windshield of my front cockpit. I raised hell but Hammond put his arm around me and explained how they knew I'd get there. Baloney. As it turned out though, I was the only one who did go all the way through first try. And that locker just disappeared once I crossed the border.

"We'd planned to do a couple of gas loads each day and make Laredo the third morning. We all took off together but lost the Cruiser right away with motor trouble. Then another Tourabout went down in Texas. I went on alone and landed at Nuevo Laredo on the Mexican side of the Rio Grande. Nebraska Aircraft had already sold the American border patrol a couple of airplanes and sent some fellows down with those. They never caught anybody because they only flew about three hours a week but we were in good with the customs people so I sailed right through. Stuck around two or three days, waiting for the other planes and figuring out where to head next.

"My only map was a page I tore out of the biggest school geography book I could buy. All of Mexico and some of Central America on one page. It showed a railroad to Monterrey, where I wanted to go next, but that made a big bulge and it was mostly desert either way, so why swing out and around just to follow some tracks? A compass was about as much use as a red silk kimono if you had a metal motor in the airplane and the ship wasn't fast enough to bother with one anyway. We could navigate pretty well by the shadow of a strut. Line it up with the trailing edge of your bottom wing to fly south. For an angle shot, pick maybe your fourth wing rib.

"I flew clear on into Mexico City that way and discovered we weren't very popular there. Wyant, another Nebraska boy, had gone down earlier to demonstrate Hisso Standards to this guy O'Neill [General Ralph A. O'Neill], who was head of their air force. It seems [General Winfield] Scott took an Irish regiment down in 1847 and a lot of Mexicans had names like that. I found out right

An LS landing at a San Luis Potosi air show, a stunt event held to make extra cash. Airmail was the stated purpose of this trip, but it was really a barnstorming excursion—pioneering new land for passenger hops or anything else that might pay.

Chris Pickup with the LS Cruiser he tried to fly to Tampico but abandoned in a tree after Mexico City. He later flew as a United Airlines pilot and was lost over the Pacific.

away why Wyant wasn't on the mail deal. Apparently O'Neill did all his flying with one wing way down so Wyant, in the front cockpit, had to throw his leg against the stick to get it back up. Then the general says Standards are wing-heavy. Wyant told them the SOB didn't know what level meant. Put O'Neill in any Mexican plane they had. He'd take a Standard and chase that general right out of the air. Did that go over big. American pilot challenges O'Neill to a duel. Wyant got out of the country to

beat hell but it was a little bit against me because I'm in a Hisso Standard too.

"Then we got an air show job right away, so I went back to San Luis Potosi, halfway up to the border. Chris Pickup, who had started out with the Cruiser, would bring another Tourabout down from Laredo and the Mexican air force would send six more planes. Those never showed up. O'Neill just stood on the sidelines all weekend and glared at us. An organ would pull the crowd in and we'd run

seesaw races. Get ahead, you'd slow up a little bit until the other guy came around for a dead heat. Those Mexicans loved the old carny hokum. I'd do an exhibition down low too. The Hisso Standard would loop off the level at that altitude." Slonnie quickly discovered, however, why wise pilots avoided Mexico City, even for level flight. "Hell, I don't think I'd ever had an airplane up to 7,000 feet before Mexico. Your ship got sloppy to handle. I tried to give some photographer a picture inside Popocatepetl once and we ground away until I was about out of gas without ever getting high enough to see in. Those planes topped out around 15,000 and Popo must be eighteen anyway."

A Standard Tourabout with 150 HP was built to climb out of just about any pasture at sea level, or land to a full stop in 400 feet. On really windy days the Standard, with all that wing area, would almost hover if its pilot tried for a propeller-saving, three-point landing. "We had to," Slonnie explained, "props cost like hell. Any nick would throw the blade off-balance and pull your motor right out of the ship. Even heavy rain could wear down the leading edge. That's why we started out with a third wheel under the nose, to keep from pitching clear forward in a rough landing. But the fields weren't so bad after all so we took those off to save drag. For an airport in Tampico we got some scrub cleared west of town and a little inland. Marked it with a big circle of lime. Rode a bus out from our hotel to the road junction and then it was only a mile to the field. One local kid walked it every day to just lean against the hangar and whistle. We just plunked in and started thinking about mail and getting some more ships.

"The Cruiser had gotten to Laredo, finally,

Slonnie (left) with Cal Niemans, another Tampico airmail pilot.

so they hired a boy named Lefferinck to fly that
turkey to Mexico City. It didn't work any better
there so he stuck his wife in front and started for
Tampico. That geared-up motor quit again of
course and he put it down alongside a little dinky
road where they had to crawl out of some trees to
reach the ground. Then start walking until they
found a couple of mules. Took them two weeks to
Tampico and by that time I'd gone up north and
collected another airplane we'd loaned out. It was a
Tourabout too, painted the same blue with silver
wings, and we needed every damn one by then. But
we left the Cruiser to rot.

"We'd gotten into this payroll business and
it was good." Oil field laborers demanded hard
coin, not paper, on payday and Mexico had no
shortage of people out to grab off payroll shipments.
Nebraska pilots found people lining up to hire their
airplanes. "Besides payrolls, land rents for well
owners went down twice a month, mostly about
100 miles south of Tampico. There was a canal
which could handle maybe sixteen-foot boats, a
very poor road, and the narrow-gauge putt-putt. As
far as I heard, no one bandit was getting it all, but
each one had a territory and some relative with
Tampico oil company connections to tell him when
a shipment was due. More than half that cash was
never getting through. "Their biggest haul came
when one outfit hit the *cucaracha*, a little three-car
train doing about 10 MPH. Their idea was to blow
up the rails out front and shoot the guards but
somebody was slow on the button. That train was
right over their dynamite before he punched it.
Killed the guards all right but the load was mostly
pesos so we had bent coins around Tampico for
months. I flew over the site afterwards and didn't

A beach landing below Tampico to make a gold delivery.
Slonnie is talking to the paymaster in front of the airplane.

see any more foliage than a tabletop for a square block. Peons had sieved that ground bare. Which is really how we got the first contracts.

"There were almost no fields outside of Tampico at first so it was usually a beach landing or sort of bombing, close to the oil fields, if they were a little further from the coast. When the first load had to go inland before they cleared a place for us to land, I figured it was only four sacks. Carry that and their paymaster in the front easy. Told them to put the gold in double bags and get guards out, all around a clearing. I made one pass about 100 feet up so the paymaster could recognize his receivers. Then had him balance a bag on the step. Slowed up so he could stand with his back to the slipstream and each time I yelled, he gave one a push. That didn't happen often. Most times we waited until tide was out. Tuxpan beach was hard as a floor so the slight angle didn't hurt us at all. "Some were pretty big loads too. The largest I ever had was close to $50,000, packed in fifty-pound bags. Kind of staggered off the field in Tampico without a paymaster even. Landed on a beach at the other end and got my receipt."

Getting an airplane down in one piece was seldom the problem. After that things might get tricky. "Our guard came running up one day, shoving his hand down like a crash and yelling: 'Laguna seca!' Cal Niemans was working for us by then and had a great big payroll plus paymaster on board, so I figured I'd better take a look. His engine had quit and he put it down okay, on a dry lake ten or fifteen miles south of town. But then he'd gone clear over to the far edge and stuck that nose between two trees. The wings were swept right back. I could land alongside with our guard and his

big hogleg pistol but there were maybe fifty natives already watching. Niemans said they appeared out of nowhere as he coasted in. His paymaster was yelling 'No hay dinero' before they even touched. I turned my ship around with the motor running and told them to grab all the money bags at once and run like hell for my front cockpit. The guard stayed with Niemans and that paymaster was just about half aboard when I left the ground. Those natives gave a big, mad yell but we were off.

"Loads of wealthy families had sent at least one son up north to school," Slonnie continued, "and they would invite us to a dinner where nobody but the oldest boy spoke English. One rancher was the son of an Englishman who married a local girl. Her father owned most of Tamaulipas state. The son was Oxford-educated and had a place up the Panuco, that big river the oil tankers used. He suggested I fly up for some deer hunting. Okay, but where do I land? They would fix that up. He chartered our plane and told me to follow the river until he hollered. Only a week after we set this up they had already cleared a spread of mesquite larger than our Tampico field and marked it like Croyden, outside London. Weren't many trips like that, though. There was one bachelor in Tampico who had asked us all to dinner about the second night after we arrived. Servants by the dozen. Next day he arrives at the field in leather flying suit, shiny boots, helmet, the works. He would stay around all day and every so often I gave that fancy outfit a ride. We stuck to old lace boots and leftover army breeches, mostly. There was too much to do, even on rainy days, to get dressed up.

"If the sun was out we hauled passengers too, for $25 each. My share was half on top of

salary." Back home that year barnstormers were getting $3 a head and scratching for business.

"Some of our weekends got really busy with people coming back two or three times. One was a fellow named William van Fleet who had flown for the French during the war. I hooked up controls in front and checked him out. Good pilot so I told him to come out Sunday and get some flying in. He said he'd take his sister up first and wipe out the whole family. There was crowd that day so I offered Bill a quarter of everything we took in. Hell, I couldn't carry more than I already had, but he just wanted to fly and used what he made to throw a party. Van Fleet was refinery superintendent for one of the big oil outfits and told me he could turn those valves any way I wanted. Hottest gasoline I'd ever seen. We'd used five-gallon cans before he took over, then it was fifty-gallon drums, but we still had to pour it through a chamois. Best stuff Hissos ever got, anyway."

Slonnie and van Fleet were a decade ahead of Standard of New Jersey in developing special aviation fuel but extra horsepower never hurt, particularly when you were giving student lessons, a job Slonnie disliked at best. "Teaching was on our own. I think we charged them a thousand, double the price back home. I finally taught a couple but they didn't learn easily. One hefty fellow always showed up in a French Delage touring car with a wood-planked body like a fancy boat deck. Six cylinders and two carburetors. If one carb went out, which it did pretty often, he only had three cylinders but that didn't bother Guzman much. Nice guy but he couldn't fly. I gave him about ten hours but he never did land without me up front, holding the stick too. He'd just come down over

The Hotel Colon on the waterfront in Tampico, Mexico.

the edge of our dinky little field wide open.

"So we'd fly over to his ranch instead. Kids practiced cape work on baby bulls there and they showed me how. Bullfighting is the most graceful sport there is, plus you're playing with death. The two big names then, Belmonte and Mejias, were both Spaniards. Mejias was a doctor who told me: 'Hell, you make ten pesos a day rolling pills. Fight bulls, you make five thousand dollars a week.' He was never the fighter Belmonte was but better than the top Mexican boys then. And clever. Except that he thought I should learn to be a bullfighter. He figured flying airplanes was too dangerous. There weren't any American fighters then so I'd be a big drawing card. I'd seen too many boys carried out with holes in their sides to go for that. I just played at it on Guzman's ranch. Then Tampico had a big fight on New Year's Day, where amateurs took

on young bulls with their horns sawed off. Just the cape work. We drew for bulls and I got the first damn one, with everybody yelling, '*El piloto, el piloto!*' It was the high point of my toreador career. And the end.

"Everybody around Tampico knew us. Just walking to my hotel I'd have little kids running behind me, chanting '*El piloto.*' So I wasn't much surprised when this American oil field hand insisted on buying me a drink one night. He said: 'I was hauling payrolls down south, right?' No use saying no. So he asks why I couldn't carry one the other way by mistake and he'd handle the U.S. end with half for me. I just told him there were a couple of places I didn't care to visit. Atlanta maybe, or a place in Kansas named Leavenworth. Suggested he learn how to fly and get my job. He wouldn't have been the first guy to arrange his own hijacking.

With an airplane then you were propositioned for everything.

"Another boy, with a gold mine, asked what kind of airplane would lift the biggest load. You couldn't even take a twenty-dollar gold piece into the States legally, so his stuff would be worth twice as much up there. Told him Uncle Sam shot too straight. Pilots got shot at easily enough anyway, even when your nose was clean. Coming back from a money delivery one time, with nothing on board except a couple of pesos in my own pocket, the paymaster up front jumped a mile and yelled that we'd been hit. I'd felt the little jolt too and could see a hole in my left wing. When the fuel pressure began to drop and we smelled gasoline I figured the bullet had gone right through our pressurized tank, just in front of his seat. Hollered at him to find both holes and hold his thumbs over them. He could only find one but we landed okay. Afterwards we found that slug inside my tank, so spent it hadn't gone out the top. I always figured some guy simply took a potshot for fun.

"Everybody had some kind of gun. I was walking down the street in Tampico one night when a couple of guys with pistols stepped out of a doorway. Took my money and told me to keep walking. Which I did. That was common and border towns weren't much different. On an El Paso trip I was eating supper over in Juarez because the States were dry and anyway, Big Boy's served quail. A little, freckle-faced redhead asked if I wanted to make a lot of money. He was a gunman who'd been run out of the U.S. with some tough woman killer and wanted me to get a long-range plane and fly them back, way inside the border. 'How much would that cost?' He wouldn't drop it, no matter how many times I said no. Finally I told him, 'Look, maybe I say fifty grand but before we take off I send a wire. You don't want any part of me. Go away.' He kind of stared hard and told me I wouldn't live long.

"What I'd been doing up north was getting some cylinder banks which I knew were hotter than hell. I could buy them brand-new from a sergeant at Kelly Field cheap as used ones. Waiting around for those I spotted a cubby off the hangar stuffed full of this ship the locals had dubbed the 'Flying Dill Pickle.' Just a tube big enough to hold an OX-5 engine, with a four-bladed prop tucked inside the pipe too. For the exhaust end they welded in a chunk of cast iron which must have weighed 200 pounds. A fan jet, really, with stubby little wings and a riveted skin smooth as anything Boeing puts out now. The guy finally got it all together and managed maybe 10 MPH, all wound up. He was thinking ahead of his time but he was a little short of power."

The Standard with a Hisso in its nose had sufficient power to take off and fly clear across the state of Chihuahua, but most of them lacked the fuel capacity for even that modest jump. "A lot of our ships only carried thirty-five gallons, maybe three hours worth. And you had to release tank pressure to pour more gas in. Then you really needed two men to restart it. A Hisso had pretty high compression and those props were tricky to swing through alone, but it also had a booster magneto with a little crank. If you shot raw gas into your cylinders so the next one in the firing order could catch, then cranked that mag like hell, it might start when somebody just jiggled your prop. Not really pulling it through like our mechanics did.

"Flying alone one day I had to go down to fill up and was just starting to pour gas in from cans I'd stuck in the front cockpit when this head came out from behind a cactus. Pretty soon there were about twenty with not a stitch on, just long hair and big machetes. They didn't speak Spanish and I heard later the Mexican military wouldn't even chase them because you weren't likely to come back. Their favorite trick was peeling the skin off the soles of your feet and sending you off across the hot sand. But one was a pretty husky-looking guy so I decided to see if he could help start my engine.

"I'd already tried to pump up the three pounds of tank pressure, set the prop just right to catch a charge and run for the cockpit to hit my switch. That was no dice. Lost the booster charge again before I could get around the wing. Your prop had to be right in the six inches where the engine could catch. So I showed my new chum how to jiggle it a little while I cranked that booster. First try I bounced up and yelled '*vamos!*' just before hitting the switch so he would back off in time. Took five minutes to get everybody back when it didn't fire. The second shot didn't work either but they only backed off a couple of feet. Third time it caught and all you saw was dust from Indians leaving. They were still pretty curious though, so I stood out in front while it warmed up to keep them from sticking a head into the prop. The boy who had helped me kept edging closer and kind of put his head against my shoulder. Figured I was in for a wrestle but he was peeking into my pocket. I gave him that pack of cigarettes and the rest wanted some so I divided up a carton in my bag, to get them all around behind the wing. Couldn't let my pal down so he got the empty gas cans too and I got

the hell out of there, to go find Tampico.

"I never figured I was ever lost in my life, but there were times like that when I maybe didn't know for sure where I was right at the moment." No pilot could ever forget that Mexico was an easy, empty land when you flew in, but maybe hell to leave in good health if you had a forced landing. When a dollar-per-mile charter came up that became an acceptable risk.

"A couple of fellows wanted to go to Brownsville, clear over on the eastern edge of Texas. A cinch. I had the coast if I wanted to swing east and it was nearly 400 miles by road so the price was good. We had to land on the American side since Matamoros didn't have a field. I cleared the ship with our customs right away. The Mexicans closed on weekends but said they would clear me Sunday as a special favor.

"I went to Mexican customs Sunday but the head man was indisposed. Not having a very good understanding of international law and caring less I just cranked up and took off for Tampico. About halfway down the motor let off a couple of backfires and started cutting out. One of the two magnetos was gone for sure. You only lost 150 revs that way but it was liable to foul the other set of plugs and that meant no motor at all. It looked like I might not make the ranch where we had gassed going up, so I began to look for any place to put it down before the other mag quit. I'd wired Tampico I was leaving and they might even take a look, although you were mostly on your own. I waited beside the ship for one day, then figured I'd have to do it alone. There was a river somewhere south and you always find people living by water, but I never made that. All I had was a quart canteen of water, my old .45 army pistol, and a few chocolate bars. If I'd known I could have gotten water from any cactus. After four days I was getting pretty thirsty and only making three or four miles a day through those flatland thickets. All mesquite, cactus, snakes, and horned toads. Tried to shoot a cow with the pistol but they were wild as deer. I could make out cattle trails though and followed those south, hoping for a water hole. When I got too tired I'd just lie down in the shade of a mesquite at some trail junction.

"That saved me. I didn't even know I'd been found until I half-came to and saw this guy holding out a fancy china cup of goat's milk. When I really woke up sun was coming through a brass-rimmed porthole set into adobe. That house had thick mud walls and a thatched roof but the bed was European boudoir. This guy who found me was the son of an Italian sailor, shipwrecked along the coast, who'd married a local girl. They got most of their furnishings from other wrecked ships. Silver on the table and everything. While I was out they had taken my cordovan flying boots off and one fellow tried them on. Then he couldn't get out of them again so I had to leave barefoot. He was probably wearing them for spats twenty years later. They said an American ran the ranch where they all worked so we got on horses and rode twenty-five or thirty miles to this big, two-story house. Same place where I'd landed to gas on the way up.

"The foreman said Victoria was another seventy-five miles, but no roads. That sounded like a long way on a horse. Then I saw this brass, Model T radiator sticking out of a shed. Somebody had broken down going through and the foreman didn't know how to drive so it was just standing there. I put some gas in and cranked. When it started with a big clank you knew a rod bearing was shot. But he said if I could fix it, and would teach him how to drive, we could follow dry creek beds into town. I pulled one plug wire at a time to find the bad cylinder and left the spark plug for that one out so things sounded all right to him. We headed for Victoria on three and fortunately he didn't want to drive after all. I caught the Tampico train and got there ten days out of Brownsville, which beat my telegram.

"It turned out to be a good thing I'd gone down. Some Mexican general up in the States was trying to set up a revolution and disappeared the same morning I left without clearing customs. Their army assumed he was coming back with me and kept guards at the field in Tampico for days with orders to shoot us both on sight. By the time I showed up he'd been spotted though, still in the USA. So we took a spare ship up and put another mag on mine and flew them home. All their generals were like that.

"While I was lost an order had come through for me to testify back home in this court case they were putting on against the two owners, Winship and Hammond, about the way they had bought up the Standard factory. When I disappeared they were even accused of fixing my ship so I couldn't testify. Near as I could make that deal out, a fellow named Wild, who was supposed to be a pilot, had been designated by Nebraska Aircraft to bid in this factory lot of surplus Standards and the rest of the plant. I'd been leery of him the minute I saw his supposed FAI pilot's license with a new picture pasted in and the number added in ink. Apparently he had set up a bunch of alternate bids and then got to the gals who would open them. A diamond watch and fur coat were mentioned later, when Nebraska Aircraft got loads of stuff so cheap: wing ribs, longerons by the thousands, even whole ships. When their trial finally started nobody could be convicted because all these vital papers for the case had turned up missing. I was damn sure they had gone into Mexico in that footlocker on my first trip. Without records their trial never came to much but nobody had done anything to sabotage my airplane. It just quit.

"Actually, I was kind of sick of Mexico by then anyway. I'd picked up malaria after about nine months and the only cure then was cognac, quinine, and wait. When it started coming once a week, I decided to get the hell out of there for a cold climate. George Rihl took over the operation later and had a pretty good deal, mostly payrolls. I got about one wire a month, asking me to come back and fly for him, but I was sitting up in God's country and didn't want to get mixed up with Mexico or malaria again. On top of that, the Mexican government began talking about taking over all the oil companies. Stirring people up. Our hotel manager would tell us not to go outdoors next Monday. Things like that.

"Then a U.S. destroyer steamed up the Panuco river. Foreign warships could only stay twenty-four hours in a friendly port but we had a couple more just outside the three-mile limit so one did its day and another one steamed in. The Mexicans couldn't say boo. They did have a couple of wood-burning ships way down at Veracruz and sent those up to show these gringo dogs a thing or two, but the crews had to stop all along the coast to chop more wood so the whole deal blew over before

Slonnie (right) with Jimmy Angel, who later discovered the highest waterfalls in South America ("Angel Falls" in Brazil), and continued to resurface throughout Slonnie's flying career.

they ever saw Tampico.

"That's when I grabbed a train back to the States. Left Tittle and Jimmy Angel to fly those pesos." Angel would eventually move his flying career even further south, to Venezuela, where he became the first white man to see the highest waterfalls in the world, leaving his name on them. Angel was a resourceful pilot with a sense of high drama as well, ideal material for Latin American aviation. Slonnie said, "Jimmy came through Lincoln a little later in a Canuck and his carburetor was all shot. I had a spare one in the garage so he begged me to just let him have that carb and he'd send a brand-new one from Oklahoma City. Then I knew Jimmy was broke again. Years afterwards he was going back to Mexico with an Osage woman who had oil millions and they stopped in Fort Worth, where I was Chief Pilot. All dressed up. Claimed to have found some place where ancient

Indians had hidden their jewels in a cave. When I asked where the hell my Canuck carburetor was he said, 'Didn't you ever get that? Tell you what I'll do, Slonnie,' he says. He's going to send me a handful of diamonds and emeralds. He held both hands out, all cupped. That many. 'God,' he insisted, 'there are bushels of them down there.' You can imagine how many emeralds I ever saw."

Slonnie returned to Lincoln in 1921, the year General Billy Mitchell shocked all of America's admirals by sinking their sacred battleships (actually some which had been taken from Germany at the end of the war) with aerial bombs, just as he had promised. A Pershing report evaluating the potential of his upstart air arm against capital ships was (predictably) anti-aviation even so. Mitchell was both too outspoken and too often right about the future of military flying to suit old-line commanders. They eventually had to court-

martial him for stepping beyond the command chain before air arm advocates subsided a little.

Meanwhile Omaha, as Nebraska's largest city, hosted the second Pulitzer Trophy air race and got precisely six entries. One racer did set a new record for landplanes around a set course however, at just shy of 200 MPH. Giuseppe Bellanca, already a well-known airplane designer, visited Omaha by invitation but discovered his hosts had more enthusiasm for their proposed airplane factory than funds. Airplane instruments were still stuck on panels wherever they might fit in 1921, contributing to forty-nine fatalities from 114 accidents that year. Hollywood heroines just loved to pose with an airplane—on the ground—and the *Baltimore Sun* bought the first plane to do newspaper work exclusively. A Canuck, of course. Eddie Stinson wrecked his Ansaldo in San Luis Potosi, trying to start a Juarez-Mexico City airline.

Statisticians insisted a family of four could live on $10 a week in the United States of 1921 but Slonnie, fresh from the Mexican gold run, didn't intend to try. He returned to Lincoln in October with a lifelong tendency to say *"Por nada,"* because it sounded more polite than "You're welcome," no particular desire to visit Mexico again, and sufficient cash to live until he found his next job in aviation. This would be based on leftover, wartime planes again, needless to say, even as late as the end of 1921. The new Douglas Cloudster, first airplane able to lift a useful load equal to its own weight, went looking for buyers that year. Only seventy-two new airplanes had been built for civilian use during all of 1920, since the best surplus ships only cost $1,500, while used Jennies went for pocket change. Not to mention that vast store of ex-Standard parts left behind in Lincoln when Nebraska Aircraft went south.

Slonnie said, "When I first got back Vic Juvenau, who'd learned to fly in France, knew that Nebraska Aircraft was up for auction. He figured seventeen thousand would take it and his father would put up the cash. I looked around and said, 'Let's take this over.' There were enough airplanes already assembled to make the seventeen back immediately. Just wheel them out to the field, rig them up, and go. But a local guy named Ray Page got in ahead of us. He started a company named Lincoln Standard and called his airplanes the same thing, except that the first ones were still Tourabouts, just like we took to Mexico. I began flying for Page, testing his ships, in the fall of '21. When we had to add them up later, I figured I'd put in 800 hours around Mexico, what with passengers to haul, payrolls, even a couple of mail runs, plus air shows and charters. There had been plenty of flying to do down there, that's for sure."

October 1921   Flying hours: 1,330:29

Chapter 6

Stunt Flying

"I always stayed ahead of my airplane."

Slonnie returned home to find much more than just a winning university football team in the Nebraska capital. Lincoln had become the undisputed center of Midwest aeronautics, according to Ray Page at least. After all, once Page purchased Nebraska Aircraft's assets and all those Standard spares, he owned the third-largest airplane-producing operation in America. Many private-plane builders would settle in middle America, including Beech and Piper, but Page was there first. In 1922 Walter Beech was only a rawboned pilot of specials like *Miss Wichita*, flying with mixed success against a show crew Page called his factory team, starring Slonnie, whenever needed. "Rest of the time I just barnstormed," he said. "A couple of us took mechanics and headed for warmer weather that first winter. You couldn't get anybody out to take a ride at thirty below. Trying to make a buck but no steady contract for a couple of years. Page already had Otto Timm for testing too."

Timm was an "Early Bird"—one who flew even before WW I—and a canny, proven designer who built his first airplane as a boy and taught himself to fly it in 1911. Following the war he built a racing job which won in its West Coast debut

with Page watching. He asked Timm to take charge of Lincoln Standard but Otto didn't want to go back to Nebraska. All that snow. Page finally convinced him. Their unsorted supplies of airplane parts were still in Havelock, just outside Lincoln, when one pilot came in with his old Standard held together by baling wire. The future factory couldn't help him yet so he decided to come back later, even though Timm told him not to fly that plane again. The man went up anyway, swooped down low, and the wings fell off. They had to get organized fast. Page had a great deal of material he didn't even know about. Some parts were sufficient to build fifty thousand airplanes, others not enough for a dozen.

Timm sorted things out and converted all their planes to Hisso engines. The company was still called Nebraska Aircraft right at first but became Lincoln Standard in short order. The planes were all called that anyway, so pilots wouldn't confuse them with eastern-built Standards which had a bad habit of catching fire. Page didn't even need hangars when they started. Planes were assembled, tested, and flown right out by some customer. At the best of times they might have three or four tied down out on the meadow.

Testing was something less than the prescribed military routine of their day, where pilots watched at least eight dials while monitoring

The handbill for the Big Aerial Circus touring air show. Included in its highlights is the D VII Fokker, a nimble German fighter aircraft made famous in WWI.

oscillation, longitudinal stability, stick forces, and wing loading (according to their Air Service handbook, at least). Slonnie said, "I just took one up and read a couple of engine instruments. Maybe it was wing-heavy, so you tightened some turnbuckles and took it up again. It wasn't a hard plane to put together right. Stand out front and you saw which wing bay should be pulled up. I don't know why the top wing was so high above the fuselage, though. Except that the fellow who designed it liked them that way. Every 'LS,' which is what we all called the Lincoln Standards, was going to be heavy on the controls anyway, compared to a Canuck.

"I don't think I flew every plane Page built but I flew damn near all of them. Other stuff too, like that little Sport. A South Dakota kid had designed and built this baby plane with a three-cylinder Anzani motor. Cracked it up trying to learn how to fly so he came down and rebuilt it at our factory. Hell, you could put it in the living room, but it was a good-flying little job. We put it together one day and it flew all right so we stuck it into the show that same afternoon. Down in Kansas I flew the Sport right through an old Army hangar for one show. Page cataloged it as a Lincoln Sport for a while. The big Ansaldo I tried was something else. A Frenchman had traded it to Page on an LS but I'll never know how he flew it as far as Lincoln. Our best mechanic finally got that big inline-six motor going though so I flew around for about thirty minutes. Of course loads of people were out to see this great big thing fly. I came in and they were are all lined up across the field, waving me off. I looked overboard and one boy is holding up a wheel. I'd lost the left one on takeoff.

That was the only one-wheel landing I ever made.

"Mostly it was straight demonstration. Customer would come in and want an airplane so I'd put a couple in the front seat to show it would carry them. Then go up alone for the loop, Immelmann, spin, and roll to prove it would stick together. I got $250 on every sale, plus salary sometimes and passenger percentage, but it was a hell of a big month if we sold half a dozen airplanes." Early Page ads also offered either an airplane or an aeroplane—same plane in both photos—which you could put together yourself at their field. Slonnie recalled one such buyer. "He was going to run in his own motor on this big parking area behind the factory to save our fee. I went out to check and he was fast asleep so I slipped underneath. The bottom of an LS was aluminum and I started pounding. He woke up

hollering, cut the switch, and ran inside to claim the bearings were all shot."

Up to 1924 that sleeper's airplane would have been an LS Tourabout, a three-place machine they sold for $2,000. Page claimed every one would climb to 10,000 feet in a quarter hour and reach 90 MPH under most favorable conditions, yet land at only 35 MPH. To turn that into an LS5, Timm kept the same four wing panels but widened the forward fuselage, something like the Nebraska Aircraft Cruiser. Empty it weighed only 1,735 pounds, seventy-five more than a Tourabout, but an LS5 would lift a 720-pound load, in part because tank capacity had been reduced, cutting range to only 300 miles. The LS5 cost $2,950, pretty good for a five-seater then. An emergency kit, sold with each plane, included two spare valve assemblies, gaskets, several lengths of radiator hose and eight hose

An Ansaldo of the type in which Slonnie made his only one-wheel landing.

The baby Sport (not designed by LS) that Slonnie flew in various air shows is flanked by two
Lincoln Standards.

clamps, six feet of ignition cable, oil and fuel strainers, a set of magneto bushes and eight spare plugs, plus extra careburetor float and tools. Those defined operations of their day. The firm's brochure touted real windows and rich maroon leather upholstery, not to mention gray, fire-resistant paint and exhaust pipes aimed straight up to reduce noise.

Timm insisted the stressed-plywood fuselage was a new design, noting steel landing gear in particular. Before long an Air Coach model was added as well. Its cabin was elaborately finished in mahogany and rich gray fabric while soundproofing supposedly allowed conversation in normal tones. Aviation was already straining to attract the businessman buyer. A wider nose made this Coach a little harder to land but Slonnie said, "It wasn't so bad. Just lean out of the rear cockpit a little more. The Tourabout really had too much wing anyway, so the bigger planes had plenty of surface left. That's why the one we called a Speedster flew a little bit better yet. It had four of the lower Tourabout wing panels, which were shorter."

Like all good designers then, Timm flew his own airplanes. He said, "I used to keep my hand in, making test flights for the fun of it. I was just about to fly one Tourabout when these two kids showed up. They had never flown but jumped right into the front cockpit. I tumbled it around a bit but Bud Gurney and Charles Lindbergh loved it. Lindbergh had a few lessons with us after that and took to it right away." The man destined to turn cow-pasture aviation into a booming business with one Atlantic crossing didn't solo in Lincoln, however. He couldn't afford a bond for the plane, which Page required of every student.

Barely a year later this same school wanted business badly enough to offer a complete set of free Standard parts to any student completing a pilot's course in Lincoln. By the late twenties Lincoln Aeronautical Institute, a successor to the Page school, claimed all it took to fly was to be clean-limbed, clear-eyed, and steady of hand. Their instructors, all high-class gentlemen with enough cultural education, according to the school brochure, would provide the rest, out over those rolling prairies where emergency landings were always safe. Slonnie, like Timm, avoided teaching, although neither thought twice about test flights. Timm admitted, "I put a Speedster into the ground too, just like Slonnie did. In my case the engine quit cold on takeoff so I cocked it into a fence and didn't hurt myself any."

Slonnie's slip was more vivid, as breathless local newspapers rushed to report. "Local flyer crashes from 800 feet—has miraculous escape," was one story. Another went: "His plane was smashed to splinters but the pilot was little the worse for his experience. The fall was probably the most sensational ever witnessed in Lincoln." Quoting Page, a journalist explained: "The pilot was testing a brand-new airplane when he turned it over and flew upside down. The ship was nose-heavy and went into a spiral which Sloniger was able to straighten out just before he hit the ground." One writer concluded: "He simply lost control of the lifting apparatus," adding, "fortunately Sloniger was driving alone at the time."

It was the only flying incident in a thirty-eight-year career which put Slonnie into a hospital and then only briefly, to repair a broken nose. He admitted: "I just clobbered that one. Came out of

the dive okay and mushed into the ground, knocking off my landing gear so it slid along on the belly. Could still have gotten away with it, except for a broken prop, but when I stuck my head up to see what's out front, there's a great big golf bunker right ahead. That's what got me in trouble. We had a witty little wing walker with the air show named McCarthy. He claimed that when he saw me going in I was yelling, 'Fore, fore!'"

Gurney, later a fine stunt pilot himself, said, "Behind that apparent wildness Slonnie had a steady head. He knew stunting so well he could do it with a flair. True acrobatic pilots go at it a different way, know what their plane will do and put the flourishes in to make it an act. I don't really know what made a good one. Reactions maybe. But Slonnie was *the* stunt pilot of our area, star of Page's show. He usually wore a bright red stocking on his head with the rest streaming out like a tassle. The girls just plain fell over."

All so-called stunt flying had begun with a level airplane and a man clambering around on it. He was Ormer Locklear who climbed out of his WW I cockpit to tighten a radiator cap and discovered he liked the exercise better than teaching cadets how to fly. Slonnie said, "I only ran into Locklear when he first started changing planes for money. He was number one at that." The ideal wing walker, as these aerial strollers were called, weighed less than 120 pounds, so most were air-mad kids trading stunt time for flying instruction. Air shows actually lost more parachutists than guys who hung by their knees from an axle spreader bar. Pilots who flew the pickup planes for them were invariably billed as skilled, ex-war aces although many "Never wanted to get their ship past a

Jerrold E Sloniger Collection

Slonnie crashed this LS Speedster on a golf course after it failed to come out of a dive during a demonstration flight. This airplane was the first and last of its kind built. Slonnie walked away with a broken nose.

twenty-degree bank," as Slonnie described them.

Top acrobatic pilots ate regularly, even though they told one another, a man was old in their game at thirty. Most were a mix of old rodeo hand, hot-rodder, and gypsy, men who knew all about fear and the control of it—then forgot the subject. Slonnie's love of the game had something to do with his single status as he neared thirty, although he had met the girl he intended to marry only a few weeks before wiping out the Speedster. He quickly discovered, however, that any kind of flying, never mind acrobatics, would make it difficult to win her father over. "I met Johnny out at Capital Beach where they had a big dance floor," he remembered. "She gave me a dance and that was about it."

Katherine John Everett, oldest daughter of a third-generation doctor in Lincoln who had expected a son, explaining her middle name, added details. "There was a boy I had dated before who took me to that dance. These two dashing young men came in and waved to my date, motioning him over, but he just danced the other way. I asked who they were and he said nobody I'd want to meet. But I certainly did. Finally he took me over and introduced us. Next morning Slonnie called and asked for a date. He would only be in town for short periods but he sent flowers at least once a week and my father thought that was overdoing things a little. Dad liked him personally but we'd only been going together about a month when Slonnie asked me to marry him and Dad just exploded. Aviation and ten years older besides. So we went together another eight years."

The Everetts were establishment Lincoln but their home was hardly stuffy. Johnny's mother rarely knew whether her husband was bringing a star of the Orpheum circuit or the university football team home for supper. On one hand he loved light music and kept a tuned piano on each of their home's three floors, on the other he and his private hospital provided free care to all Nebraska players. It was only unconventional within proper Midwest limits of course. Slonnie said, "Blackjack Pershing was a great friend and Doc Everett always had a supply of good whiskey so Pershing would be over pretty often. Doc told him I was a flyer one day and Pershing told me there was no future to flying. Army pilots would never be anything but the eyes of the ground men. Of course he was the old military expert but I told him we'd both live to see another world war and the side which controlled the air would win it. Doc didn't think a punk, ex-2nd Lieutenant should tell a General of the Armies how to fight a war. He kept his temper but I could tell he didn't like it much and figured that would be my last date."

It wasn't. Johnny liked handsome, attentive men with minds of their own, although it never occurred to her to cross her father directly. "I certainly never flew before we were married," she said, "because I had promised my father I wouldn't. Dad was very proud of Slonnie and after we married he acted as if he had invented aviation for Slonnie's express use, but he worried always. Slonnie would dive over our house whenever he got back to town. I knew any ship that low was him but my father had the house insured against falling airplanes. Dad had said I couldn't date him two nights in succession, and I had promised to finish school anyway, but I never thought I'd marry anybody else. I did learn about all sides of flying in the meantime. Out in Topeka, Kansas, once, their parachute act for that

day had never jumped before. Just as the plane was ready to go up he ran over and asked me to take his mother's address and his watch. If the parachute didn't open I could send it to her. It opened though."

Most air shows still managed nicely without fancy equipment. Recycled wartime designs like the LS were a cheap favorite for aerial circus work, although new models were finally beginning to push in too, particularly for the sports-pilot market. These were much less cumbersome, even when powered by the dated Curtiss OX-5 engine or its OXX successor. Bellanca actually built the first U.S. monoplane with enclosed cabin in mid-1922, backed at last by Omaha businessmen jealous of all that activity in Lincoln. Slonnie recalled it as "A very good-performing ship for five, but the cabin was so wide he had his pilot sitting over left of the keel longeron, where he was blind to the right. He couldn't have seen out either side from the middle. It was an awful light job so it flew well but Bellanca went back east soon after that so maybe Nebraska wasn't quite ready for cabin monoplanes."

Speed was one clear index of a good airplane, and a certain LS dubbed the "natural wing" had that. This was the plane Slonnie generally flew for Page. "Just a three-seat Lincoln Standard job, really, but one of the best-flying airplanes Page ever built. Balanced just right, by chance. We called it natural wing because there was no color in the dope. I always used it to carry wing walkers and as pickup ship for plane changes." Its performance led them to stage a few races for the crowds too.

"A fellow named Beeler Blevins had developed this act where he'd amble out on our field in the farmer hat, chewing an oat straw. They'd push him back into the crowd a couple of times. But one

airplane would be running and Blevins would sneak into that and off he'd go. One wing down, nose straight up, the announcer hollering for him to come back. He had his own plane for hopping passengers as well and one day he told me he didn't think that natural wing was any faster than his LS. Well, I'd tested his before he bought it so I bet ten bucks the natural wing was faster. Next day they put us into the show—'Pilots Argue about Their Airplanes.' I took the outside lane around a couple of pylon points we'd figured out and won my ten bucks, but it was an attraction so we left it in. Usually start three ships, with me on the outside. I'd stick pretty close to the bunch until the third time around, then pour the coal to this baby and win. I had a skinny little toothpick prop on it too, which let my motor turn a little faster than those with a fatter, standard propeller.

"When I had to do the pickup on a plane change I needed that extra acceleration to overtake the ship below and take a boy off his top wing right in front of the crowd, not way off somewhere. Your pickup pilot did all the work on plane changes. Tell the other guy to hold his ship steady and I'd get the wing walker off. He had a rope and handle attached to the top wing of the lower ship so I'd bring a rope ladder hanging under my plane down and try to give the guy two or three rungs. Dick Hazelrig was my 190-pound wing walker originally. He was a mechanic who wanted to do the plane change but I had to keep my knee braced against the cockpit side to hold a wing level with this great big guy out at the end. One time he was hanging from a trapeze below my landing gear and didn't come up and didn't come up. I hadn't felt a jerk so I didn't think I'd lost

The Lincoln Standard 5, an Otto Timm rebuild with the pilot in back and a half-cabin over the front cockpit where four passengers could sit in facing pairs. Pictured from left to right are Slonnie, Augie Pedlar, and Ray Page.

him. Finally he climbs into the front cockpit sucking a finger. Been down there trying to light a cigarette in a sixty-mile wind. None of those boys used any safety harness at all. McCarthy would even stand on his head on the top wing. Just hook one arm over the leading edge to grab hold of a strut." Pilots figured wing walkers were sure to go early.

"There were always air shows somewhere on a weekend so we saw all the new tricks. A couple of wrestlers worked up this idea where the pilot would let a guy down at the end of a rope to drop off on the ground. I thought that was the craziest thing I ever saw but when you stopped to think, that Standard landed at less than forty. He'd hang with his legs crossed until his feet touched, then let himself down the rope and slide on his back. One wrestler told me 'Hell, it's easier than working the ring.' Next weekend a couple of our mechanics wanted to do it too."

By mid-summer, 1922, Page people were billing themselves as the biggest aggregation of planes and plane stars in America, to hype a weekend in Tarkio, Missouri, and that had to mean a good parachute act. The Page troop had Lt. Charles Hardin, introduced as the man who jumped with six chutes and had a patent on the idea. His main rival was Sgt. Encile Chambers, credited with the world's altitude record for parachute jumps, the man who dropped a thousand feet before opening his bag. Slonnie said, "They didn't have pack chutes then, just a big round ball tied out at the first wing strut, near the leading edge. You kind of throttled back when he climbed out, to keep the blast down. Then he grabbed the ball, sat backward, and fell off the wing before

Slonnie and a passenger make the tricky climb to board an LS 5.

The personnel of Page's Aerial Pageant, including Charles Hardin as a parachute jumper, Eyer Sloniger, designer Otto Timm, and Bud Gurney, a close friend of Charles Lindbergh and the man who later brought Slonnie to Robertson Aircraft Corp.

When they landed this guy was hollering, 'He didn't loop the loop,' so I told Ray to stick him in my ship and gave him a loop all right. Speed Holman held the world's loop record for a while, later on, and told me he had to use bungee cord to take the pressure off his control stick. Run it all on the throttle and just help along with the stick. He didn't have the strength to keep pulling that ship around a thousand times. And Speed was no midget. With our old Standards you mostly did a sort of descending series anyway, losing altitude every loop because they didn't have enough power, unless the motor was really hot. Coming off the top of one, even with the dive, I started the next one maybe 300 feet lower. Look out after a while and decide to quit after the next one. Maybe ninety percent of the people watching were parked outside the fence anyway. They could see the show just as well without paying a dollar. We made our money on rides. Usually Page tried to tie in with somebody like the American Legion for a percentage of ticket sales. Sometimes we'd share a weekend with some auto show and give away a three-seater LS Tourabout as gate prize for someboy who paid to get in."

With business booming Page hired an advance man with a busy imagination. Both Bill Langley and his wife Bab came straight from New York newspaper desks. Bill was called the press agent. Fifty dollars a week and the soda pop concession. When he found a good pasture he made a deal with the farmer and hunted up his well, if any. Removed the handle. No water? More soda pop sales. Bab drove their old Model T ahead of the show troop so pilots would have rides to town. When Bill drove the crew in one day, two

pulling the string. Gurney was billed as the youngest parachute jumper in America and he'd go in those three-chute races for the ground which Page advertised. I even had to do a double jump once. We'd advertised this big multiple jump and Hardin was injured. His wife Kathryn was supposed to be a jumper too. But I took her up and she wouldn't get out because the field was right next to a river. She

kept saying she couldn't swim.

"Another show, we were busier than hell, hopping passengers with me taking them up for stunt rides after the acrobatics, and two more boys giving regular rides. Some drunk wanted a loop but I was in the air and three or four more waiting so Page stuck him in another plane. Figured the fellow was so drunk it would be enough to dive and pull up hard.

got out to walk before they were halfway there. Here they were, risking their necks in what he called baling-wire jobs (where the public couldn't hear), but too scared to ride with him in the Ford.

Slonnie had already dreamed up a name for their show before Langley arrived: Page's Aerial Pageant. New towns would be well-primed with full-page descriptions of these flying fools in the local paper, illustrated with drawings of tumbling biplanes and photos of the stars. A typical story might begin: "It is hard for us mortals who trot around on terra firma to imagine the thrill of satisfaction the daredevil craves who daily laughs at death in an attempt to satisfy the curiosity of the multitudes." It couldn't have been easy for pilots to live up to that kind of publicity.

The *St. Joseph Gazette* in Missouri insisted, "These superhumans seem not to care for money and aren't payed (sic) the huge sums many suppose." This was also the article which first presented the tale of Sloniger being used by awed superiors in France as a teaser pilot, occupying the enemy while slower pilots discharged their solemn duty in eliminating the enemy. Slonnie only snorted. "That was a publicity man's idea for sure. There was no such thing as a teaser." This same story continued, more accurately, that "His loops were over when he settled calmly to the field with no more tremor than you or I would work up in hopping across the smallest creek." The feature closed with several paragraphs listing stunt pilots and wing walkers killed at their game.

If the papers faltered Langley was ready with a good tale. "During one trip with Slonnie," he recalled, "he asked if I had ever done an outside loop. When I said no, he warned me to hold tight

and damned if we didn't do one. Barely. When we leveled off and I returned partially to normal I tapped him on the shoulder and asked, have you ever done an outside loop before. His answer was a laconic, 'Nope.'" Slonnie's response to this story is a fair indication of his flying approach versus his reputation. He said flatly, "I never tried an outside loop in my life." Indeed, the first one recorded in America wouldn't be performed for several more years. He was game for most other tricks though. One Page promotion promised Eyer Sloniger would light the sky for miles around, in a plane illuminated by flares. The pilot said, "I had done very little night flying at all then. The only thing we could try was to wire an airplane with kits from the fireworks people. Put somebody in the front seat to punch the button when I hollered, so things would all start sparkling and burning. It was a beautiful sight." Particularly from the cockpit of a wood and cotton airplane when you didn't wear a chute, but Page still had that ample stock of LS parts to get rid of.

Timm was beginning to realize there was little chance for brand-new airplane types from Lincoln Standard until those spares were used up. He discovered early that Page was really more intrigued with exhibitions than new designs. He never liked to spend much money and that included not wanting to pay Timm at times. Page had far more fun with a plane he billed as "the captured enemy Fokker." This German-built fighter soon had a corner on what the newspapers called "handsome silver trophies" and Slonnie described more accurately as, "all those tin cups."

He liked the airplane itself though, saying, "That Fokker D VII was a honey, a real honey. It was an attraction too, the only one in the Midwest for

sure. Of course I could only take one passenger up at a time in the Fokker, even after Timm rebuilt it with a front cockpit, so stunt rides had to cost double. After we got that Fokker I never lost another stunt meet, but that was just the way it flew, even using a Hisso engine just like the Standard. The German engine it came with was all burned out so we put in a 150 HP Hisso. There was no airplane to touch it until I got into the *Mystery Ship* a lot later. There were no special stunt planes then. We could only do so much upside-down flying in any of them before the float dropped down in our carburetors and the motor quit. You had to give yourself plenty of time to roll over and let some more gasoline flow in." Lincoln papers loved his new plane too, claiming: "This little Fokker had proved a hit wherever it was flown. It was fast, agile and in the hands of a clever pilot like Sloniger, performed wonderful evolutions." Promoting a Nebraska State Fair appearance, one paper said: "Eyer Sloniger in his Fokker biplane does everything a creative mind can think of."

Actually, getting the plane was no more than a lucky draw by Page. Slonnie said, "Ray didn't go out and buy one, really. It just came with a bunch of other stuff he bid on." Some 140 of these D VII model Fokkers reached America after the war, for Air Service evaluation in theory, since a D VII outperformed every other WW I airplane, built by either side. U.S. military pilots liked them so much most were still being flown regularly in the late twenties, until spares began to wear really thin. The original D VII had faltered badly during initial Imperial German trials, in fact. Baron Manfred von Richthofen said it was directionally unstable. And it was, although other German military evaluators,

Jerrold E. Sloniger Collection

Ray Page bought a Fokker D VII, and Otto Timm added a front cockpit to permit stunt rides at double the going price. Slonnie (in the rear cockpit) called the Fokker one of the two or three best-handling planes he ever flew. The Fokker was so good in stunts that other pilots refused to compete with Slonnie.

vacationing in Berlin on Tony Fokker's supply of wine and women, hadn't noticed. Overnight the designer welded in several extra inches of fuselage length and even Richthofen approved, although he would be shot down before flying one in combat. It was a remarkably clean airplane and despite much later caveats about ground loop tendency in restored Fokkers, Page's stunt ace felt, "It wasn't bad for that time. Taxi on the throttle and use a lot of rudder. If you wanted to get in close, a mechanic would grab one wing and hold it so you could turn sharp around him. Ours was painted gold, a snappy little job. Besides, it was one of the few airplanes then which could always loop without losing altitude.

"Tarkio, Missouri, was the first meet where I flew it and we got the acrobatic prize first time out. FAI rules said you had to stay above a certain height in official stunt contests but when I got through up there I'd bring the ship right down over the center of the field and pull it over into a loop from fifty feet. You didn't want to miss, working that close to the ground. Usually the formal contests were three days, with $75 day money for acrobatics. With that Fokker, if some guy would roll, I'd roll twice. Next day nobody would start. They figured, why the hell burn gas. Give me the money. So the organizers would say: 'Nobody is going to compete against you and we got a crowd out here. Will you just give us a show?' Sure. For $75 I'd do twenty minutes down low.

"St. Jo was one of those demos. We were all up in my room after dinner with a bottle of corn and inevitably got into a crap game. But before that, in Detroit, Page had brought along a girl he later married. Shooting craps and I made twelve straight passes, doubling after each one. Got into the hundreds and this gal wailed she couldn't pay. I told her, 'Listen, as long as I don't quit shooting I'll fall off eventually and the score is clear.' Think that impressed Ray. After I made seven or eight passes in St. Jo, he figures I'm a natural at craps. Which I wasn't. But we did get to where I was rolling fifteen hundred. Actually, I wanted the natural wing. Make some money carrying two at a time on stunt rides. But he wouldn't lay for the natural so I put a fast price of three thousand on the Fokker and rolled double or nothing. That's how I won a D VII.

"Owned it about a year and won some of those cups marked 'National Champion.' It was like wrestling. One national Champion over here and another in the far corner." Even so, when asked about this era decades later, Lindbergh still remembered clearly, "I was a flying student in Lincoln and he was an accomplished pilot. He was an acrobatic pilot of great skill." The Fokker had race-winning speed as well. More precisely, it was maneuverable enough to outfly quicker planes around the pylons. Slonnie said, "The St. Jo race was something like 100 miles against the clock, around a triangular course. Walter Beech brought a special Swallow with the wings chopped off and a Hisso in the nose instead of an OX-5. I'd just won the Fokker and we were out for blood. There was real money —$750 for first when we usually broke our necks for a damn tin cup.

"Couple of days earlier we'd gone up for qualifying trials but hell, the minimum speed was set low enough that we got our plain Lincoln Standards in too. Beech was qualifying when we got to the field so we cranked up the Fokker, but he didn't land afterwards. I'm on the back leg when I saw his reflection in the little glass windshield. Pacing me. So I started shoving the motor up gently. I couldn't give it the gun all at once or he'd see the black smoke. When I landed our boys wanted to know, 'What about it?' Well, his special was a hell of a lot faster but the catch was, that clipped-wing Swallow wasn't near as maneuverable. In the hotel that night Walt was telling this good-looking Serbian gal behind the desk how he was going to whip Sloniger the next day. Caught me listening and his face got all red. 'Tell you what Walter,' I said, 'You're going to have to pat that baby on the back all the way around and a Hisso won't take that. Besides, I'm going to pull one of those wings off and fly as a monoplane. I haven't decided which one yet.' Actually, Fokker spars went clear through so I could never take a wing off that plane but he hit the ceiling. Claimed I couldn't do that. I'd entered as a biplane and by God, I'd fly as a biplane. He went off looking for the judges and we just let him stew.

"Got all ready to fly next day and mine wouldn't start. We had two damn good mechanics though and one said, 'Let's get another carb on there fast.' I had to go within an hour. You had a diving start across the line and then did five laps alone, for time. Beech was about halfway through, making big wide turns at the pylons, before I got going. After the first turn where I stayed in tight I could see I was gaining but then my damn motor stuttered on the backstretch. She picked up, missed again, but I figured to hold on. Hell, motors were cheap. Just made the last lap and did a chandelle to come around and land but that prop stopped over the wires and I landed dead stick. Left the Fokker in a field and started walking back, not feeling too happy until I saw Page running towards me with the biggest grin. He patted me and said, 'You won it all.'

"I could beat Walter Beech any day. Another time in Missouri, we had an efficiency race, depending on speed and the load you carried. We left the ramp with just McCarthy and a little parachute jumper up front, like the two in his plane. But we loaded in two more guys at the end of the runway, on their knees with their heads in the first pair's laps. We ran about the same speed but I had four passengers to his two and he got out of that Laird madder than hell. Then the Fokker got hit with hail. Poor thing looked like a polka-dot dress after I cut little cotton disks and pasted them over the holes. I didn't want to recover and sold it back to Page for 1,100 bucks. He put new cloth on and when some movie company wanted a camera plane for *Hell's Angels* he for sure got a good price."

The Fokker had already proved especially handy at jobs like flying exposed photo plates for newspapers. The *Chicago Examiner* had been first with airborne photos from newsbreaks in 1921, part of its running battle with the *Tribune*. The Post Office owned most of America's longer-distance airplanes then so the *Examiner* talked President Warren Harding out of an executive order which let them use one. Before long Slonnie was flying for the *Trib*. "Those jobs came through Page. The Fokker would go about five hours at 100, good range when most OX-5 jobs cruised around 85. Even before the Fokker, newspapers would wire everybody for bids on some job. Ray always figured mileage, added my expenses, and doubled the bill. No guarantee. I had to get the pictures in to be paid. If I lost a motor we were out of luck but those old Hissos rolled right along if you didn't crowd them.

"We never missed a delivery but they might have a slower, backup plane behind me on big jobs. The Fokker had them all whipped for speed over the distance. Give another paper a head start if his photographer got to the field first and still beat them in. At one Indy 500 two planes got away ahead of me but we were first into Chicago. I'd leave before an event finished and be sitting in the cockpit with the motor running when the photographer dashed up. The thing we had to watch for—another paper would try to slip you their films if you had the fast airplane. I was coached to know our boys. First trip to Indy I landed in the infield but they chased me out because my plane would block the view. Moved about a mile away, to a little pasture. That Fokker only needed a quarter-mile to take off. Half a mile was a big deal. Only saw the Indy race itself twice and it was about as thrilling as traffic on the freeway.

"At the Chicago end the *Trib* got me permission to land in a park right next to the Loop. Told Page to get a couple of big sheets and pin them to the ground where I was supposed to land. Got in about dusk but he had a can of gasoline too. I could see the flame and smoke showed where the wind was. Taxied over close, right up to a police car where a guy from the *Trib* grabbed those plates and jumped in with the Chief. Off they went with the siren on like Capone was right out in front. Page turned me around and I flew out to 63rd and Cicero, the Chicago field. Rolled in, cooled the motor off, tied down, and the *Trib* had a cab

waiting. In front of the hotel there was a guy selling papers with a picture of the Indy winner. Paid a nickel for pictures I'd brought in maybe two hours before.

"When it was the Kentucky Derby I didn't see any of the race. Too short. For the Gibbons-Carpentier fight I was using an LS5. A guy in Chicago had bought two planes from us to fly pictures and sent two pilots down to be checked out. I don't think one of them had ever been closer to an airplane than the passenger seat. The other was a wartime pilot who was only a little sloppy. I told Page we couldn't let that first guy out, he didn't know which rudder to kick. So they hired me to fly one ship back and help out for a couple of months. The fight was down at Michigan City, Indiana. It was drizzling and I was sitting inside the hangar while a mechanic warmed up the ship when this Cadillac rolls up, carrying the nicest-looking, rosy-cheeked fellow, plus a sort of sharp-looking little guy, a big, rough-faced bozo, and a blond babe. The sharpy came over and told me: 'Look, we can't get to the fight. Roads are bumper to bumper around the end of the lake and it's starting in an hour.' I explained I was on charter and had to leave right after the fight, or sooner if there was a knockout. Couldn't be waiting for passengers going back.

"He didn't care. 'If I got them down there, they'd get back okay. How much?' I said $200 but it could just as well have been $2,000. He pulled out a roll bigger than my pocket and peeled off two bills. The chubby one with a diamond stickpin the size of a dime just smiled. Never said a word. When I got over Michigan City there were seven or eight other planes about four miles out of town at the regular

field. Well hell, I'd landed on a lot of sand down in Mexico when we didn't have anything else so I swung back to a good solid beach on the lake front, maybe two blocks from the arena, and we walked to the fight. Standing in line together to get in and my pal pulls a pint from his pocket. Offers me a drink out in front of God and everybody, with Prohibition on. I pointed to a policeman right behind us but the big, gaunt guy just says, 'To hell with him,' and the cop walks away.

"I had promised, if they got to the beach before I cranked up they could go home with me too. Put all four in the front and flew back to Chicago. My hangar was a hangout for the motor-cycle patrols who could put their bikes up on the stand and run their wheels instead of riding around out in the cold. When I pulled up this one sergeant wants to know who my friends are. I didn't have any idea. Turns out Dion O'Banion was the smiling fellow and Hymie Weiss, the mob banker, was the sharpy who did all the talking. The hawk-faced one was Dapper Dan McCarty. The toughest people around Chicago but just as polite to me as you could want."

Slonnie always got along well with policemen. In Lincoln, on a later occasion, he took a motorcycle patrolman up over the football stadium during a big university game. Naturally, they spun down for a better look. "We found out later everybody in the bowl was watching us and nobody saw the only touchdown of the game. I was really working sort of part-time for Page by then, when I delivered a ship to this outfit about to start an airline between Kansas City and Wichita. Ed Bern, the guy behind it, offered me a job paying more money than Page gave me because he would cut me in on the profits. There never were any, of course. But I stayed in Kansas a while to fly for them." His aerial circus days were drawing to a close.

In his autobiography Charles Lindbergh commented on various pilots from Lincoln, identifying each by an initial. Included is this: "S. was a wonderful acrobatic pilot but he held no reserve for something going wrong; sooner or later he'd probably be killed." Could Slonnie have been 'S'? "I don't have any idea," he said, "but I was the only one doing much acrobatic flying around Lincoln when Lindbergh started there. If he did mean me—I sure fooled him on that one. I always stayed ahead of my airplane. I think that's why I lived so long. I knew what I could do personally up there and after a little practice, that was it. I was ready to go that far." By 1925 he was also ready to figure the odds a little differently. Slonnie couldn't know Kansas City Airways would involve him in a pioneering night flight, but he was more than ready to admit the time had come to try a steadier side of the flying game than aerial pageants—regular passenger schedules in place of pickup stunt flying.

July 1925   Flying hours: 3,000

Chapter 7

Sweet Corn and Pineapples

"He handled his airplane like he had been born with it stuck on his tail."

America's pilot population was sternly winnowed out during aviation's first postwar decade, well before flying became an accepted profession. Most who tried barnstorming became discouraged long ere 1925. Even the natural, meaning unworried, pilots among them were likely to fly a very limited while before choosing more stable mid-twenties professions, once they married. A few might still fly on the occasional weekend; the rest bowed to family fears.

Slonnie was a clear exception, already fixed on a cockpit career by the time he made the swap from stunt champ to hopeful airline pilot with a pioneer Midwest air service.

He said, "Ed Bern was a salesman for sure. He sold this fellow some trucks, then promoted him for $30,000 to start an airline between Kansas City and Wichita, the main city and the oil town. Bought two LS5s in Lincoln, plus a cabin job which was a real turkey. I took one plane down to them and he gave me this sales talk. I'd get $100 a week and share in the profits. Hotels were maybe $2.50 then, a damn good dinner a buck. Anyway, most of the people who wanted an airplane ride had already been up."

When Congress passed the Kelly Act in early 1925, it looked as if private mail contractors might hope to make some money at last, flying approved Post Office routes taken over from the Army. Henry Ford went into this new business early and Wall Street money followed. Ford's Detroit airline already boasted pilot uniforms and metal cabin airplanes designed by Stout.

Bern's Kansas City Airways would be more modest. He announced the first flight for June 1, 1925, although they weren't sure yet which town would be at the other end. Either Tulsa or Wichita. Bern promised that the first of eleven airplanes ordered by his company would be making regular passenger runs from the first day. Instead Bern put his cabin plane on view at the Kansas City airport that day and mailed 2,500 trial-flight invitations to local luminaries. A surprising number accepted, perhaps soothed by the news that every passenger could be covered by a $10,000 life insurance policy for only ten percent above the fare of ten cents per mile.

Unfortunately, KC Airways was a little premature. Airlines in Europe only survived on heavy government subsidies. Aeromarine hadn't even been able to make a profit between dry Miami and drinking Nassau in 1920. It would be mid-1926 before Western was launched as the first U.S. airline destined to be permanent.

The land which invented airplanes only managed to sell $100,000 worth—six planes and twenty-one engines—for export in an especially good month of 1925. The Russians might plan a China run to cross the Gobi Desert in twelve hours, versus 160 by car, but Wichita was almost too close to Kansas City's three airfields, including a mail field north of town where Bern's operation was based. He clearly hoped that passengers would quickly be followed by a KC-Chicago mail contract, when bids provided for by the Kelly Act were opened. Meanwhile, Bern's company stated clearly that its business was not barnstorming, even though visitors would also be given rides over Kansas City at $2.50 a person. They published a schedule too, skipping Tulsa. One ship would leave Kansas City at eight each morning, stopping in Topeka at nine and Emporia at ten. The return flight would leave Wichita at four P.M. Fare was $30 one way, $55 round trip. That included taxi service into town at both ends, by arrangement with Yellow Cab. Flight time of two and a half hours was five quicker than the train.

All this publicity and planning failed to attract a single Wichita passenger for the first return flight, so it terminated in Emporia. Worse, this truncated inaugural carried only KC Airways employees. Wichita's newspaper was quickly lined up to promise that the second trip would definitely

Jerrold E. Sloniger Collection

Ed Bern bought these airplanes from Ray Page and hired Slonnie to fly them for Kansas City Airways off grass fields like this one.

reach their town, whether it had return passengers or not.

Slonnie didn't actually fly that first complete trip until July 7. Bern's publicity described their lone aviator as a former experimental pilot with 3,000 air hours to his credit. No mention of acrobatic cups. The sole passenger for that first complete round trip in their open, four-seat, front cockpit was a *KC Star* reporter who filed from Wichita to tell his readers that "an eager crowd was waiting when the air stage from Kansas City glided down out of the sun-swept sky." He rated his first flight as fairly smooth and even enjoyed pounding along at a low elevation over the river, right after takeoff.

Slonnie knew better. "Kansas City starts on a hill just across that river. When I had to take off south, with any load, I couldn't climb over the city so we had to turn right and go under the north bridge to get out."

This passenger was well primed. Admitting that he had looked for helmets and other air paraphernalia, he passed on Bern's explanation: This was a businessman's conveyance. Nobody needed a uniform to do a day's business in Wichita. Just wear a straw hat. Slonnie agreed. "We never flew higher than a couple of thousand feet, following the Rand McNally map for railroads and towns. No wind in the cockpit, really, so you would open a map, smoke, hold the stick with your knees. We knew where all the airfields were without a map. Then check the nearest smokestack for wind and land."

Editorial Wichita wrote enthusiastically that they were now on the air map of America. Slonnie said, "They did have a pretty good grass

A free cab ride from the city center to the airfield was
included in the KC Airways fare.

field there, even a couple of hangars. Hell of a lot
better than the cut-alfalfa field in KC. We added
our own, open-face hangar with room to get two
planes in. Anybody my size could pick up the tail of
an LS and wheel it out. I made the one run each
day easy and never remember four passengers all at
once. Half the time I went alone but maybe
Wichita had sold a ticket coming back. There were
no ticket offices so we went to all the hotels and
you could buy a ticket through them. Or just come
on out to the field and ask if we were flying that
day. We always had space, that's for damn sure.
Bern never did try for that mail contract but he had
a deal with the state of Kansas. If we operated three
months they would give us a lifetime exclusive on
that route."

This promise was never tested, despite a
sharp fare cut at the end of July. Ads read: "Three
hours to Kansas City, 220 miles for only $20. This
is the opportunity you have waited for. Time is
Money—Save It." Apparently there weren't many
people eager to save some time.

When they ran out of willing reporters, a
ride was offered to two officers of the KC Business
and Professional Women's Club. One of them
gushed that she "never knew how to appreciate the
earth she lived upon until she viewed it from the
air." Kansas City's Postmaster and wife received a
free round trip too. He told the press it was his
chance to get firsthand information on flying
conditions so that he could write and talk about
aviation and know what he was saying. He added
that despite the fact they returned after dark there
had been no trouble whatsoever. Of course the pair
weren't told they had provided a minor footnote to
Midwest air history.

Bob Cochran stands by the Timm-modified cabin LS which Ed Bern bought from Ray Page.

"There was a rodeo on in Wichita," Slonnie said, "so we went to that and didn't get back to the plane until dusk. I called Bern and told him to go out to North Field in KC with a couple of cans of gasoline. Put them on the downwind side of my landing. We kind of navigated home by the stars until I picked up the glow from KC. The plane had no landing lights so I sort of felt for the ground. Bern always claimed this was the first night flight with passengers. Of course they weren't paying passengers."

Freight did them a bit more good. KC Airways announced that an Emporia booster had picked a basket of tomatoes, sweet corn, and cabbage from his garden and delivered it to the *KC Star* office two hours later for auction. "Mr. Bern vouched for the fact that this was the first shipment of corn by an air route in the United States," as the paper put it. The promoter also managed to mention that his planes had covered 3,600 miles with no arrival or departure more than four minutes late. Bern spoke bravely of a new airplane which would carry seven in the cabin but this was ominously offset by a note that ships would cease to fly on Saturdays or Sundays. Furthermore, they would abandon air service entirely unless Wichita supported it. Free Yellow Cab rides were dropped.

Bern soon shifted his aim to a route through Parsons, Kansas, to Tulsa and Dallas, discontinuing what they still called the Wichita Division. The paper there conceded, at the end of July: "As the situation stands now, KC Airways is ready to quit Wichita, although they are in aviation to stay." Imminent airmail contracts would only go to established lines and Wichita had barely a week to decide whether it would throw its

air future into the ash can. Bern still promised to fly to any town in Kansas City's trade area where they received support.

Officially the next move was a search for new airline territories but Slonnie said, "We left to barnstorm again, really. I told Ed you could still make a lot in Mexico if we could get the planes across, so we went on tour with two ships, still hauling passengers for $2.50. Any clerk could afford that. But we couldn't get the planes cleared into Mexico. Instead Bern sold the Laredo Chamber of Commerce this idea of advertising them as the gateway to Mexico.

The name KC Airways had become Airway Transportation Company and KC was painted off the ships' flanks. Bern also kept his Mexico option open with a proposed route from Kansas City to Tampico, a trip of only fourteen hours. The year closed with no takers, although American aviation was almost ready to take off properly, at long last.

Aviation, calling itself the oldest American aeronautical magazine, reported proudly in 1925 that the court martial of General Billy Mitchell for pushing military aviation too bluntly had aroused more general interest than any military tribunal since Dreyfus. Common people were becoming aware of flight. The Packard car company already boasted ten years of aviation engine experience and airmail not only moved three times faster than regular letters, it was surer as well. When the Postmaster General signed contracts for the first five private mail routes it marked government acceptance of flying, even though KC Airways hadn't survived to benefit.

Slonnie returned to Lincoln and promptly

met another man who needed a pilot. "Jack Story's family had bought this Alexander Eaglerock airplane for him," Slonnie said, "so I went up to Omaha to fly the thing. A typical job would be throwing $3,000 worth of checks out to launch a new theater. Anybody who picked one up could cash it for the face value. About three were $100, which Jack stuck in his pocket. He only tossed out the one- and two-dollar kind.

"I did teach him to fly that Eagle Rock though, and next time I ran into Story he was flying for National Air Transport. Got a Travel Air into a snowstorm on the NAT run and just stepped out. Let the mail go. Jack quit flying, finally. Announced air shows for a long time, then he was a rodeo announcer. There were a lot of people like him around aviation in the twenties."

Regular pilots were always looking for profitable new fields. For Slonnie that meant Flint, Michigan, in 1926. "We'd gone up there the first time because they had advertised a big show and Page might sell an airplane or carry some passengers. It was a good meet and Bill Malloska, who had cut-rate gas stations all over town, was giving free gasoline to everybody. A couple of us stayed on, until the weather turned bad. Then worked south. But you wanted a base like Flint where General Motors was."

A local flyer there recalled that Slonnie and his friend responded to his call for help, handling demand for rides. "Day after day. Pile them in, circle the field, dump them out." As this Flint man explained, "They were heroes to almost everyone except themselves. Stories seldom mentioned the punishment dealt out to stomachs or backsides. And Slonnie was the best of them. A

Hisso Standard was clumsiness personified in the hands of most pilots but even with legs and arms stiff, tired, and aching, he handled his airplane like he had been born with it stuck on his tail."

Historians would eventually decide that this 1926 season marked the effective end for flying circuses and barnstorming in America, although a few, including Slonnie, could still do quite well, hopping passengers, by picking their towns carefully. That year did produce the first enclosed plane, called a Monocoupe, ignoring a general conviction that every pilot must have wind on his face. And Edsel Ford's boat designer took a very close look indeed at a three-engined Fokker transport that year and sketched the famous Ford Trimotor, a corrugated metal indestructible which pilots dubbed the "Tin Goose."

Pratt & Whitney built a nine-cylinder radial engine and Daniel Guggenheim donated $2.5 million to civil aviation because there was so much still to be done in this new field. America had uncounted cow pastures but fewer than 100 registered airfields and any working pilot was sure to know or meet almost every other good flyer in any given year.

Slonnie first met Speed Holman in Michigan. "I was flying out of Iona and you didn't even need to sell tickets. They were lined up in fours like a squad front. Two of us timed it so I could empty my ship and reload while he was halfway around, then get out of the way. About the fourth day it started raining. I'm sitting there to unload and load without even an umbrella. So I just shut that motor off and went into the tent.

"While we're waiting, in come a couple of two-place Standards. We had passenger rights for

A Flint, Michigan, filling station chain became an ideal promotional tie-in for Lincoln Standard. LS planes were painted with the name "Lincoln Oils" in exchange for free gas and oil.

that show so when I said to hell with sitting under a shower bath, we tried to buy tickets back. About a hundred wouldn't play so I asked these new boys if they wanted to haul some passengers. This great big tall fellow said, 'Hell yes.' I was getting five bucks. If he brought the tickets back I'd pay him the five. He wanted to give me part but I was just trying to keep those people quiet. When it got dark we went into the hotel and Speed Holman came up for a drink. He had about $65 worth of tickets and told me, 'You know, I had less than five bucks in my pocket when I came in here and about ten gallons in my ship.' Here we'd been up in the clouds making plenty and he had the worst airplane...I wouldn't have sat in the damn thing, let alone fly it. But he sure could. One of the best stunt pilots I ever knew.

"We stayed pretty close to Flint as long as we could. Malloska was an old carnival man who said if we'd paint "Lincoln Oils" on those ships—that was the name of his chain and it tied right in with Lincoln Standards—why, he'd give us all the gas and oil we needed. Paint it on. The ships won't weigh any more."

Barnstorming still looked easier than flying the first civilian airmail routes. Lindbergh was a pioneer of those, carrying letters for Robertson, which had won the St. Louis-Chicago bid for a route numbered Contract Air Mail (CAM) 2. Flying aids were marginal. Transcontinental airways lighting was only completed in August 1926. Airmail time between California and New York would be reduced to two days.

Up to then around-the-clock mail had only gone clear across the country once, while Slonnie was still in Mexico. And only because a

pilot named Jack Knight had a very special sort of guts. Congressmen of that day doubted that any airplane could move at night and the Post Office found itself committed to a single, make-or-break trial run in the depths of winter, long before guide beacons were put into place.

A pair of lumbering de Havilland biplanes started from each coast but one westbound plane promptly fell out with mechanical trouble and the second was stopped by snow in Chicago, far short of its proposed turnaround in Omaha. One eastbound pilot crashed to his death and the last airplane aloft was flown by a man in deep pain, his ribs tightly taped from an earlier crash.

Knight was only scheduled for the Cheyenne-Omaha leg, over terrain he knew, but engine trouble delayed him in North Platte until midnight. Exhausted, the pilot struggled into Omaha to discover his relief was cozy in Chicago, grounded by the same blizzard Knight now chose to battle over totally strange country in the dark. He followed a road map to Des Moines but the snow was too deep to land. When he got to Iowa City the storm was so thick they had closed the field and gone home. By the time he buzzed a watchman awake to light one weak floodlight, Knight was flying on dry fuel tanks and raw nerve. But he pushed his mail on into Chicago where a fresh pilot could take it east, completing the first transcontinental mail run in America.

Slonnie, who would be flying winter mail himself by the end of 1927, never mentioned his drinking buddy without adding, as if it were part of the man's name, "Jack Knight, the guy who saved the night mail."

In 1926 Orville Wright said airplanes were

developing faster than he'd ever expected, yet ninety percent of all trained pilots were out of work and seeking jobs in other fields by playing down their flying experience. Pilots remained soldiers of dubious fortune to most and only 5,800-odd passengers would fly over all U.S. routes combined during 1926. Still, mail pilots were carrying 40,000 pounds a month and meeting better than ninety-three percent of their schedules.

The Air Commerce Act, law since May, amounted to the first time a private industry had sought government oversight for its own good. Airplanes came under government control if they crossed a state line and every new design must seek an air-worthiness certificate. Even pilots would need a license now and have to start keeping a logbook record of their time aloft. Slonnie only escaped the regulators that first winter because he was flying hard all over the hinterlands.

"Mostly piecework," he explained. "Charters for Lincoln Standard and that stuff. When spring came it was back to Flint and full-time flying. We had two LS5s again, with a boy named Bob Cochrane to do the teaching if there was some." Slonnie took the specials. "Like that wedding out of Lansing. Young couple and the preacher up front with a second witness. The preacher rode backwards so I could read his lips, since I was supposed to be a witness too. Throttle way back to cut a little of the motor noise out."

Thirty years later fellow pilots still talked about a landing from this same era. Slonnie said, "I had four riflemen going to some kind of shoot and it was raining like hell, so I'm right down over the treetops when the old Hisso just quit. There wasn't an open piece of ground anywhere and I couldn't

Slonnie promoted the Buhl airplane with its dependable Wright J-5 Whirlwind engine to fly the Dole mainland-to-Hawaii race. The *Miss Doran* was lost in the Pacific with pilot Augie Pedlar, his navigator, and Mildred Doran (niece of owner of Lincoln Oils, for whom the plane was named) aboard.

glide far, being that low. So I took it down and just before we touched, went into a stall and eased it into the treetops. The wings broke but there wasn't a scratch on any of us. Except that the four up front got all excited and every time they moved the ship would settle a little further and tip more. We were still a good fifty feet up so I hollered to hold on. Told them to get out onto a limb which had punched through the wing, one at a time. Each guy worked down to the ground before the next one went. We were only a quarter-mile from some highway but never did go back for the ship."

Slonnie and a new partner, a very aviation-minded city councilman named Lovejoy, had a growing fleet for 1927. "He already owned one Waco, bought another and finally the two LS5s from Page. Offered me a very good deal to take over the four and do charters. We didn't have a name. Or need one. The Waco was a new job, lighter and much nicer handling. It only carried two but when you didn't have many passengers it was cheaper to fly. Main thing, the Waco had a self-starter which worked off of compressed air."

It was a popular time to expand in aviation. The *New York Times* gave every inch of its first five pages in the Sunday edition of May 22, 1927, to one pilot, a quiet kid named Charles Lindbergh who made it possible for American flying to turn its biggest single corner since the Wrights. When the whole world went wild over this modest hero, the king of Hawaiian pineapples decided to reap a little glory too, offering a $25,000 prize for the first mainland-to-Hawaii flight. James Dole hoped the New York-Paris flyer would enter, so he added a second prize of $10,000 and made it an outright race within set dates.

Hawaii had talked statehood ever since becoming a territory in 1898 and Dole was frankly seeking attention for this cause. Some thirty pilots captured immediate headlines by announcing entries for the August 1927 event, although a $100 registration fee reduced that number by half. William Randolph Hearst told his son on the west coast to buy a duplicate of the Lindbergh Ryan and see that it won. Ryan pleaded no time to prepare another ship so Hearst bought a Lockheed Vega. This plane would become the propeller equivalent of later corporate biz-jets, although the new firm's prototype was lost over the Pacific in this same Dole race.

Slonnie pointed out, "Lindbergh had quite a time getting his airplane too, and had to settle for the Ryan. I'd never thought of trying that Paris deal because it wasn't as well publicized." Once Lindbergh succeeded, funds became available for almost any ocean crossing. Slonnie was offered backing from his hometown initially. Two men, unofficially representing the Chamber of Commerce, understood that Sloniger would be happy to fly for Lincoln, Nebraska, and glad to turn any prize money he might receive over to the city.

Their original plans ran to a new airplane and Wright Whirlwind motor, the same power plant Lindbergh had used. Slonnie settled on a Buhl, a buxom, five-place cabin airplane costing $12,700. The only multi-wing plane in the Dole race, it carried Approved Type Certificate (ATC) number 12 as one of the first designs certified under the new Air Commerce Act.

"A Buhl was the only thing we could get in time," Slonnie said. "Put extra tanks in the cabin, right under the wing, and the navigator could ride in back. Communicate with the pilot by a voice tube or string pulley. A sesquiplane, really, not a biplane. There were some very funny airplanes in that Dole deal. Some only ran down the runway, dropped a wing, and spun around. The Buhl was pretty heavy but it had a Wright motor."

This was the famous, nine-cylinder radial known as their J-5 model, a synthesis of the best engine knowledge available. Wright demand boomed once Lindbergh's engine performed so smoothly, although the company had originally refused to risk its name on an unknown mail pilot.

When Lincoln, Nebraska, fell through as a sponsor, Bill Malloska became prime backer, figuring the red, white, and blue of his Lincoln Oil Company should grace the Dole winner. "He put up the cash," Slonnie said. "Then one of the people working for his gas station chain was the father of Mildred Doran, a school teacher Malloska had kind of adopted, and she wanted to go along."

Easily the most-photographed contestant at the eventual California start, Miss Doran was actually only another in a long line of paying over-ocean passengers. At least she had the distinction of riding in an airplane named for herself. On June 4, 1927, the *Flint Daily Journal* headline read: "Girl to Make Journey with Local Airman." The story added that the twenty-two-year-old girl was learning to be a pilot and looking forward eagerly to a Pacific journey, following a nonstop trip from Flint to San Francisco, to test their airplane.

That was very much Slonnie's idea, although he was out of the Dole Race, following the flip of a coin. Slonnie's recollection of losing his Pacific chance was barbed. "Augie Pedlar had been my wing walker out of Lincoln and those

Slonnie (right) with Bill Atwell (left), a second pilot in Flint, Michigan, and H.F. "Pop" Morris (center), who was always referred to by Slonnie as "just the ticket-taker" for their Page passenger hops.

fellows usually rode along when we moved from one show to another. They'd hook up controls in the front cockpit and you'd let them practice. He finally picked up enough time to go out west and get a flying job. But he cracked up pretty badly and was very crippled, with one leg turned way under. An awful nice guy though, who'd heard about my Buhl and was hanging around Flint, where we had this 'Pop' Morris who was just a ticket taker for the show."

Souvenir cards with a photo of the pilot and a place for filling in altitude reached on your flight called the operation "H. F. Morris Aerial Navigators," however, indicating Pop had more say than Slonnie wanted to remember.

"My ship was due in a week or so," he continued, "when the papers got hold of Morris and asked who would fly it. He told them he didn't know. 'Guess we'd just have to flip for that.' When I heard about this I said, 'Flip hell. That's my airplane.' Morris said the newspaper boys were coming just to watch us flip. I yelled, 'Tell them we couldn't wait and I won.'

"Pedlar didn't want to go for that. He said I'd fly the rest of my life but he was all crippled up. Couldn't ever make enough money flying but he might get something out of this Dole deal to start a little business. Hell, Morris had already told the papers and I couldn't talk Pedlar out of it. It was my half dollar and I never flipped it on anything else. It ended up on Johnny's charm bracelet and Pedlar flew the ship."

We have to wonder if Slonnie was really that determined to go—or how much influence he had over the crew of this Buhl. He doubted if Pedlar had 200 hours in his log and more than one

reporter around the Oakland carnival start wondered if the Pacific Ocean was really the best place to practice your first instrument flight.

"Pedlar didn't give that plane a fair shot," Slonnie said. "I told him to fill it full of gas and fly clear to the coast in one hop. Get a feel of what it would do and how much fuel it needed. But Malloska, with his carnival ideas, rode out to California in *Miss Doran* and they had to keep landing for some more publicity."

At twenty-four Pedlar was the youngest pilot in the Dole Race. The oldest was still in his thirties although several had flown in the war. Slonnie, just thirty-one, would have been among the most experienced. Instead Cy Knope, hired to navigate the Buhl, was easily the best-trained person on board *Miss Doran*. Reporters noted that radio beacons were strung clear across the Pacific on Navy ships, without adding that only four starters carried receivers and only one, Art Goebel in a Travel Air, had two-way radio to call for help. Two Pacific flights had already lifted off that 7,000-foot runway on Bay Farm Island by Oakland anyway, before 50,000 gathered to watch these racers try. Experienced crews in both made it to Hawaii but left before the starting date and couldn't claim Dole's money.

Those who dared question the qualifications of certain racers were told Lindbergh had no overwater time before his flight either. And anyway, the 2,439-mile Dole distance was only two-thirds as long as his trip. True, but Lindbergh could divert to land at several points along the way, whereas there wasn't a rock between Oakland and Honolulu.

An overstrained power plant would be one

Jerrold E Sloniger Collection

Johnny Sloniger's charm bracelet with the half-dollar that was flipped to select the Dole Race pilot, a *Hindenburg* crew pin, Quiet Birdmen wings, and various other memories.

theory for the disappearance of the *Miss Doran*. In an interview shortly after the plane was reported lost, Slonnie said cautiously, "Pedlar's luck would save the plane. He had come through before when the cards were stacked against him and I know he will be rescued."

The Buhl had gotten off fairly easily, unlike some starters, but returned within an hour, suffering spark plug troubles. They dumped some fuel to lighten the landing load, fixed their ship, and Knope begged the school teacher, still smart and jaunty in her Sam Brown belt, to stay behind. Reporters remembered that a rather grim-faced girl refused and Pedlar was too busy to care. Later, nobody could be sure his tanks had been topped up again, to replace that jettisoned gas.

Another guess at their fate, and that of other lost airplanes, was based on the recent discovery that a pilot without visual reference has an inherent spiral tendency. This could have caught the inexperienced Pedlar unawares during the long night. Some who did arrive spoke of spinning down, often more than once, and only barely regaining control before they hit the water. What's more, carburetor ice always lurked some 700 miles off the California coast, where warm air meets the Humboldt current. Pedlar might not have known the trick of blowing the carb throat clear by backfiring his engine.

In the end, ten pilots lost their lives before or during this so-called Pineapple Derby and the U.S. Navy mounted the costliest search in aviation history without finding any of them.

The race itself, won by Art Goebel of Hollywood flying fame, with Hawaiian Marty Jensen second, had turned from gala to what headlines insisted was a major blow to aviation. Dole was blamed for leading young aviators astray, although he hadn't formulated the actual flying rules. Cutting corners to meet a race-start deadline was a more likely culprit.

Aviation itself was too firmly established at last to fall in the face of one tragedy. The Duponts were willing to back Bellanca in the plane-building business while several passenger lines ordered Ford Trimotors to offer the appeal of an enclosed cabin, even if it meant the noisiest airplane ride in the land. A Ford only cost $42,000, without toilet facilities, although film star Wallace Beery had one in his private Travel Air.

There was another rush to break records. A pair of Germans took the endurance mark away from America with a flight lasting better than fifty-two hours without refueling, whereas Jimmy Doolittle of the U.S. became the first man to do an outside loop. Air races drew good crowds once again and flying schools flourished. Radio station KOA in Denver broadcast fifteen minutes of flight instruction every Friday night while Boston University offered an evening course in Aviation Business, a suggestion that barnstorming was a thing of the past.

The Robertson brothers in St. Louis continued to operate CAM 2. Lindbergh didn't return after that Paris flight and Bud Gurney, the second Robertson pilot, couldn't fly both ways alone. St. Louis-Chicago mail still moved in rebuilt de Havilland biplanes, powered by surplus Liberty engines, a combination even the parsimonious military had retired following a last Marine sortie in Nicaragua.

"Most boys didn't like to fly at night," Slonnie said, "but I told Gurney I'd help over the winter of '27. Then I got intrigued. Didn't make as much from the mail as on your own and you had to go out when it was your turn, whether you felt like flying or not, but I wanted weather experience and liked the idea of ground help. Plus the fact, it was a year-around job and we did get about $450 a month when I began.

"We'd kept the four planes in Michigan though and I meant to go back there. Then, just about the time I got to St. Louis, Cochrane came in over the wires at Flint with one of the airplanes and didn't he set it right on top of another one. Wiped out half my fleet right there, so I stayed on

the mail."

To fly mail across state lines you needed a pilot's license. Slonnie grabbed his on the way through Lincoln. "On such and such a day some inspector would hit town and people would bring their planes from all over." Nebraska would boast 235 pilots by late 1927, highest percentage by population between the Mississippi and Pacific. And every single one of them believed any pilot who could land without killing himself had proved the point.

Inspectors were not so sure. Slonnie said, "The guy they sent to Lincoln wouldn't go up with me. Didn't know if I could fly. So I used one of Page's planes to make some figure eights and a spot landing. We had a written test too, with a separate one for aviation mechanics. That covered rigging and engines but I'd learned it all in ground school. Those were the first licenses I ever had, except for that Fédération Aéronautique Internationale thing we needed to fly races."

Pilots were also required to estimate hours already flown, as a start on logbooks they would never again escape. Few of the older men had bothered to keep track since leaving the Army. The national average was estimated to be around 2,000 hours for war-trained pilots who had flown whenever they could since 1917, whereas Lindbergh had built up 1,800 on the mail run in just over a year. Slonnie estimated his total at 6,000 by late 1927.

"I'd been flying damn near every day it wasn't stormy for ten years. Some days we'd start at nine and fly until dark, with a sandwich in the airplane for lunch. So I figured 600 a year. I think that was actually conservative."

When he joined Robertson, operating

CAM 2 with one flight a day each way, five days a week—stops in Peoria and Springfield—business was only a little better than it had been in the earliest weeks when they lost $100 a day and a couple of part-time post office clerks could handle the loads without strain. Registered mail remained the windfall. Washington paid by the pound and that brass padlock on the registered bag was a bonus.

Maintaining Robertson's first-year reliability record of ninety-eight percent, despite winter weather, would be basic to business survival. Robertson was hardly a large firm, even among generally modest U.S. mail lines in 1927. Boeing and National Air Transport both operated trunk runs with ten feeder routes and every major city in the land except New Orleans had air mail service, while Robertson struggled along its single route. Western Air actually built its own weather stations, with aid from the Guggenheim fund.

Robertson pilots would have welcomed those. Gurney recalled, "Twenty-seven/eight was a bad winter. Seemed like a forced landing a week. You faced that, as well as jumping from a sick ship three or four times a year." Hardly surprising that Robertson lost pilots to lines like NAT, which paid twice as much. Gurney only added, "I was very careful about introducing Slonnie to the de Havilland. Told him, there is your airplane and Chicago is up there. It was our standard check-out."

Before they could afford better flying equipment Robertson had to use up a vast de Havilland store, with planes stacked around "like corncobs," as Slonnie put it. "They didn't bother much about airframe maintenance and gave me a brand-new airplane of my own right away. Those wartime Liberty engines were much bigger than the Hisso but not long-lived. If you cracked a wing spar or something fairly serious they wouldn't even bother to change the engine. Just roll out another plane and paint your name on that."

When Slonnie arrived on October 1, 1927, St. Louis was eager to call itself one of the most air-minded cities in America. Drive out to the suburb of Bridgeton and you found a floodlit field named for Albert Ball Lambert, early aviation booster and balloon man. They already had both boundary and searchlights, while the Robertson Flying School brochure insisted their home base would soon rival Le Bourget, Croyden, or Templehof, Europe's finest.

The new mail pilot wasn't quite so internationally impressed as all that. He still had to climb into standard leather flying suit, knee-high boots, helmet, elbow-length gauntlets, and face mask, all fur-lined, before every winter flight to Chicago in a Liberty-DH. But E. L. Sloniger was finally a part of scheduled, commercial aviation, a field which would occupy him for another quarter-century and more.

October 1927   Flying hours: 6,000

Chapter 8

Biplanes to Trimotors

"The only guy who ever smelled his way into an airport."

Aviation historians would eventually assure each other that a single flight in May 1927 turned an entire nation into aviation fans overnight. It would be more accurate to say that Charles Lindbergh's famous solo to Paris lit a slow fuse which sputtered into 1928 before U.S. aerial transport took off properly. At Robertson in St. Louis, the winter of '27/'28 was history before the brothers who owned the struggling airmail line could even contemplate new equipment, however keen they might be to promote aviation. Bill Robertson, the prime mover, came from an aviation family and soon had the name of Anglum, a one-store town alongside the airfield, changed to Robertson, Missouri. Four of eleven children organized and/or flew the mail. Their sister sewed patches on ripped wings.

Slonnie had switched from gypsy barnstormer to the airmail—soon to be airline—cockpit with his usual well-timed luck. "Almost as soon as I got to St. Louis," he said, "operations managers for both Boeing and NAT came over. 'Hey, how about flying for us instead?' I told them I was just down there temporarily. Maybe I wouldn't feel like flying whatever day of the week they told me to. In the end I was glad I stayed with Robertson. It wasn't long before we became one of the main blocks when American Airlines was formed and went way out in front of everybody. Besides, there were only three of us flying for Robertson to start with. Boeing or NAT—hell, there were a jillion of you."

Robertson's own brochure, advertising "the oldest flying school in the Middle West" (a point Page might have debated) claimed there were 900 firms in aviation, 141 of them building airplanes in the U.S. alone. Twenty-two airmail routes served sixty-three major American cities and provided Robertson's best hope, although their own route, Contract Air Mail 2, had a doubtful future at best during the first winter Slonnie spent flying their open mail planes. Pilots did get paid whether the brothers went short or not, but it was still a marginal operation. Slonnie said, "Our St. Louis office was a shack really. Little, two-room place for Frank and Bill Robertson, Doll McTeague, the only woman, and George Rutledge, who was office boy when I first went to work there and later the longest-serving man with American Airlines. They all worked across the road from a tin hangar where nobody ever oiled the sliding-door wheels so you had to push them open with a little donkey tractor. When it was time to fly, two or three boys would slip a dolly under your tail skid and push on the wing struts to wheel that plane out.

"St. Louis had a long, thin field then with hangars on the north side and a good-size creek on the south. No ground rules. Just angle around if the wind was a little too strong from one side, take your turn, and land. The schools made a lot of traffic but we didn't leave St. Louis with the mail until about six in the evening. We always had to land in Springfield and Peoria both, in case there was anything to pick up. At least they had the whole route lighted by the time I got there. As easy as day flying in good weather. You could see three beacons ahead. One every ten miles and a landing field in some pasture about every third beacon, which flashed white and green. White and red meant no landing. Those fields were all a quarter-section, so it gave you half a mile each way.

"There was no dispatcher. You knew when you were due out. Drop by the field an hour ahead of time. Chat. Get in your airplane, which had been warmed up for you. The mail man would come down in his Model T and throw the bags in. Chicago was up there, sort of north-northwest. Like driving home. You know which lighted road is your own turnoff. We bought a Rand McNally road map and drew a line on it. That gave railroads and towns, plus where your line crossed some river." The first Department of Commerce airways strip map was barely three months old and didn't cover Slonnie's route anyway. "Our schedule was based

The Robertson Aircraft team in front of a DH-4 mail plane, ex-government, with Liberty engine. Charles Lindbergh had been their first pilot. The sole female employee was Doll McTeague, standing at the center below the propeller with Frank Robertson, one of the two founding brothers, to her right. Slonnie is the second man on her left.

on 90 MPH plus two landings. We were always on time unless the mail truck blew a tire. Southbound out of Chicago depended on the transcontinental mail arriving with our stuff to take down.

"Chicago's new airport was out at 63rd and Cicero. Right south of it was the Argo starch factory with seven tall chimneys they had lighted for us. Stay near those and you'd find the field. One trip, when visibility was not too good, I got onto the canal which ran along there, staying on the west side because I was already below the level of those stacks to the east. I'm keeping this canal under my right arm and smelled the city dump which was about five miles too far up. I'd overshot in the murk so I turned around and followed the canal back until I smelled starch, picked up the Argo lights, and landed. When I apologized for being ten minutes late our station manager claimed I was the only guy who ever smelled his way into an airport. If we put that mail in on time it saved a whole business day over the train. Money for those big guys could draw interest an extra day. Most of the airmail was bank clearances." Pilots seldom discussed their close ones but they knew the ground people kept score. Was that Robertson or Northwest which got into Chicago on a bad day?

"We didn't get a hangar in Chicago at first, but there was a Post Office right on the field. We'd taxi to their vacant lot, across this little bridge over a ditch. Our station man would hold one wing to keep you from dropping a wheel off the narrow place."

Cicero, the new municipal field where fourteen mail runs converged from 5,000 miles of airways every day, was not only larger than its predecessor Maywood's half a square mile, it even boasted a single, cinder runway some 2,600 feet long. Slonnie said, "Municipal had a revolving beacon too but no field lights right at first. Your mechanic spotted his man and called for the generator to power floodlights at one end of that runway. You had to land pretty close to those, they didn't shine out very far. Get real near the ground and use landing lights bolted to a spar under your bottom wing. But they ran off batteries so you only used them at the every end. The DH wasn't really a very nice airplane but it had a fairly good gliding range if you misjudged those runway floods a little bit. Otherwise we just had running lights at the end of each wing. On a clear night you could see them quite a ways. That's how I knew when some guy was trying the old trick of turning his running lights off as soon as he saw you and trying to sneak up behind to fire his landing lights. They were pretty powerful and you were about ready to jump overboard if you didn't expect them. But I could spot the running lights way off and give my engine the gun. The guy couldn't catch up and next trip he might ask where I ran my engine. 'Hell, cruise RPM, like the book says.' Everybody was up to stuff like that, whereas we seldom talked about the weather unless it was exceptionally bad. Then you might tell the other guy.

"Mostly we'd just go on through, in weather that was really stinko, but the pilot decided. Usually we read a newspaper for their weather map. See where the low was. Then take off and if you got down to clipping treetops, maybe it was time to turn around. Rain wasn't so bad. Or snow, unless it got so deep they'd call and say, 'Two-foot drifts here, don't land tonight.' We'd fly over that stop and send the mail back by train. Drifts hurt. That DH axle was a hell of a drag down below the snow. I got to carrying a four-foot lath in the mail compartment too. When ice built up, go into an emergency field, leave the motor running and pound it off. Struts and wires would pick up a load and start the whole ship shuddering until it felt like it was coming apart. Had to watch those emergency fields though. When they froze after a soft spell you landed alongside the ruts. Drop a wheel in some big rut and it would put you right up on the nose. When snow was too deep at our main fields, either end of the run, they'd drive automobiles up and down to pack it. Up to about a foot, you just leaned way back on the stick and when the wheels touched, poured the power to that engine with the flippers pulled back to your stomach to keep the tail down.

"Bud Gurney caught a rut in Springfield once. Broke his tail skid so they called me to take him another airplane. And I was on the way to Lincoln for Christmas. I wanted to say, put that mail on a train—but that was a no-go of course. We had one of those St. Louis fogs too. The old DH was pretty stable at least so I climbed up on top and figured I'd go back, but I couldn't find our own field either. I'd just come down from Chicago and knew the weather was open up north so I picked up a course from the North Star and headed for Springfield. We found a hole and saw a beacon at the bottom so I put the ship into a steep spiral and broke out underneath. I figured it was the second beacon north of Springfield. We went back and gave Gurney the good airplane. Fixed his skid and flew back to St. Louis to start my vacation a day late.

"Springfield was grass when it hadn't snowed but narrow, so you had to land kitty-corner if the wind was bad. If you had bucked a head wind

Jerrold E. Sloniger Collection

Slonnie stands in front of a Douglas with ex-Page wing walker and parachutist Bud Gurney, who had learned to fly. Gurney eventually flew for Boeing, which later became United Airlines.

down from Chicago they might pump some more gas in from a couple of fifty-gallon drums. Otherwise, I never even shut the motor off. You didn't dare let some stranger pull the prop through to start it again. The best system with that great big Liberty motor was three guys in crack-the-whip style. The man in front, holding the prop, took the chances so he gave the orders. On three he pulled the prop through and his helpers tried to throw him over the fence. Peoria was another sod field but more active. Half a dozen private airplanes at times and quite a nice little building. Kind of a lounge with offices out back. Stove in there and a telephone. They had field lights and a beacon but if there wasn't anybody around at night the boy who came out to pick up our mail would get there enough ahead to turn the lights on."

Even those winters which remained ever-fresh in pilot memories, like '27/'28, finally end and Robertson was doing well enough by spring to hire more staff, including new pilots. Slonnie said, "We decided to station one boy in Chicago so Les Smith, one of our original three, took that end and bought his own car. He'd meet me after a trip and then I'd drive him out to the field next morning and keep the car until I left that night." A second Robertson route, CAM 28 from St. Louis to Kansas City and Omaha, was added next, so Slonnie called on a flying friend, much as Gurney had tapped him. "That was George McCabe, a great big guy. Taking off from Omaha once, when the snow was pretty deep, he couldn't get the plane up. Of course, his ship was 100 pounds heavier than mine so I said, 'Tell you what. I'm not so fat. I'll just take your mail to St. Louis.' You never heard such language. Another time he'd broken his back and got so he

Slonnie himself captioned this one, "just another mail flight."
Some days pilots wore a business suit, complete with parachute.

could fly again but still couldn't climb in and out. Two of us could hardly lift him in so we got out a motor hoist and hooked that to his chute harness. McCabe was not amused."

They all wore parachutes by now, mostly to pad the bare metal bucket seat. "I never owned a chute until I started on the mail," Slonnie said. "They were expensive and had to be dried out and repacked every thirty days. But Robertson furnished ours and we might jump one for fun. Got into an argument with Gurney one day and bet five bucks I could beat him to the ground. Our chutes both popped right away but I pulled my risers so I only had half a chute and won the five. Les Smith got into rain once and thought his chute might be wet so he flew mine instead the next night. It was about due to be repacked but I rode it a couple more times. The National Guard would put them on dummies and dump them out over the field to open good before repacking. Gurney was watching and one didn't even begin to open so he rolled the dummy over and that chute was mine. The good one I'd loaned to Smith. I never had to jump in thirty-eight years, though. Just did it for fun."

Robertson's glossy new school pamphlet played down these pilot games while lauding the firm's own flying club where students and those same, presumably staid pilots could gather— convenient to the field, in a simple, homelike atmosphere, including a library of aero books and magazines. Room and board cost $9 a week, a dollar cheaper than private accommodations nearby. Hotels cost some $6 a week that year, without food. Slonnie soon rented a one-room apartment anyway. "The trip out from town was no special problem. I bought a Ford coupé and if it

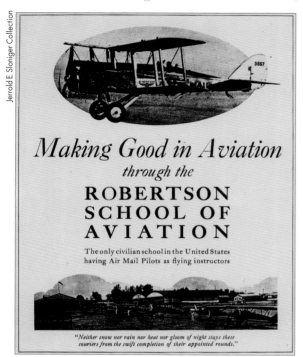

Robertson was a diversified operation, so Slonnie made sure there were no teaching responsibilities in his mail contract.

The Robertson Flying Club offered room and board for students.

wasn't working there was always somebody around with a car. Came in one day and Frank Lambert, a gentleman pilot with his own plane, was on the field. The Lamberts owned Listerine. He wanted some acrobatic instruction but thought I must be tired. Hell, I'd only come down from Chicago. Told him to crank up his plane and I'd show him a loop, an Immelmann, how to get out of a spin. Afterwards he asked if I ever took a drink. He was giving a party that night. I met loads of people there and from then on I always had something to do in my time off."

He certainly wasn't teaching regularly

though. Slonnie, described in Robertson's publicity as a youthful veteran of 6,000 hours, with boundless experience in cross-country flying and exhibitions, was no more eager to teach than the line's second veteran with the next-highest log total: 4,000 hours. Both found the mail safer, whatever might happen.

Robertson's rebuilt de Havillands no longer carried fuel in a tank directly ahead of the cockpit, like the military version dubbed a "flaming coffin," but a newspaper item in his first year did report that Sloniger, who was alive because he lost a coin flip before the Dole race, had been caught by fire near Springfield. They assumed the plane would not be a

total loss and the pilot had saved his mail. Slonnie said, "I landed across the furrows of a corn field and all we saved was the wings. The people who stopped and drove me back to Springfield had seen the fire before I knew about it and followed me. Couple of minutes after it started I smelled rubber burning and my motor quit about the same time so I put it down quick. It was a clear night and we carried flares. If you couldn't get to an emergency field, pull a flare and circle to get in behind it. Whatever you had out in front when that motor quit, you landed there. Those engines weren't any too reliable." The Liberty V12's prime asset was cheap availability. America had built thousands during WWI and gotten none to the front. Due to welded cylinder jackets, any Liberty leaked a good deal of water but ran reasonably well if not pushed. Pilots could expect fifty to 100 hours before an overhaul or junking. "Cruising speed for a Lib-DH was about ninety and you didn't dare run one wide open any length of time. Bucking a head wind you just sat there and waited.

"Pretty soon we got some new planes anyway. Lighter than the old silver and maroon DH." Robertson's 1928 fleet had expanded to five active de Havillands, an equally surplus Standard, a Waco, and three Douglas mail planes, pride of any line which could afford them and clear proof CAM 2 was picking up. Slonnie recalled, "We only used those Douglas jobs on special occasions. They had a little jump seat in the mail compartment which folded up against the wall. Better than sitting on mail sacks. If we got a passenger once a month they'd roll out the Douglas. Much nicer ship to fly than the DH by a long shot. Much faster. When we did that special Lindbergh anniversary flight Phil

Love, Tommy Nelson, and I used those. Think Gurney flew a Ryan and Smith got a DH. Lindbergh flew our new J5 Travel Air. Nice little airplane."

That was far more than Slonnie would say of Ryans. "A fellow named Phil Ball, who owned the St. Louis Browns baseball team, had a big interest in Robertson too. Then he bought out Ryan and moved it to St. Louis. They weren't selling very fast so he turned some over to us. They called me one Sunday morning to do acceptance tests on a couple of them. I didn't want to test an airplane that day to start with and didn't like Ryans much anyway, but I went out. One of Lindbergh's original backers and I were leaning against the trailing edge of a DH wing in the hangar, talking about Ryans, when a little fellow in a derby hat, long coat, and gaiter shoes came in and just stood listening. I said, 'The greatest thing Slim Lindbergh ever achieved was to keep a Ryan flying thirty-three hours. They are turkeys. I wouldn't try to fly one for three.' I got a kick and this little guy scowled and walked away. That was Ball and I figured I'd better look for another job, but nothing was ever said."

That special flight was a promotion called 'Lindbergh again flies the mail,' where each and every one of thousands of envelopes would supposedly be flown personally by the famous, ex-Robertson pilot in May 1928, one year after his New York-Paris flight. Slonnie said, "Slim came in after his personal appearance tour around the U.S. It was just our regular night mail run except that it took six of us to handle the load." The Post Office counted a quarter-million pieces of mail that night, nearly 4,300 pounds of it. Despite assurances that

The six pilots who took part in the 1928 commemorative St. Louis mail run each addressed special Charles Lindbergh covers to themselves and had the other five sign. This one is Slonnie's.

Lindbergh would swap planes to carry every piece, Slonnie said, "We kept our own airplanes all the way. None of us made every stop and he couldn't have flown six airplanes that one night to begin with, on a route with only three legs. We each got our load, taxied out, and took off. I don't know the departure sequence. I had Frank Robertson on the jump seat in my Douglas. We skipped Springfield and went right into Peoria. Slim landed at Springfield because the postmaster was an old chum. He left St. Louis without too much mail so they could put it all in at Springfield. Of course he landed at each stop because he was the one they all wanted to see."

When Slonnie reached Peoria 10,000 people broke through the ropes, thinking it was Lindbergh. "I shut the motor off right away and hoped the prop would quit turning before somebody got chewed into hamburger. I guess they were pretty disappointed so they got behind the ropes again and I taxied over to the office. Of course there were a jillion people out in Chicago too, but a hell of a lot of policemen, so I could taxi right up under the big

floods. Not Lindbergh so they weren't interested. Pitched the mail out and took my ship to the hangar. There wasn't a banquet afterwards or anything. We went down to the Robertson apartment and I got a speakeasy to send up two jugs of beer and a couple of bottles of whiskey. A restaurant on the first floor sent in some food. Quiet. Just good friends who had flown for Robertson that night, a guy from Boeing who had taught him to fly, a few more."

With the Travel Air properly baptized, it was put on the regular mail run and Slonnie became very fond of this lighter, faster, more maneuverable ship. "That DH was a heavy plane for a little guy like me to move fast. I couldn't snap one up on its side, for instance. The Travel Air was much nicer. We shared that apartment in Chicago with three pilots flying for Northwest. It turned out Speed Holman and I were scheduled against one another. He had a Laird and I flew the Travel Air. Both Whirlwind motor jobs. We were both due into Chicago about nine so I'd watch for his running lights and edge over towards his course.

Legend has it that when Charles Lindbergh returned to Robertson Aircraft in May 1928 to fly the commemorative St. Louis mail run, he flew every special letter. Actually, covering the route took the entire Roberston crew, pictured here from left to right: Tommy Nelson, Frank Robertson (who flew as a passenger), Lindbergh, Phil Love, Les Smith, Bud Gurney, Slonnie (almost hidden except for his cigarette), and a Robertson official.

The Robertson mail division also bought a Whirlwind-powered Travel Air for the mail. Col. Halsey Dunwoody, executive Vice President of Universal Airways, congratulates Slonnie on completing a million air miles.

Then we'd put on a dogfight. You had to work against Speed. Morning after the first one the station manager raised hell. He wouldn't have any more stunting with the U.S. Mail. But the ramp had been loaded with people out watching so two or three nights later Speed and I put on another show. It wasn't the only deal which got me called onto the carpet.

"The Post Office was way off at one end of the field. Then you had to taxi down a long ramp and out along this little strip to get onto the one runway Cicero had. Just idling your motor and getting wetter than hell when it rained. Here was this big concrete ramp in front of the hangars when I had a south takeoff one night. Not a soul around so I gave it the gun and took off from the hangar ramp. Got hell for that too. Pretty soon John Paul

Riddle, another WWI pilot who had talked Paul Embry into starting an airline that also became part of American Airlines eventually, was standing in the Post Office with me. He got his mail first but it's raining like hell again. I said, 'Know what I did a month ago? I just took off from the concrete there.' So he jumps in his airplane, revs it up, and goes right down the ramp. The manager's office was above this terrible restaurant in the terminal building at the other end and Riddle was about level with the guy's window as he passes the building. Next time John Paul gets to Chicago it's up to the office. Riddle claimed I told him I always took off from that ramp. The manager says, 'Don't listen to that Sloniger, he'll get you in trouble for sure.'"

Mail remained the mainstay for all these little lines, despite increasing passenger-airplane

fleets. Will Rogers wrote, "What pilots these airmail babies are. Lindy came from a great school. These mail babies go through...in weather most people couldn't find their way from the house to the garage. Good planes, good pilots." Robertson, using more outdated equipment than other lines, lost fewer men at their task than most. American headlines regularly tolled the latest aviation death count and newspapers monitored earliest radio frequencies, ready to rush reporters to the field if some plane reported trouble. That aroused Rogers's ire too. "When will papers give aviation an even break? Eight are killed in all America in planes on a Sunday and it's headlined in every paper. If a single state didn't do as well (in cars) it was only because it fell below the average that day."

In figures: 1928 brought five commercial air accidents with insurance claims paid, versus 6,761 for cars and twenty-five for the horsey set. Gurney announced in the pilots' new newsletter, at the end of that year, that Robertson had presented all its boys with a nice block of insurance, making them feel the firm appreciated their striving to get those Lindbergh souvenir letters through. He didn't mention how rare any insurance still was for pilots. Most airline bosses believed implicitly in surveys showing that forty-five to fifty-five percent of all accidents were due to pilot error. Weather, darkness, and terrain accounted for twenty percent in the first half of 1928, less than nine percent the second half. Pilot experience would remain the chief factor in reducing accident tallies, although long odds could catch even an old hand out. Les Smith was killed on June 28, 1928. Robertson lost one of its canniest flyers on a special deal which Slonnie turned down flat. "Phil Love had gotten in wrong with the Robertsons so they fired him and Nelson quit in sympathy. They had been classmates in flying school, along with Lindbergh. Love was a quiet redhead and a top pilot. He would be killed in an Army transport during 1943, when he wasn't doing the flying. That was the same year Bill Robertson was killed in the St. Louis glider smash, as a matter of fact.

"We started hiring one guy after another and they never stayed. One wouldn't fly after dark. Said, 'Hell the birds don't fly at night and I won't either.' Another boy didn't like weather. When this special came up we were back to Gurney, myself, and Les Smith, who was a damn fine pilot. A St. Louis newspaper made a deal to fly morning editions to the Democratic convention in Houston. Lots of money per mile. Gurney told me he thought the two of us better fly this. I said, 'I think you and anybody else better fly that. Someone is going to get hurt on that damn run. No radios, no lights, no nothing. Five hours at night and blacker than hell over east Texas. Count me out.' 'Well, would I fly the mail every day instead?' Up to Chicago one night, back the next morning. I said, 'Sure and you can tell the Robertsons they're crazy to take that contract.' They started on it while I did the mail and on the third day we lost Les Smith. He didn't come home from Little Rock and it took us a week to find him." The army even sent a dirigible to bolster twenty search pilots. Slonnie said, "Smith was gone though. Just clobbered it in a forest.

"While they were still flying those newspapers we had three nights running when Chicago weather was pretty sticky and Robertson was the only one of five lines to put the mail through. That sounds like bragging but it hap-

Slonnie readies a Whirlwind-powered Travel Air to carry a couple on their honeymoon—the pair wearing helmets and goggles.

pened. And we lost a hell of a good boy on that special because the odds were ten to one against him. I'd take my chances with an even break. But when it's stacked against me—well, I was maybe a little smarter than that." Passengers couldn't know the odds but even so, Slonnie recalled, "We mostly only got people in desperate circumstances like a death in the family. Or a drunk who'd have a couple too many and wanted to fly to Chicago."

One desperate rider was opera singer Dorothy Speare who wrote a Hamilton watch ad about their trip. "She was my most famous passenger that year. Said I told her we were always on time, which was not the whole truth, but you wouldn't tell anybody that." The singer-lecturer described her pilot as "an element-defying god riding the wings of night," and Gurney rushed that into their newslet-

ter, commenting that Slonnie said he got a new Hamilton watch out of it and they naturally hated to question him further. To catch any who missed the double-page ad, Hamilton printed booklets titled *My Flight with the Air Mail*, telling about this beautiful singer stranded in St. Louis with a Chicago concert deadline which no train could make. The lady wasn't too rushed to notice her pilot was young and very attractive looking.

Slonnie did agree, for different reasons, with Speare's enthusiasm for flying above the land by night. He said, "I always liked night flying for two reasons. Your motor ran better and the air was smoother. Maybe it was a little bit harder to navigate but you always had some kind of stars. A look over your shoulder for Polaris was enough going south. You did it by towns mostly anyway, because you knew their sizes and when you were due. Nothing but little places between Peoria and Chicago though so maybe I'd remember the filling stations. Two right south of such and such a town. Low clouds were the worst until we got working radios, but that wasn't really until 1932. No decent instruments in '28 either. A compass, but it wouldn't read within fifteen degrees of the right course so mostly we didn't bother to watch it. The only cockpit light was a little car-dashboard thing. Pull it out and twist it around. There wasn't much to read with it anyway."

Many pilots were not what Slonnie called "one-hundred percent sure" of their instrument abilities yet either. As one claimed, if you had the right equipment maybe instrument flying wouldn't be so bad but he felt it was a doggone good way to keep from growing a long white beard.

Radio ranges, which pilots might follow by ear when vision disappeared, were still toys in 1928, largely because the radio itself was heavy, hard to operate, and mostly useful for deflecting the magnetic compass even further. Thoughtful pilots really cared more about a standarized instrument panel, since almost all their employers seemed to have one of every airplane built. Universal Airways, to be formed shortly as a step between Robertson and American Airways, would even comission a standard board of dials for its first Fokker transport, but that cost extra. A pilot could scan this vertically and horizontally at a glance. All needles pointed to the center when their plane was straight and level, with its engines healthy. There would even be a rheostat for dial lights and reflecting nickel trim was banished.

With hindsight, 1928 marked the thresh-

Slonnie and a helper resupply an airplane on an endurance flight. The resupply plane fed a hose down and lowered fuel, oil, food, or other supplies the endurance team needed.

old to a decade in which pilots could move from open cockpits to passenger cabin airplanes with eight or ten dials, along their way to the Douglas DC-3 with duplicate instruments for pilot and copilot, further than any flyer would have dreamed a year after the Lindbergh flight. One of the first changes which came to the Robertson Division of that new conglomerate called Universal Airways was blind flying instruction, keeping your eyes inside the cockpit, and maneuvering by dials alone. Slonnie said, "They closed in the rear cabin of an old Fairchild with the check pilot left outside in front, in case you got way off course. Put us in back with all the new ideas and we had to fly it by the needles. I believed in that very much." A few visionary pilots actually suggested they would not only be flying blind but even landing without seeing the runway within a few years, something no airline was willing to do with passengers on board more than half a century later.

A trend towards fewer, larger airplanes of only one or two types on each line was already clear. The more rigid old-timers still wondered about flying from inside, others shied away from the responsibility for twenty other lives. Even if full loads weren't likely to begin with, could they justify blind flying with passengers? As 1929 approached, these various U.S. airlines were finally hauling respectable numbers—nearly 18,000 paid passengers in 1928—and pilots were expected to acquire what their lines called a "new corporate mentality." This was open to interpretation. At some stops the pilot still drove fares to the field in a company car. One got a guest who was too loud so the pilot hauled him out of the car bodily and dressed him down vigorously. Challenged by management he

admitted: "Sure I shook him. You can't expect me to take such talk from a damned passenger!"

Universal proved a lucky airline mix, put together from many small lines such as Robertson. Their routes meshed in most cases, even if the fleet became even more various. H. R. Dunwoody was named Executive Vice President. He was a West Point man and an efficient organizer who even knew what an airplane looked like. Officers of many lines being formed and merged then never saw their own equipment and shuddered at the mere thought of going up in such contraptions. New departments called Sales or Publicity were no closer to flying reality. They often thought any man who applied for a job with a white scarf was some European ace who should grace their cockpits. Most proved lousy flyers. Colonel Dunwoody, however, actually believed true flying ability should be the primary pilot consideration. There were a lot of pretty weather-beaten men on his routes but they made their runs with good regularity. Once Robertson became part of a million-dollar corporation and bought its first Ford Trimotors, trips might even be made in approximate comfort. This was the first airplane which moved U.S. lines in general along the path marked respectability.

Introduced as early as 1926 on Ford's own routes out of Detroit, this early metal classic quickly carved an enviable niche, although it owed much of its flying ability to engineers who had secretly measured every inch of the rival, but cloth-covered, Fokker. Ford's aluminum-clad version was so loud pilots who scorned earplugs would have trouble passing flight physicals for years afterwards. The cabin was always too hot or too cold. The plane had no deicing equipment and an open hole as its sole

passenger toilet. But metal felt safer at a time when selling security was the main preoccupation.

Slonnie recalled, "Robertson bought Model 4 AT Fords with J5 Wright motors first. Those carried twelve and cruised about 85 or 90 MPH. Lumbering old tubs that would lift off a short runway. But Trimotors were big stuff then. Actually, people weren't so air-minded yet that we would have twelve going at one time very often. Maybe Springfield would call and say they had ten for Chicago though, so we'd take the Ford. We did loads of advertising too. Frank Robertson figured I knew a lot of people around St. Louis. I should ask some couples to fly to Chicago and back on us. I invited some that same evening and right away the rest were lining up to go too. Take four out to the field and if the ship was full they had to go back home. But it looked better for some guy who had paid if more than two people rode in this great big Ford."

Universal Airways had its distinctive insignia—a nude man with wings—and a good slogan, "Man's desire to fly is Universal," but no rush of customers. One obvious solution was another free press ride. The *St. Louis Star* reporter duly recorded the fact that they had to buck a head wind, which he took to be the jinx of every flight, but also said it wasn't so many years since the same trip had taken two days, with luck. He noted that passengers could lean back liesurely in leather-covered chairs as the ship glided along. A young man had taken their tickets, then gone to the controls and lit a cigarette. A company spokesman explained that smoking was cetainly allowed, since these ships were all metal.

And no great problem for old hands to fly.

Slonnie with his St. Louis-built Robin, used as a refueling plane for one of many late-twenties endurance flight attempts. The dangling hose visible under the airplane was lowered to refuel the endurance airplane.

When Gurney collected Robertson's first Ford the factory tried to insist he stay three months for full indoctrination. He told them it was just another airplane. Flew it around the field and said okay, he was checked out. For Slonnie he said, 'That's a Ford. Then he was checked out on Fords, too.' Slonnie added, "Instruments were out on the nacelles for the two side motors so you had to stand up and go look at the right-hand ones. They were inside for the nose motor. Set that one first, for the RPM you wanted, and when the others got out of synchronization you heard about it damn soon. The Ford would fly on two motors but you had to hold the rudder against all that drag if one of the outboards quit." On some lines pilots even cut the center motor on clear nights to save fuel. Heat? Yes, on rare occasions when the pilot could get it working. Mostly passengers just put their coats on.

"When we got the first Fords we put a mechanic in the right-hand seat, just in case. One day I took our night watchman along instead. He wanted to see Chicago. Up in the morning, back that evening. But the southbound was actually full for a change and a late passenger came up besides so I went out to talk to him. That's how I met Rogers Hornsby, the big baseball star. Anybody with a name like that had to go of course, so I arranged to bump the watchman off. Government wasn't very strict in those days. But I would have to take care of him, put him up in a hotel. Hornsby said he'd pay anything. Just get him to St. Louis. Buckled him into the right seat and told him to put his feet flat and cross his arms, with his hands in his lap. Touch nothing. It was probably Hornsby's first and last job as a copilot."

Sheer survival economics had dictated these Fords. Hauling people in single-engined, five-passenger ships cost airlines fifteen cents per passenger mile with every seat taken. With one of the larger Trimotors (eighteen seats eventually, when bigger motors were fitted) they could fly a full load for seven cents a mile. Of course trimotor pilots cost more too. Regular pay behind one motor was $2,500 a year while base for a trimotor pilot was $3,000 and top men averaged $7,500 a year with flight pay. When proper copilots came along they added another $200 to monthly cockpit costs.

As more pilots became settled and even bought shares in some lines, their need for a common voice led to the National Air Pilots Association. Slonnie remembered that as: "A couple of bucks in dues a year but the newsletter was worth it easy. Kind of a loose club with no meetings or anything. Carl Egge started it when he got out of government mail." NAPA, most impressive of several pilot groups founded in or after 1926, was nothing like a union. That came later. This was a fraternity for a land where there might be 7,000 current commercial pilot licenses but only some 200 holders of them working full-time in aviation. A scant 110 of those were airline pilots and they all knew one another, passing the jobs around. Classified columns carried dozens of pleas from experienced pilots for every job which came open. One man could fly twice as many people in the new equipment so that even fairly senior flyers might have to ride in the right seat like a new copilot. Many moved into operations instead and some even edged into top management. A good many junior captains put the fur-lined flying suit back on, preferring open mail planes to copilot rank inside.

Senior pilots donned blazers and company caps for these new passenger runs. Their NAPA newsletter insisted uniforms were inevitable, although most members who wrote in disliked them. If pressed, pilots favored a common uniform for all lines so anybody could tell them from taxi drivers at busy airports. Also, a man was going to have to buy his own and could take it along when he changed lines. Most-vocal opponents were one-time Post Office pilots who had been thrown out of speakeasies when they were mistaken for Prohibition agents. Robertson's men donned uniforms soon after the line acquired Trimotors and came close to blows over their design. As Slonnie described the attire, "It was a double-breasted blue jacket with brass buttons. No sleeve stripes, just little wings. In the summer, white pants and a white cap cover. Black tie. In winter it was all blue. Universal picked up the same combination."

Pilots were wary of all new ideas from above, particularly from the sales side. They vehemently debated whether advertising should be sent by airmail, or would that lessen the unique value of fast mail service. This came up when a car maker decided to launch its new model by shipping promotional literature by air. In the end, bad weather grounded all first-day loads and customers would have gotten their blurbs sooner by rail. Slonnie was involved in that job too. "Willys Overland wanted to ship all these pamphlets and NAT had the Chicago-New York run which was the main route for them. There wasn't any competition on your own route then. They used every spare airplane to haul the stuff into Chicago and got all the connecting people like us to take a ship up too. It happened Holman had a Northwest Ford but his carried Wasp engines with twice the power I had. It was a nasty day and no real runways so I said, 'Damn if I'm sure I can get this load off that soft ground.' He picked it right up and said he'd just show me how. His wheels were sinking six inches into the mud, roaring down the field until he saw he couldn't make it and cut the gun. My load was ready so I jumped in and put it right into Holman's tracks so my tires weren't pushing all that mud ahead. Got off in good shape and Speed just laughed."

Robertson soon bought more powerful Fords as well. Everybody wanted new-engine glamour to pay for bigger staffs. When 1929 opened eight men were flying for the Robertson Division out of St. Louis alone, none of them aware that pilot rosters had peaked at a level they wouldn't touch again until 1936, when passenger demand finally began to fill new airplanes. Universal's crew would be short one of those men for most of 1929, however, and Slonnie wouldn't get to fly improved Trimotors for a while longer.

He said, "That advertising load was my last trip before a leave of absence. When I got back into St. Louis Gurney came running out and told me I was going to China. They had a deal coming up and I would sail in a couple of days. I didn't even have a passport but Dad got one mailed to the hotel in Seattle and I jumped on the train. Bill Robertson had gone with Curtiss when they started building these private jobs called Robins in St. Louis. C. M. Keys was a big financial man in New York who controlled Curtiss and backed the Robin factory. Then he got the idea of going to China to get the mail contract. They were sending two Robins, a Falcon, an Ireland flying boat, and a Ford Trimotor. There weren't so many trimotor pilots

around with flying boat time too, so somebody said: 'Tell Slonnie he's leaving tomorrow.' I hadn't been in that direction, so why not?"

The NAPA newsletter for February 1929, noted, "Sloniger has gone to China to teach the Chinese how to fly American airplanes. Somehow or other friend Sloniger is always one jump ahead of the rest of the boys. He says he went to help sell Robins and what not but we who know Sloni (sic) know better." The same man who had declined to fly over the dark wastes of Texas without reasonable odds now seemed happy to try a land where pilots were still considered either some kind of god or dragon. Frequently both. In 1929 China was still provincial enough that one hour of flying could carry you so far the best interpreter became useless. Mostly, it was one more land where he hadn't sampled the flying.

February 1929   Flying hours: 6,836:25

Chapter 9

The Orient

"Hell, I'd never seen China."

One Midwest mail pilot visited at least a small part of China in 1929 because an eager player among the new breed of air-minded conglomerates, North American Aviation, wanted one foot or more in every flying door. Founded in December 1928 by a Canadian named C. M. Keys—at various times classics professor, editor of both railroad and financial pages, banker, broker, and (since 1920) president of Curtiss—North American Aviation was a leading player in the new merger age.

Some 300 companies were building airplanes, engines, components, and even dirigibles during 1929, a clear temptation to forge more combinations. Keys quickly gathered Curtiss airplanes, Wright engines, Curtiss Reed propellers, and nearly a dozen suppliers into a company capitalized at $25 million. Aviation stocks had become a favorite speculation for people who wouldn't go near an airplane. Instead they bought $400 million in aviation shares, giving manufacturers money and incentive to go after foreign as well as domestic markets.

The Orient itself had beckoned western dreamers ever since a prehistoric emperor supposedly flew his throne on eagle power. Charles Hamilton took an American airship to China in 1909; Thomas Baldwin's *Red Devil* became the first heavier-than-air effort by an American in 1911. One Chinese government even ordered a mail plane from France in 1913, while Christofferson booked an order for twenty-five U.S. models in 1916. Katherine Stinson made sixty flights in oriental air space during 1917 alone. Chinese airmail between Tientsin and Peking finally got off the ground in 1920 and an air link with Russia was also contemplated in 1925. A thousand miles in sixteen hours, versus ten days by car, underlined the need for air routes over such vast distances, but it was never easy to line up the players who could make a decision which would stick in that land. About the only Chinese constant was potential military advantage. It was no coincidence that the so-called mail flight from Canton to Hankow, Nanking, Peking, Tientsin, and Shanghai in late-1928 was flown by one General Chang.

Exports of any kind had always been a favorite Curtiss territory. The original company sent a pilot named Tony Janus to Russia as early as 1915 and put representatives into Shanghai, proposing a ten-million (Mexican) dollar corporation which would operate a Chinese airline, flying Curtiss equipment of course, a good year before Slonnie became involved. Chinese who weren't given their cut called that imperialism. A decade earlier different local cliques had signed parallel contracts with British, Japanese, and U.S. interests, all seeking to build wireless networks, but endemic local payoffs muddled communications. Identical interministry jealousies plagued aviation dealings in the late twenties. The fractioned state of anything called central government meant Slonnie would start yet another mail route survey from square one. Canton might have been designated the main regime in 1917 but local warlords still tended to heed whoever happened to hold Peking. When Sun Yat-sen died in 1925 he left Chiang on the right but Sun Fo, his son, held both a key ministry and his father's heritage as George Washington of China, enough to dazzle foreigners.

Slonnie disembarked in the spring of 1929 to find Nationalists and Communists alike fanning antiforeigner hatred whenever it suited. Keys's people discovered the real trick would be identifying some person or group permanent enough to sign contracts with any pretense of legitimacy. The financier had given Major William Robertson, the onetime mail-route pioneer from St. Louis, now working directly for Curtiss, guidelines for making deals or contracts with the "Nationalist government of China and others." Those last two words suggest Keys was not entirely naive about Oriental factions. Robertson could draw on $10 million to operate a transport airline or other

92

aviation activity and Keys might say for publication that he had no desire to dominate with American capital but no other kind was suggested. Robertson's real goal was a mail network between major industrial centers. He may or may not have known that a Shanghai-Tientsin venture, flying German airplanes and thus beholden to their builders, had already been financed by merchants of those two cities in 1928. Even Keys admitted it would be ridiculous under prevailing conditions to establish too many routes. His field team should confine itself to places where fuel and oil might be available. Furthermore, they should start using Chinese personnel from the beginning. If possible.

Keys hardly sent a first-class fleet initially, promising to ship more and better equipment later, which indicates he was aware of how often loose airplanes were appropriated by local warlords. When it came to picking the team, Robertson apparently exercised a free hand. Slonnie had already flown mail for him but he too was told clearly that anybody who proved out of sympathy with the project would be sent home immediately. First the Nebraska pilot had to get there, a task which engaged most of the Sloniger family's time because Moorefield hadn't bothered about birth certificates in 1896. Brother Perry was swamped with long-distance calls for more papers and local ones from Johnny, who wanted to know where her fiancé might be. Perry could honestly say he had no idea. They finally used school records to obtain the passport. A fraternity brother had become county attorney and could swear he had gone to school with Slonnie, who therefore did exist.

The pilot said, "My papers and train got to Seattle together so we sailed for Shanghai just fine.

Guess it took about twenty, very rough, days but we did get off in Japan to see Tokyo and picked up the ship again in Kyoto, so there was a break." Looking back from retirement, Slonnie realized those three weeks were the longest spell between 1917 and 1955 when he didn't fly some sort of airplane. He reopened the log early in March, when the Keys airplanes arrived.

Their party included Robertson and wife Majorie, her sister, a lawyer, an ex-Naval officer named Roland Riggs, and a one-time missionary named Jim Wilson, taken along as interpreter. Another pilot named Arthur Caperton had arrived by the time they got something to fly. Slonnie added, "Robertson liked to be called Major then, but when we stopped in Japan they questioned him plenty, so I figured it was just as well I'd let my National Guard reserve status drop." Settled into the Palace Hotel they found little to do in Shanghai at first, except watch small-boat traffic. "So Wilson and I decided to go up to Hankow by river boat, then train to Peking, on to Tientsin, and back via Nanking, just locating possible landing fields and facilities. I knew we were really there to pick up a mail contract. Selling airplanes was a blind but they did have to send at least a few out to show around. Four to start."

Four was rather less than indicated in an April *New York Times* item saying an entity called Curtiss-Robertson would ship forty airplanes and several trained pilots to inaugurate commercial aviation and fly under Chinese government sponsorship. This suggests a more permanent operation than Slonnie intended to join. His Shanghai calling card didn't mention a Chinese airline, saying only: "Chief Pilot, Aviation Explora-

tion Co." Surveying new routes would pay him $500 a month, about what a corporate pilot back home might expect, but less than a man flying night mail.

During his stay their fleet remained modest, although a clear improvement on surplus Breguets, Avros, or de Havillands at the local Hungjao Aerodrome, not to mention what Slonnie recalled as, "Something the Chinese themselves designed. They were getting the wings all fixed when we landed, using wax, not dope. I doubt if anybody flew it and for sure, not very far. They didn't like to fly much over there anyway. When we got going a little in Shanghai I made sure our own mechanics assembled my planes. We had an OX-5-powered Robin, another with a Challenger engine, and since Keys owned Ireland amphibians, they sent one of those, plus a Liberty-engined Falcon. Reason I went to begin with was my Trimotor log time but the Ford never arrived. At least I had hull time too, to fly that amphib."

The basic Robin was still a good short-field airplane, despite its aging OX-5 engine, but refused to remain level if the pilot let go for a moment. It did have an enclosed cabin, handy for what became Slonnie's chief task of giving rides over the city. A reporter for the *Shanghai Times* was most impressed when the pilot explained it was "next to impossible to make a Robin spin," a considerable retouching of fact. E. L. Sloniger even demonstrated how he could fly it hands-off, "in a straight line or even in a circle," the scribe added. He obviously hadn't noticed feet on the rudder pedals. "Durable" described any Robin better than "dashing." With the more reliable, air-cooled Challenger radial engine, "another one of the

Jerrold E. Sloniger Collection

Wheeling the Challenger Robin into a Shanghai military hangar. The airplane mysteriously disappeared into the China interior, and the field commander, General Chang, offered no explanation.

things Keys made," as Slonnie said, it even managed a cruising speed of 100 MPH. "The Challenger was easier to start too. It had a crank off on one side, just like an automobile. But I did all our survey work with the Falcon, on account of its range. That was built originally as an observation plane for the Army. But Curtiss owned National Air Transport as well, so they closed the front cockpit up and made a mail space. We stuck in a jump seat for the interpreter. Cruised maybe 125. Very nice airplane."

As for the rest of their fleet, "That Ireland boat was a turkey. Only advantage, you could land on water too, all the way up the Yangtze. But it didn't have the range to go from Shanghai to Nanking. Wasn't the fastest thing in the world either. Nor the most maneuverable. It was only sent over because we were supposed to be selling airplanes. Nobody would have bought the damn thing. We left it down on the Wangpoo river and some local guy who was supposed to be a boat pilot took it up. He landed right between a couple of fishing boats and the Ireland was all shot to hell. I didn't care much. Later they sent over Loening amphibians—a single-motor job as well but it carried more people. Amphibs wouldn't take open seas but somebody figured they would be good along the rivers. The Loening wouldn't have been a bad idea but I never flew one over there. When I got to fly at all."

Since they were in China chiefly "to sell a bill of goods," as Slonnie put it, "we seemed to wear dinner jackets a lot. Plenty of entertaining. Rest of the time, twice a week at least, it was somebody's home, from the Consul General on down. I went to one big dinner with about forty-four courses, where everybody helped themselves from central dishes.

And they had mussels. When I reached for one it began to slip from the chopsticks. I squeezed harder, which you certainly shouldn't do. That mussel hit the ceiling and back down and not one person at that table except the Americans even batted an eye. Afterwards I bought a pair of chopsticks and a bag of little round peanuts and practiced. Most of the passenger hops were people we met at those dinners."

Slonnie turned to regular survey work with the Falcon, which put just over ninety minutes into his log over the Shanghai-Nanking route. "To get there? Just head west. The Yangtze is a great big river so you followed it to Hankow. Getting anyplace was dead reckoning. Look at a little pocket map for the general direction, then turn either right or left at the coast. We didn't do any night flying though. Not even Shanghai had lights on its field.

"Our local interpreters couldn't spot towns from the air either. None of them had ever been up in an airplane. At best, they could talk when we landed, make arrangements for gas maybe. We had a deal with Standard Oil and anyplace I landed I had the name of the right man to get in touch with. But the place is so big, all speaking different dialects, we had to keep changing interpreters. Mostly, it was one smart boy who was a Harvard graduate and spoke northern Chinese. When we cut back down to Canton he knew somebody who spoke that so we put his pal in the front seat instead.

"A lot of time was spent on some kind of political situation. That's why I took Sun Fo to Nanking the first time. He was our boy. The deal was, we would go the next morning and he would

Slonnie (left, center) with his local helpers and an unidentified man. One reason Slonnie had been sent to China was his experience flying hull planes like this amphibian.

Jerrold E Sloniger Collection

telegraph ahead so the right people would meet us. We got there right on time and everybody rushed out in surprise. His telegram arrived later."

Since this was the first such air trip for a cabinet minister, Slonnie received full honors too. "I wanted to stay at the field and take off next morning but no, I must go to some hotel, as guest of the government. I was escorted by a Chinese pilot who had trained in St. Louis. He registered me as a guest of Chiang and got a houseboy who was supposed to understand English.

"After dinner I was in the room with a couple of magazines when a fight started next door, between about five males and females. The walls were plain, quarter-inch boards and the cracks were good so I could stand on my bed and watch. They were slugging and chopping and kicking and I was having a hell of a good time when there was a knock on my door. A couple of soldiers with a big damn scroll I couldn't read. But they pointed to it and wanted me to go with them. To hell with that. They left and I went back to the fight. The wall was so thin, a bunch would hit and sort of bend it my way and I'd push back.

"In ten minutes the soldiers were back with a couple of friends, showing this scroll again and trying to pull me out of the room. Figured I was batting a sticky wicket for sure, but I got out on the balcony of this rotunda hotel and yelled down into the court. 'Anybody speak English?' A voice said, 'Righto.' 'Do you speak Chinese?' 'Righto.' He came up and explained who I was. The Military College would verify it. The soldiers finally left and he asked me to have a spot of tea but I said 'Scotch.' Found out I was down for a Russian spy because of the name. I never did discover how they got that

Jerrold E. Sloniger Collection

In China, Slonnie typically gave rides to sell prominent groups on flight. Pictured with this Challenger Robin is Dr. Sun Fo (son of Sun Yat-sen) below the propeller with his hat in hand.

idea, for a guest of the government, but I was still damn glad to get out of Nanking the next morning."

Slow telegrams were the norm. Before leaving on another trip to Nanking, to demonstrate the Falcon to their army, Slonnie wired he would arrive over the walled military post at noon the next day. "When I got over the parade ground I thought I'd have a little fun, show what an American plane could do." Describing it later, during a guest appearance on the Jack Armstrong radio show, he said, "I dove, zoomed around, and did a few tricks, which probably seemed pretty hairraising to men on the ground in those days. Finally I landed, and what a mistake. Soldiers with rifles, bayonets, even clubs, rushed up jabbering and threatening. I crawled up on top of the fuselage and yelled the couple of Chinese words I knew and all my simplest English and waved wildly. Finally some officer who had been in St. Louis saved my life. The wire arrived nine hours later." When not on radio he would say, "They just weren't used to thinking in flying terms. Set a ship down and they'd flock in from miles around and sort of edge closer and closer until one guy would get brave enough to sneak up and touch the plane. Then he'd run off a couple of hundred feet and laugh like hell."

Military flying status was reserved for the elite, of course. As late as 1932 another American advisor would find that only twenty-seven of the fifty pilots on their list of the land's best could even fly solo. He demoted the lot. When Chiang discovered an Italian mission would graduate every Chinese candidate his government favored, he sent that American home. Slonnie wouldn't have

passed any of the ones he met but he carefully avoided trying to teach them any new tricks. His own stunts were reduced to winning the odd bet. "Majorie Robertson had invited some people for rides one day. The Shanghai field was kind of small but we had painted a white circle in the center. I bet her a buck I could do a dead-stick landing and stop with two wheels or the tail skid—either one she wanted—inside that circle. Cut the motor at 2,000 feet and glide right in. We stopped smack in the circle and she handed over the dollar. That night she asked Bill what my chances had been and he said, 'One in ten.' She told him I'd offered two to one and Bill said he sure hoped she'd taken it. She said she had and it cost her a buck."

Slonnie found tame stunts about his only relief from official deviousness. Robertson dealt primarily with Sun Fo, not only Sun Yat-sen's first-born but also Minister of Railroads, a non-military fiefdom. The pilot felt, "His guys were all for our deal." The Americans would accept gold promissory notes up to two million dollars, so long as their projected airline operated at a loss, and advance Sun Fo another million for hangars, airfield surveys, and incidentals. Robertson knew he was dealing with a Harvard man but may not have realized Sun Fo was also only one of five ministers either related to, or married into, the Sun Yat-sen family. By April they faced an impasse, based on civilian versus military aims. Riggs's contribution was General Chang, director of the Chinese aeronautical bureau and avid procurer of any airplanes which might serve in battle. Chang wasn't getting warplanes fast enough and failed when he tried to fly the Ireland to Nanking. Its top wing caught fire. Slonnie did take the Falcon there, for Chiang's

government to use, but General Chang had to go as passenger in the Challenger Robin.

Caught between the supposedly neutral U.S. State Department and Keys, Robertson cabled one last message. "It was very clearly brought out by Mr. Sun Fo as well as Col. (sic) Chang that if we were to assist their government at this time, with the sale or use of our airplanes, it would materially strengthen our position with them and greatly accelerate action on our contract." He didn't add the obvious: This also meant taking sides in a civil war. Sun Fo next suggested selling the airplanes to his Ministry of Railways, rather than the War Department, since they seemed the only new airplanes handy during a week when war was outside the gates of Hankow again. Having control of something which actually flew would give him a considerable edge with the military.

All these maneuvers probably explain discrepancies in Slonnie's log. That record puts him in Hankow, doing airmail surveys, on dates when both Robertson's report to Keys and the Shanghai newspaper have him flying the Falcon to Nanking and turning it over to the government. Actually, that same Falcon appears in his log for ten further days before turnover and a bit of check-out. Slonnie said, "They got their number one pilot out and I explained everything. He had supposedly flown a DH like our St. Louis mail planes. The Falcon was a little nicer flying but it had a narrow landing gear and very sensitive toe brakes. Put your big foot down and you had a ground loop. I told him all this very carefully and there was an interpreter, so we explained it to this joker both ways. He would nod his head. I couldn't ride with him since it only had one set of controls. He took off and flew around maybe thirty minutes before he came in to land. They used to joke that those boys closed their eyes, counted to ten, cut the motor, and pulled the stick back. You were supposed to be on the ground by then. Guess he didn't count high enough. It was a little faster than the DH and you never saw such a landing. Somebody said, 'Oh my, I hope he isn't killed.' I sort of hoped he was.

"Between survey trips I also had to sit in on negotiations quite often. One time they asked about regulations. I said we would be under American rules and since we were applying for a mail contract and passengers, the one thing we could not handle was any opium whatsoever. There was dead silence. Everybody looked askance except Robertson, who gave me a very dirty look. Afterwards I told Bill, 'If we're going to have to run this thing until they can take over we're going to have to obey U.S. rules. Never mind what Chang may want.'" That particular general and Slonnie were not fated to view the world alike, although they had actually met earlier, in Lincoln. "I was flying for Lincoln Standard when three Army DHs came up for an air show and Chang was in the front seat of one airplane. He'd been sent over to learn how to fly and seemed a hell of a nice guy so we took him out and around and got him some corn whiskey. Get to Shanghai and here's little Chang as top man in their air force, which consisted of maybe five beat-up airplanes. Anyway, they had a general in charge. I went up to his office for a cup of tea and we were chums.

"Until we got our contract. Then billboards went up all over: 'China sold her air rights

When the former General Chang, now a senior Chinese government official, landed in Burbank, California, on his way to Washington to request funding during WWII, Slonnie recognized him as the man he'd threatened to have jailed for stealing a Challenger Robin if he ever came to America. Reporters listened in, but wouldn't risk running a negative story on an ally.

to foreign devils.'" The Minister of Communications, a Sun Fo rival, urged pilots throughout the land to rise up at Robertson's takeover. They had fought a revolution to win back their railroads and now Nanking had given away the airline. By no coincidence, Communications was about to start its own airline, using Stinsons purchased outright but also flown by foreign pilots. A sign found in the tomb of the Ming Dynasty's founder even proclaimed that airlines came under Communications. Their Minister interpreted it that way, at least.

"After things quieted down a little," Slonnie said, "I was out at the field to give some ladies a ride and just about ready to take off when

half a dozen soldiers blocked my ship, guns all cocked. The interpreter said we couldn't fly because of the contract and soldiers had orders to shoot if we tried. About then I saw Chang walk out of his office without looking around and drive off. All I could do was apologize to the ladies. Next morning I was burned up but Chang denied ever being at the field the day before. I told him again, if he ever came to the U.S., I'd have him thrown in jail. I'd made the same threat about a plane he stole. That was the Challenger Robin they were supposed to bring back in a couple of weeks. But that Robin was gone. 'Where's my Robin, Chang?' He looked all around, even under the desk, but he didn't have any idea. Robertson told me not to make a fuss. Months later I saw a photo in an aviation magazine of our Robin way up in the interior some place with Chinese characters all over it. At least they hadn't wrecked it yet.

"Last time I saw Chang was during the war [WWII]. We heard some guy was coming to America to borrow a few more millions. I was taking a trip out of Burbank for American Airlines about the time his ship came in so I looked through the fence and here's Chang. I must have told some reporter I knew the guy because they grabbed me for pictures. AA uniform and all. That was the photo of me shaking my finger under his nose and asking if he remembered I was going to have him thrown in jail if he ever got to America. He's standing there with his mouth hanging open saying 'No, no.' Wasn't a paper dared print that.

"Keys had tried to sell me the idea of staying over there to run the show in '29 but I was going to get married and couldn't be bothered." Johnny finally said yes, seven years after they met, but when she called to tell him the news, Slonnie was under contract and had to go to China. He was sure she'd change her mind again before he got back but she said no, she was going to tell her family this time. Johnny said, "I always told people I meant to marry Slonnie but nobody believed me. He was never around. Now I walked in on Dad and Mother—having read all these stories where you tell your family and everybody gets all excited. Dad asked, 'What's new with you?' I said 'I'm going to get married.' Dead silence. Mother finally asked, 'Who are you going to marry?' 'Why, Slonnie of course.' Dad said, 'I'm not surprised,' and went right on reading his paper. Later he did ask when all this

was going to take place. But I didn't know because Slonnie had left for China that morning."

He was ready to return soon enough. "One night I met the Consul General and he said: 'Don't put a dime into China. You'll never get it back.' But he wouldn't be quoted. Then I ran into an American who had built them a very fancy train and been out there about five years trying to get his money. Several months after I got back, I went up to New York to see Keys and told him all this. He looked at me very coldly and said, 'If I want to invest a million dollars, I think that is my business.' So I kind of dropped that subject quick. I was still with Universal and they wanted me to take over the terminal manager's job in Kansas City. I didn't care much for that but, okay, I'd help out. It was a seven-day, twenty-four-hour job and I preferred to fly. We were married in January of 1930 and by Thanksgiving I wanted back on the regular run."

Johnny added, "Dad didn't really make it a condition that Slonnie quit flying, he just fussed about it. So Slonnie thought, rather than stir things up…. They needed somebody to run Kansas City anyway." In theory he gave up flying for his bride. In fact, he flew more hours over strange routes and in curious airplanes as backup man during the winter of 1929/30, than he would have logged as a full-time line pilot over familiar territory.

In China, meanwhile, a dozen firms continued selling airplanes, airlines, or aviation wonders to various Chinese, for civilian use only, of course. By 1937, when Madame Chiang Kai-Shek was head of the air force, her land had 600 airplanes on its books. Only 91 were fit for combat but no machine could be removed from the roster for

any conceivable cause. Loss of face. Even before Robertson pulled out, negotiations had become so involuted some reports claimed Mrs. Robertson ran both William and the firm. Rational people wondered why anybody might care. Pan American followed Curtiss into China with a full management team and still failed to make any profit for years. Their man on the spot was Harold Bixby, who later told Slonnie how he had run into Bill Robertson just before leaving for China but never said a word about his new task. He didn't want to start his Chinese career lower than scratch by having Roberston recommend him. Bixby felt the Curtiss man had made his deal with a notorious crook who had no right whatsoever to sign a mail contract. It was repudiated and when the Minister of Communications set up a rival company, both lost money. A merger was finally worked out, giving Communications fifty-five percent and Curtiss-Wright forty-five, the share Pan American purchased in 1933. At the first board meeting the Chinese director only had one idea, declaring bankruptcy. Bixby managed to talk him out of that and eventually established regular routes, up the Yangtze river and into Canton.

Thus the routes Slonnie surveyed were flown in the end. But when all this became a line called China National, an airline destined for well-deserved fame, its planes were flown by Westerners to start with. Even their first Chinese pilot, in 1934, had been born and trained in America, as were the next two. When CNAC finally hired a locally trained pilot in 1936, he became the highest-salaried man in the land. During WWII Chinese flew the Hump alongside Americans and the Oriental roster included characters every bit as skillful and colorful as those Americans from the twenties, "who made their own rules and promptly proceeded to break every one of them," as Bixby put it. Slonnie only flew some eighty hours in three months over China. But he was always glad he'd gone. "Hell, I'd never seen China."

May 1929   Flying hours: 6,943:50

Chapter 10

Early Airlines

"When Slonnie returns, we'll get this airline on the track."

Slonnie returned to St. Louis and the airmail routes which would occupy him during the rest of 1929, before marriage and what was supposed to be a stable ground job. But 1929, especially the second half, proved to be the most hectic aviation year of a frenzied decade. A standard headline might read, "Lindbergh ties the lands together," meaning mail from Brownsville, Texas, to Mexico City. The man who had done something very similar nine years earlier hardly noticed. For him, it was enough to take up regular American flying again, shrugging off inscrutable Chinese as easily as he had revolutionary Mexicans. Prior to the stock market crash nobody around aviation realized their next five years weren't going to be that simple, although their problem was not necessarily the shortage of funds which plagued most American businesses. The early thirties, when old aviation groups reformed and new airlines sprang up or merged almost weekly, were barely contained chaos. This air business looked like money but nobody was really sure just how to tap the vein. Route rights changed hands on a whim and pilots seldom knew from one day to the next if they would have a job tomorrow

and what kind of airplane they might be flying if they did. An extensive list of different airplanes in Slonnie's logbooks and the almost constant shifts from one town and task to another were a clear reflection of the aviation industry's own uncertainty between mid-1929 and the watershed cancellation of all civilian mail contracts nearly five years later.

Since the mails flew regularly and increasing numbers of passengers found their way to the terminals, commercial aviation seemed to have a future. Especially during the summer of 1929. Robertson Division of UAL (Universal Air Lines) was only one cog in Aviation Corporation of America or AVCO—but eager. And short of experienced personnel. One pilot recalled Bud Gurney saying, "When Slonnie returns, we'll get this airline on the track." When they bought up another line, for instance, its pilots remained so loyal to the old management they might carry mail pouches past their stops. UAL needed Slonnie badly and the China traveler was happy to fly the Chicago run again, for the last few months before his wedding.

He also became entangled in yet another of those endurance flights which had become more popular than ocean leaps. Slonnie had already been involved on the fringe of the first successful marathon, when a young Army crew went after the

record aloft before his China trip. They flew a Fokker trimotor dubbed the *Question Mark,* to veil its foreign origins. "Phil Love and I shared an apartment before China and Pete Quesada, who was pegged to do the team's night flying, was an Army chum of Love's. I was on night mail then, so Phil suggested Quesada should come by and chat. They would be taking off from San Diego but I told him: 'Don't stay over that coast because the fog rolls in every damn night. Take your ship a hundred miles east where there's loads of flat sand and the weather will be wide open if you have any trouble.' That's about all. I didn't know anything about endurance flights, really, but they sure did because they set a record."

Almost everybody else with a broad-wing airplane took his own crack at new eternities in the air that year as well, so Slonnie was bound to learn a little more. Dale "Red" Jackson and Forest O'Brine used a St. Louis-built Robin to circle above that city for 420-plus hours during July 1929, (setting a record they broke by going 647 hours without landing a year later). "Jackson and O'Brine had been flying around 200 hours when somebody decided to send another Robin up and got Joe Hammer to fly it, along with Gent Shelton. I was refueling them. Just an advertising deal. How long a Challenger motor would work. They weren't up so long. I think Shelton, who was really more of a

Slonnie models the dapper Universal Air Lines summer uniform, used once the closed-cockpit Trimotors and their like came into service.

sharp hunting knife in the back of my ship and I'm yelling, 'Cut the rope,' but this dumb kid wouldn't do it. I finally jerked loose, but he was so scared by then he couldn't pull the can up. We went on in and landed with it dangling. I walked into the office and told Bill Robertson to get himself another refueling pilot. I say cut and he comes back, 'It might foul their prop.' 'So what? They were right over the field. Hell, I'm in a stall, struggling like mad not to spin right down on top of them. If we hadn't jerked free he wouldn't be here now. Nor would I.' That was the end of my refueling."

Slonnie moved to Kansas City instead, as terminal manager for a new, transcontinental plane-train route. This was really something of an endurance test for passengers who spent more time on rails than in the air. Frank Hawks had launched a year of cross-country records by making Los Angeles to New York in eighteen hours, twenty-one minutes, then in 17:38, so he predicted that twelve hours should be possible. The Postmaster General wanted to know why mail and people took so much longer, ignoring the fact that Hawks always flew east for the tail winds, in planes so full of his sponsor's fuel there was no spare capacity for a very thin letter. Even so, airlines decided to hasten the mail, cutting schedules from forty-eight hours to thirty-six, while faster passenger service became a publicity match between Transcontinental Air Transport (TAT)—about to show the world's first in-flight film on a Ford Trimotor—and AVCO's Central Division. Working with the Penn and Santa Fe railroads, TAT managed to lose $2.8 million in the first eighteen months but reduced passage time from 100 hours to forty-eight for those

gentleman pilot, just ran that motor too hard. He was sure taking on fuel too damn often. They would radio the field for more and the night watchman phoned me about four this one morning. Shelton was running out of fuel early. I said, 'Tell him to land the damn thing.'

"This was a sideline for me but I went out about daylight and took the gas ship up. We had a tank in it with a hose out the back. They'd grab the nozzle and open a valve. Then my refueling boy would let down five gallons of oil in a slim tank with a spout. Dump that in and we'd pull the can back up. This time we hit a bump and the spout hooked under Shelton's longeron. There was a big,

Loud and far from fancy, the Ford Trimotor was used by Universal Air Lines for its first regular passenger flight on the St. Louis-Springfield-Peoria-Chicago run.

Brown, shown in white overalls, was Slonnie's mechanic for the Ford Trimotor. Mechanics, rather than copilots, accompanied pilots on their flights.

who could afford $345 one way. Universal started a week later with a sixty-seven hour schedule which tied into the 20th Century Limited between Cleveland and New York, plus the Santa Fe west of Garden City, Kansas. Their more-roundabout route only really benefited Chicago and New York businessmen who could cover that leg in one night.

Nevertheless, 175 booked the whole trip during the second half of July, an encouraging 750 more in August. Slonnie said, "Probably eighty percent went clear through and we were about to fly them all the way, no plane-train transfers, when our Chicago hangars burned in 1930 with a whole bunch of new Fokkers inside. The first real, all-air, transcontinental service went up in that smoke." During its short reign this plane-train idea improved passenger service slightly while adding Universal's words, "enplane" and "deplane" to the dictionary, but Slonnie had too many side duties in Kansas City to care much what the details were called.

He said, "That Powder Puff Derby deal with gals flying all over America was typical. My job was out in the middle of the airport with a watch and a fellow holding a big flag, to get each of those lady racers off for their next leg on time. Without exception, every one swerved right for us, taking off. A couple of times we even had to hit the dirt and I told the flagman, if we got that bunch started and stayed alive we'd be okay for life." Universal paid $500 a month for such chores, not to mention managing all operations and flying whatever came along, when no other pilot was available. Still, some lines only gave station managers the same eighty bucks teletype operators earned. "I was about the only manager who was a current commercial pilot so I flew reserve too. Any leg of the plane-train. Or somebody might go down with a mail ship at 2 A.M. We'd crank up a spare airplane and take that to him to complete the mail run.

August 1929 proved a good month for

commercial aviation. Universal carried 14,000 profitable pounds of mail at $1.377 each, when only seven of twenty-three routes in America earned better than a dollar a pound. Pilots flew a half-million miles on CAM 2, the original St. Louis-Chicago route, completing ninety-nine percent of all schedules. The Central Division through Kansas City replied with 99.8 percent reliability in September, despite worse weather. As a measure of how sporadic passenger loads could still be, the ex-Robertson leg only carried 500 people on 190 August trips, plus 3,000 sightseers over St. Louis Airport. Yet they also had to send out what the trade called second sections—another airplane for the same schedule—to handle overload on three days of that same month. Col. H. B. Dunwoody, canny boss of UAL, insisted that modern aviation had to be based on the time function. Called a colorful guy by old hands, Dunwoody was such a dedicated expansionist, his flying into town for a drink was enough to start automatic airline merger rumors. All this occurred under the wing of the AVCO conglomerate. It had absorbed at least eighty-five airplane builders and airlines, while losing $38 million—more than its capitalization— in the three years up to 1930. One acquisition towards the end of that period was Southern Air Transport, which extended AVCO's route map west to El Paso and brought them another eighty miscelaneous airplanes, plus grand plans for a fourteen-story headquarters skyscraper. Most important of all, it added a local manager named C. R. Smith to the national team. Flying had also become attractive to non-aviation, financeer types, if only because they would have top pilots on call for special trips. Dan Jones, a St. Louis banker and

Slonnie and the chief mechanic shown with a Wasp-powered Lockheed Vega, luxuriously
outfitted for airline president Dan Jones.

Universal president for a short spell, was an early example of that breed.

Slonnie said, "I was out in Garden City, flying vacation relief, when this wire came. Jones and friends were going to the Cleveland air races and wanted me to fly them there in our new Lockheed Vega, a pretty fancy ship. It was really Jones's private job, right down to padded pigskin seats. In Cleveland he said the hotel suite was in my name. He had another room, where people wouldn't bother him. The first thing I found in mine was six cases of Prohibition whiskey but that moved right out. We were really there to meet Eddie Rickenbacker, Sales Manager for U.S. Fokker, and buy some trimotors for Universal. Beforehand, Jones bought a whole bunch of Fokker stock cheap. When we announced an order for fifteen airplanes, which was one hell of a fleet in '30, Fokker shares went sky-high. Jones sold off and Universal got its new airplanes practically free.

"After a couple of days at the races they decided to fly over to Watch Hill, beyond Boston. But they fooled around until we were so late out of Cleveland that I told them we could only make Albany. It was nearly dark and I didn't have instrument lights, landing lights, or running lights. Nothing on that Vega. One guy's wife was waiting with a big dinner though, and her husband knew the way. Just pick up the New York-Boston beacons and cut across to Newport. I didn't really want to get anywhere near Boston after dark with no lights, or it could be no license. Even so, when I saw those beacons, it was an awful temptation to swing over. Figured I'd find the coast first though and see how it went.

"Plenty of gas and I'd borrowed every match on the ship. Light one every quarter-hour to check oil pressure. Down about 500 feet it was darker than hell but I took a course to come in a little south of Watch Hill so I'd know which way to turn at the coast. We found the right highway but my guide couldn't tell one light from another, of course. After dark I could smell whiskey in back. They were getting more worried than I was, but I had that old ace in the hole. Back to the beacon line and into Boston. Then I spotted a bunch of airplanes tied down in a field so I just swung around, cut the gun, and landed short. Jones asked where the hell we were and I had no idea, but we were down safe. 'And I am glad to be on the ground, gentlemen.' Taxied over to a hangar, opened the door, and here's the guy's wife. Right away Jones comes up with some money. Told him I got paid for flying but he stuffed it in my pocket. Then the other two. Hundred-ninety bucks. It was the best tip I ever got for sure. But I'd have bet it all at a hundred to one we'd never find Watch Hill. Next morning, when I looked at that field, it was pie-shaped with the wide part by the road. I'd have hesitated to put a Vega in there at all by daylight.

"We went to a big Newport party that Sunday and pretty soon they began to run out of applejack and couldn't find any in the neighborhood. One guy asked how long it would take to fly up to Boston. I figured an hour and got some argument, so Jones laid a big bet on me. I headed for Boston, hell-bent for election. Sunday, and this Lockheed was a very fancy ship, so everybody crowds around when we land. Jones took a fur coat over his arm and sort of strolled over to the bootlegger's car. Tucked a five-gallon jug under the coat and ducked back into the plane. Taking off we stayed down about 300 feet over the bay and out past Boston, until they couldn't see which way we turned, then made a swing back on course and finished with a big zoom over the house. Everybody insisted we couldn't possibly have been clear to Boston but there were five gallons of applejack right between Jones's legs, so the party picked up again. Maybe Lockheed sold some more Vegas."

Universal's pilots flew Fokkers on most normal runs, happy their line had AVCO ties in this case since they pretty much had to fly equipment built under the same corporate umbrella in the era before operators were separated from builders. And Fokkers were solid airplanes. Anthony Fokker, Dutch designer of Germany's best WWI fighter—that same D VII stunt champ Slonnie had won in a crap game—had already progressed from self-taught, 1911 pilot to a character the newspapers dubbed "Tony the egoist, playboy, and aeronautical genius." He would die at age forty-nine. Late in 1923 Fokker founded the Atlantic Aircraft Corporation, so named to sidestep wartime memories. It was turned back into Fokker Aircraft in 1925, the year his plane design named the Universal was introduced as the first American-designed Fokker, ignoring a strong Dutch heritage. The Super Universal followed in short order. Eighty of these, delivered between 1927 and 1931, made it the most popular plane on U.S. routes. Slonnie chiefly recalled dual pilot seats and pedals, but a single control column in the middle, so that even pilots flying alone had to do it one-handed.

Fokker's firm passed through the hands of Richfield Oil to AVCO and by mid-1929, forty-one percent belonged to General Motors, who brought in Eddie Rickenbacker. Unfortunately their F 10 trimotor would become the first U.S. airplane officially grounded (for two weeks), following the Knute Rockne crash in 1931, although its suspect wooden wing was fully exonerated. With neither cabin heat nor belts for its wicker seats the F 10 was past its passenger prime well before safety became a common topic. One suggestion from its era was a parachute fixed to each seat, with a button to drop customers out the bottom before they could panic. Alternatively, a giant parachute was proposed, to let the whole plane down safely. Race pilot and showman Roscoe Turner responded with a mini-chute for his lion cub named Gilmore, during publicity flights for that oil company. Pilots would mourn the three-engine Fokker when it was phased out, chiefly because it could remain aloft on any two of its three, nine-cylinder, radial engines, cruise at an honest 118 MPH, but land at only fifty-five. In short, "It was sweet to fly," as Slonnie noted from Kansas City, where Universal's F 10s were based.

Proclaimed the hub of the nation's airways by the local *Journal-Post,* Kansas City was busy preparing Fairfax Airport for an international air circus in late September 1929. After all, they had the only airport east of California with its own ground hostesses. Not to mention vague plans for a new runway. Fairfax had progressed from a 1925 weed patch to a single hangar in late 1928, then to nine, including Universal's new, $100,000 building, a year later. They even kept a man called "traffic manager" downtown, selling about one ticket per day. This city was also the base for Saunder's pioneer rent-a-plane fleet, from the same family which had originated rental cars in 1926. With all that glory, Kansas City could afford to be only

mildly irked when Universal chose rival Wichita as hub for its thirteen-town bus and interurban feeder network. Kansas City was more interested in plans for its aerial extravaganza, to be climaxed by a record-setting dash from Mexico City. Air fans could marvel at fifty events, including America's largest passenger airplane, acrobatics, and balloon busting. Or they might try to overhear what René Fonck (seventy-five WWI kills for France) said to Ernst Udet (sixty-five for Germany) at the International Aero ball—spectators welcome. About all the Missouri River metropolis lacked of that fall's aerial attractions was Fritz von Opel, who prefigured the future by covering two miles in seventy-five seconds over Germany, flying his revolutionary rocket plane.

Aviation had gained such momentum by late 1929, it would be less devastated than most industries by the Wall Street crash. The 1926 edition of a book called *Transport Aviation* was already deemed obsolete, even by its author. He now decided dirigibles would rule the air lanes with air/rail links the only viable alternative. This must have surprised lines eager to drop costly train hookups. UAL did fly much of the crowd which visited Chicago to view the Graf Zeppelin on its globe-circling trip, however. *Transport Aviation* also noted that most people had overcome a reluctance to fly, now that airplanes went in all weathers. Its author ignored one airline president who always traveled by train. When Judge Kenesaw Landis, baseball's first czar, was cancelled by Universal for weather reasons he was gracious enough to congratulate the line's officers on knowing when to keep their ships on the ground. Publicists found a prominent doctor willing to declare that the thrill

of an airplane ride was conducive to longevity. *Flying Fool,* starring William Bendix, opened as a full talkie and flying replaced sex appeal in general magazine tales, if the comments of no less than seven aviation publications can be believed.

Air was in. Some forty-one states debated nearly 250 aviation bills, enacting 106 of them with surprising uniformity, in the absence of federal controls. The first, $100, *Chicago Daily News* prize for meritorious transport flying went to one UAL man, while three more were among six honorable mentions for sober U.S. flying.

Then Travel Air's new airplane star appeared for the Kansas City show, fresh from its National Air Races triumph, and Slonnie proved a little less restrained in a cockpit than his stance when preaching to the line's pilots as station manager. This was the first civilian racer capable of completely outpacing military planes, winning the Thompson Trophy at 194.9 MPH. Officially called Model R, it was dubbed the *Mystery Ship* because nobody, including Travel Air, was quite sure of all details until a few weeks before their debut win. In 1931 a pal of Slonnie's would get one up to 252 MPH before suffering two separate fires, which prompted him to make one of the lowest successful parachute jumps in history. Even so, he too insisted every Model R was a beauty to fly. Slonnie agreed completely, after one short flight in this monoplane with an engine hopped up to well over 300 rated HP, supported by less than thirty feet of wingspan. He said, "They certainly put together one hell of a good airplane there, with plenty of power. A real honey, it answered every control like a race car. A fellow on our train-plane run flew for Travel Air in his time off. Universal fixed up service for them

When Universal Air Lines hosted air races, Slonnie took the opportunity to perform the first snap rolls ever tried with the Travel Air Model R, called the *Mystery Ship*. Five of these airplanes were built, using 420 hp modified Wright engines. Along with the Fokker D VII, this was one of Slonnie's favorite airplanes.

during the KC show so he said: 'Why don't we let Slonnie fly this thing?' They looked a little askance, but okay. I took it up high to practice, then down to about a thousand feet and thought I'd snap roll once. But I was on my back the second time around before I could stop it and just let it roll on over for a second one, like that was the idea all along. When I landed they said it had never been snap rolled and they didn't even know if those stubby little wings would stay on. I didn't have a chute either. But you can sort of tell if an airplane is going to fly."

When Slonnie later declined the chance to fly what he called, "A damn little racer you could have put into my office," its designer needn't have felt hurt. For one thing, Johnny had heard of those *Mystery Ship* antics and told her new husband he wasn't getting into any more racers. Slonnie said, "The *Red Head* was a Gordon Israel job he wanted me to fly in the Nationals. A sweet little ship but one of his backers decided to try it first. He nearly dug one wing in, just taxiing out, then the other side, but finally got it up. Then he bounced that thing so high, trying to land, he should have spiraled down again. It went over on its back but they fixed it up before the race. I never had any idea of flying it."

In October 1929, he had turned down an airplane and designer of considerably more impressive pedigree. Fokker's F 32 would remain the largest transport aircraft in the world until Russia's eight-engine Maxim Gorki five years later. It was the four-engine American ultimate in an age when very few, apparently including passengers, believed people absolutely needed enroute meals and panoramic windows. This flamboyant Fokker was

Universal Air Lines did not buy the Fokker F 32 (with four engines in tandem pairs) for service because both Slonnie and Fokker's own test pilot refused to fly it with a full load. The plane was ahead of its time but underpowered for its size.

nominally a thirty-two-seat giant—hence F 32—actually designed to carry thirty by day, plus two pilots, or sixteen in berths. Pilots were treated to a full, dual-control cockpit with all possible dials lit electrically for night flying. To propel all this, Fokker mounted four engines in tandem pairs, but four times 575 HP was not really enough to take this behemoth to the claimed 145 MPH, even if the rear power plant in each pair wasn't chronically overheated. One hundred twenty was more likely. Fokker had simply overreached, with seven-plus tons of luxury, including four mahogany-trimmed compartments to cosset a negligeed lady in their ads who peeked out of picture windows on her way to one of two lavatories. True range turned out to be barely 500 miles, carrying a 4.5 ton load, much of it fuel.

Rickenbacker showed off the first one in full UAL paint at that same Kansas City show. He was testing it before turning the plane over to the airline, as Universal's company newsletter reported, in ecstasy over owning the country's first four-engine airliner. Johnny saw the tapestry walls and was thrilled but Slonnie told her, "Forget that stuff. I've already turned that turkey down. You don't want to drive a truck at Indy. Most of the F 32s ended up as hotdog stands, after Western bought a couple at a very reduced price. Universal didn't. Apparently there had been a whale of a party one night and our man woke up to the fact we had signed for five. Paul Goldsborough, our VP for Operations, and I went back to New Jersey to collect the first one, all silver and maroon with our flying jalopy insignia on the side and the history of aviation embroidered above the coat racks. Looked like a harem.

"They cranked it up so Hughie Wells, Fokker's test pilot, and I could fly around, with just Goldsborough and Rickenbacker in the rear. And it still needed the whole length of a dry grass field to get off the ground. I wasn't intrigued about that, with four big motors and only four people on board, and told Goldsborough I wasn't so crazy about this airplane. Plus the fact, I wanted to see it fly fully loaded. And one more thing. I wasn't going to be in it when they tried. Rickenbacker said they would spread thirty people's worth of sandbags in the back but Wells said he wasn't going to fly it that way and Rickenbacker hit the roof. He had three more pilots, goddamn it. He'd get one who could fly. Goldsborough spoke up then and said he wasn't going to ride in it either. Ended up, nobody would fly the thing fully loaded so we took the train home. Fortunately Universal had been smart enough to order on specs. It had to take off with such and such a load in so many feet. We were out."

Slonnie had more pressing projects anyway. As the local paper mentioned, "a veteran mail pilot and KC manager" was moving to Cleveland as operations manager. He said, "Universal had hired this efficiency expert who wouldn't have known an airplane if he found one in his soup. He decided each manager would take over some other guy's job for a while. The day after I got to Cleveland this so-called expert comes around. My place in KC had been cleaned up like a million bucks but somebody had thrown a lot of oil mops into a closet in Cleveland and this old Navy boy raised some hell. 'Tell you something Mr. Frederick G. Coburn, I belong in Kansas City.' He finally left us for National Distilleries. Guess he made sure they filled the bottles right. At least I got in a little more flying boat time in Cleveland. We'd bought up some airline with a water run to Detroit, using Sikorskys, a hull job with two up front. But we never took a copilot. You didn't check out in those days. With any new type, somebody would ask if you wanted to fly it. Just had to remember, there were absolutely no stall landings in a hull job or you'd push that light skin up around your ankles. All you really had to worry about was junk and logs in the lake. We hadn't seen that in China because those people took anything that would burn right out of the water.

Slonnie was back in Kansas City shortly before 1929 ended but didn't stay long. "I was out at the Garden City end again when they wired me to deadhead right back to Cleveland. We had three pilots flying night mail up there, including Roy Mitchell, who kind of ran things and flew too. Until he broke his back in an auto accident. Next night Waldo Roby got tangled up with a hill. That left Jap Lee and he couldn't fly both ways every night. I got into Cleveland about six in the evening, but really beat, so Big Mitch said he'd take Elmer "Red" Caine off Fokkers for the mail that one night. I could go out the next. Well, they called me before daylight. Caine had clobbered it too. I jumped in a mail plane with a mechanic and went down to make arrangements for shipping his body home. Then flew his mail to Cleveland. Left the mechanic to dump the rest of his ship into a creek." UAL lost two men in a few hundred miles, versus their 1929 average of one fatality per million miles flown, shading to perhaps one in 100,000 over unknown territory at night, the conditions Slonnie now faced.

"Actually, my worst trip was one with a

Packard diesel engine. It was like following a bus with your nose up the exhaust. If you didn't get sick those four hours, boy you were tough. That Packard was good and dependable. It even set an endurance record without refueling, but nothing for an open airplane." Packard's compression-ignition radial had been released to a very few lines on trial but it shook instruments apart and only provided worthwhile fuel consumption cuts on flights of more than five hours. When their own designer was killed in a diesel-powered crash, Packard lost interest and closed out the program in 1933, after winning a Collier Trophy for it. Slonnie had dropped the idea a lot sooner. "I told Mitch, to hell with that airplane. Next time I'd walk with the mail. He said it made all of them sick too, so I got a Whirlwind Stearman. Lee and I flew one of those every single night for a full month, except once when the weather was really stinko. It was winter and pretty rough work for thirty straight nights without ever seeing my route by daylight. When I got back the doc put me into a hospital for three weeks. Nothing particularly wrong, except I needed a rest."

By this time, pilots drew $2,500 a year plus mileage pay—more on trimotors—and since that added up to eleven percent of an airline's budget, management began to watch over their health. A little. The country's thirty-four regular airlines had doubled route mileage since 1928 and needed 442 airplanes to carry 159,751 passengers over 22.4 million miles. The airlines weren't prone to hire one more pilot than necessary when planes also cost real money: $15,000 for a single-engine Fokker, triple that for a small trimotor, and up to $60,000 each for big, new airplanes which needed three times as many engine spares.

Recovered, Slonnie was flying relief again as 1930 opened. "Until mid-January," he said "when I went back to the terminal manager's job in KC, then home to get married. We got as far as Chicago on a honeymoon and were called right back. I was supposed to be out of flying but that didn't last. On January 25 I had to fly a second section to Chicago for some convention, since we had a spare airplane but no extra crews. Took a stock clerk with a fifty-hour license as copilot and Johnny in the back. About 3,000 feet over Chicago I called her up to see the field. She looked at our wings and that little bit of field down there and didn't think I'd fit it in. Chicago airport was only half a mile square." His bride said, "That was the first time I'd ever flown because Dad wouldn't let me before we married. They called us very early next morning, to beat this storm back to Kansas City, and I was the only woman on board with some spare crews. Right down over the treetops. I kept looking out and saying, 'Isn't that snow beautiful?' The men didn't say a word. In Kansas City people rushed out to tell us every other plane had been grounded by snow." Slonnie grinned at the memory. "She thought it was a ball. I wasn't quite so crazy about things but nothing happened."

Snow was the main enemy, taking most of the twenty-eight lives lost per 100 million miles flown around America during 1930. One of the first crashes that year dropped into Slonnie's own lap, a few days after he returned from that abbreviated honeymoon. Kansas City morning papers on January 27 carried photos showing scattered shreds in the snow—all that remained at dawn of Central Airlines wreckage which took five lives the previous day at Fairfax Airport. Slonnie said,

"Central belonged to Universal and had a second section from Wichita. Somebody looked out the big window by my office and hollered, 'My God, it's going in.' I rushed out but it was still burning. We tried to keep the crowd away but they came from all over, even grabbing for a shaving brush that was still glowing. Nothing to do so I called the government inspector. He had tickets to the Orpheum that night and told me to have the ship picked up and roped off in a hangar. He'd be over in the morning to find out what happened. They never did. It was a good airplane and we took good care of them. But I got hell for moving that ship."

Johnny added, "Next day all the papers got nasty. Even Senator George William Norris wrote that Mr. Sloniger should be put in the penitentiary for destruction of evidence. The Congressman read a little bit about the crash and didn't bother to check a thing." The debate came down to a missing tail wheel, which was never recovered but couldn't have influenced the accident, and the stolen carburetor which Johnny remembered vividly. "Our apartment bell rang and two young men with a great big gunnysack asked if Mr. Sloniger lived there. I wouldn't have been surprised if they had him in the sack, at that point. But they just said, maybe they had gotten Slonnie into trouble, taking the carburetor, so they were bringing it back. I was so flabbergasted I didn't even think to get their names. I just called Slonnie and told him I thought I had his carburetor. It filled the front hall. We were out to dinner with two local men a little later and one asked how I liked Kansas City. I said there were things to like. 'But not the *KC Star*.' And got kicked on both ankles. I was talking to the editor. But he made me mad. There wasn't a word of truth

in their stories but they wouldn't retract. I broke up that party."

Slonnie wasn't jailed and shrugged off the press. He had enough to do with smooth operations in an era when pilots still decided basically whether to fly or not. Universal's men were known in the business as very sharp bad-weather men although the best advice they might get came from calling some farmer along the route who'd probably say, "Kinda cloudy around here." One mail pilot who called in to ask for a clearance through the snow was told, "You're out there. Fly on in if you can. Or want to." In this case the pilot came around next day to tell the operations clerk, they weren't supposed to do things that way any more. Others preferred an operations man who had been a pilot himself, rather than the inherited wealth and banker crowd who were taking an interest in the glamour of aviation ground jobs. A fellow pilot could appreciate the limitations when he had to sooth a passenger caught by bad weather. "Strangler" Lewis was on one flight UAL cancelled that first winter and the desk thought it was going to get a little tough here, telling this bruiser he was about to miss a rich wrestling match. The muscleman just said it made no difference.

This wasn't the reason Slonnie was still toying with the idea of operations. He said, "I always thought, one day I might get too old or some doc would find my pump had a funny tick. So I'd take an operations job, usually with flying too. The only time supposed to be just ops was early '30 and that didn't last long." Could the new wife of a man who had already spent nearly 7,500 hours at flying really think he would stay out of airplane cockpits? She said, "No, but I was neutral on the subject. I

met him when he was flying and believed he was an excellent pilot, knowing absolutely nothing about it. After a little while I realized he wasn't going to be happy not flying. That had been my father's idea. I wasn't going to marry a pilot. But Dad never mentioned it when Slonnie went back to regular line flying about four months after we were married."

Pilots who wanted to fly that badly were generally credited with the good safety record achieved by lines using outdated airplanes. "But heaven help them," as one pilot/ops man put it, "if maintenance failed to send out near-perfect equipment." Slonnie faced that problem often enough. "We had an F 10 come in about four P.M. one day with a motor shot. Due out at eleven the next morning so I rushed over to the overhaul shop. Perry, my head mechanic, said he didn't even have a spare built up. There it was, on those shelves. Rods, pistons, everything in a row. I figured somebody on the field might have a spare Wasp. It was the top engine so we all used them. But old Perry said to let him handle things. He'd keep a crew on all night, putting ours together. I went home and hoped he knew what he was talking about. About seven the next morning he called to say he'd just turned that motor over to maintenance to install and they would run it up in the airplane. I could test it around nine. Took the F 10 up for maybe thirty minutes and everything was fine. That's how we kept operating then. That and a sense of humor."

Winter flying suits with long-pile fur linings were irresistible to pilot jokers. Slonnie said, "Universal's hangar porter was a good worker but kind of a nervous little guy. Somebody told him the local zoo was missing a gorilla so he should keep an eye peeled. Then they turned one of those winter suits inside out, with the long black fur showing. Gloves too. When our boy went for a mop this arm comes out of the closet and makes a grab for his neck, with a big growl. He burst into my office just about dead white. 'Gorilla loose in the hangar.' When I got out there—no gorilla." Not even Tam, the Sloniger Scottie who got loose regularly just so the porter could carry him back. "When Johnny started working at the field too we just let him roam. Our hangar was maybe a block from this fancy new terminal. When they taxied a ship up to load, Tam would hop in and ride to the passenger ramp. Open the door, he'd jump out, visit her, and run back to the hangar."

Johnny said, "My being at the field began when somebody suggested I help the decorator pick things for this new lounge. We bought soft, blue-leather furniture with silver wings set into the backs, to go in front of a bay window that went up two stories, looking out on the field. Afterwards I ran the switchboard and even ticketed some of the little airlines. Or filled in for the cigar desk and coffee shop cashiers. I got to know all the guys who flew into Kansas City that way."

About the only job she skipped was flying, although many pilots taught their wives. Slonnie said, "I never even thought about it. Only time she rode up front was in the Dutch wing." Johnny picked up the tale. "He called and said he had to take this Fokker with a special thick wing to St. Louis. I didn't know Slonnie was the only man who really liked to fly it. In any case, I'd been learning aviation words around the terminal and wanted to impress him." Slonnie said, "We got about half way

and Johnny wanted to use her new lingo so she leaned over and asked, 'How are your ailerons?' I rolled that wheel full left and she let out a yip. Whipped the ship over on its other side, then leveled off and advised her my ailerons were just fine. She told me she'd never ask a question like that again. It was a nice smooth ride the rest of the way."

That same summer he called Johnny to ask if she wanted to fly to Garden City in the Monocoach. She thought, why not? Slonnie knew why they wouldn't have company. "That ship was supposed to be a good performer but ours took off, cruised, and landed at one speed, about ninety. A turkey, even with the 225 HP Wright engine." Universal's sole Monocoach lived up to its reputation that day. Johnny was sitting in back and getting sicker and sicker, until Slonnie decided they were low on gas anyway and had better land. There was an alfalfa field by a roadside gas station so he filled up while she walked around until she felt better. Climbed in and got sick again. Later they found a big gas leak. Worse, they hadn't wired for a room and she would always wonder why they called the place Garden City anyway, without a single tree in sight. Temperature that day was pushing 112 and no rooms left with a bath. Slonnie went on west about some beacon argument and she camped in the lobby until they opened somebody's room for a bath and promised her one of their own that same afternoon. When Slonnie got back, looking beat, she announced proudly she had a bath but he just said, "Fine, but go up and pack. The Chicago hangars burned down.

"Heading back east," Slonnie said, "the engine lost all its oil pressure and I wasn't too sure

we'd find open country to land. I told Johnny I didn't think we were going to make it and she thought I meant we wouldn't get down. I told her never to worry about that. Gravity always took care of getting down. I was thinking about making Kansas City." They landed in the Flint Hills where the pilot worked on his ship a while, then had her get out while he started the engine. She wasn't really much of a pilot if it had run away from her. Johnny finished the tale. "Flying was certainly one thing I was very sure Slonnie could do far better. A couple of months later he called to say he had to finish the beacon deal and did I want to go? No thanks. I didn't care for forced landings. Or that Monocoach. He took a Super Universal instead, along with my brother-in-law, but they got back over the Flint Hills, and went down again. I just said, 'See.'" Aviation might be a quarter-century old but pilots who could fix their own planes on the spot were hardly out of date quite yet. This time the engine quit over a bunch of washed-out ravines but Slonnie lifted it over a barbwire fence, dead stick, and set it down in a pasture next to a schoolhouse. The minute they hit, school let out. Turned out it was no more than a throttle rod detached from its socket so the engine could only idle. Slonnie spotted one kid with high-top boots. Before he finished saying, "Son, will you sell me one of those laces," that boy had it off. He got a quarter and Slonnie fixed his engine with six inches of whang leather.

Johnny didn't mind airplanes headed anyplace other than Garden City. "Every once in a while I'd go along," she said. "One 3rd of July, the hottest summer Kansas City ever had, we went out to watch the mail go through. George McCabe was the pilot and he came in with an awful headache so Slonnie sent him out to our place with the Ford roadster and Tam. We found some overalls for me, took the lid off the mail compartment, and pushed some sacks around to make me a seat." Slonnie added, "She'd never been up after dark or in an open cockpit and you could see three or four beacons ahead. Our first stop was St. Jo, a very small field with a bluff at the edge. You had to get right over the fence and ride your brakes hard. Johnny had to see it all so she stood up and leaned over the right side. About the time I moved left, she changed sides too. I had a newspaper in my lap, kind of nibbling on the news with a flashlight as we went along. So I rolled that up, reached forward and batted her over the head. She ducked like I'd thrown a rock and we landed with no more trouble."

Such casual, wife-along flights with the mail were not to last. President Hoover had a Postmaster General named Walter F. Brown who strongly favored fewer, financially stronger airlines following stricter rules, to attract more passengers and eventually reduce the need for mail subsidies. His goal was faster schedules with bigger airplanes to replace outdated open ships, as well as the queen-bee Ford. Brown wanted order and prestige above all so he ignored shrill screams from little lines being squeezed out, just as he missed the message of Aeropostale in France which had come under vicious attack in late 1930 for the wrong kind of government aid. A typical Brown move was to transfer the Kansas City-St. Louis route from United Air Lines to American Airways, with only a brief sublet clause as sop to United. Universal became one part of American Airways (or AA) in

This Ford Trimotor bears the American Airways company name, used until President Franklin Roosevelt cancelled civilian aviation mail contracts in 1934. The company was called American Airlines thereafter.

Jerrold E. Sloniger Collection

August 1930 and celebrated its new status by adding copilots on some runs to hand out box lunches. With Brown's connivance, AA could finally fly clear across the continental United States, following a route almost as patchwork as its Alaskan arm, which carried mail in competition with dogsleds.

Pilots still worked, in theory, for their old divisions, but most were proud to be part of a proper airline too, even if size didn't bring immediate profits. As one Universal Division man explained, mixed companies like theirs lost money in large quantities and it was only tenacity which kept them going at all until the wheeler-dealers moved in with merger cash. Then the new American Airways went transcontinental and lost even more money. Slonnie said, "Pretty soon we bought up people like Delta to get the Dallas-Birmingham run, or Standard for San Diego-Phoenix. Ended up with eight or ten little outfits which had been flying just about one of every known airplane from Pitcairns to the Temple, a high-wing job with J5 engine."

The government installed 3,000-plus miles of new lighted airways in 1930, making 13,504 miles in all, but many lines like AA had to fill the gaps. American put in its own beacons and emergency fields west of El Paso. This lack of unified fleet or plan for almost any airline was another reason theirs became the first American industry to actually ask for federal regulation. Washington's answer: the Air Commerce Act. The year ended with thirty-eight government-rated carriers flying 497—mostly different—airplanes and a continued steady, if slow, rise in passenger totals. Planes were still slow and noisy too, but then, 40 MPH was good for a car on contemporary roads. Nebraska, for

example, had only 310 paved miles and trains stopped at so many way stations, even slow airplanes got there first.

Postmaster General Brown's vision of passengers traveling in aerial luxury was going to take a while, but most lines did respond by grouping staff as well as airplanes at hub airports. To go with what was billed as its "Skyline Ltd," Chicago-St. Louis service at $3 extra, with no stops, Robertson Division of AA bid on another contract air mail route, CAM 28 to Omaha, which tied in with the transcontinental mail through Kansas City. Slonnie said, "I took that because we had all been taken off salary and were only paid a straight ten cents a mile. But double at night. So I decided to go back on the night mail. It had beacons all the way by then. There was no seniority list for picking your job yet, but older men got first choice, which

meant the same thing. And we still flew regularly. We moved again, on Thanksgiving , and had a hot dog holiday dinner on the way to St. Louis."

During the Depression working pilots flew more hours than ever—happy to have a job. Slonnie logged his first 1,000-hour year in 1931, despite a rare, two-week vacation, opening with 105 hours in open mail planes that January. Such flying would continue until the '34 airmail shuffle, with 1,122 hours logged during 1932 (no vacations) and five months above 100 hours each, much of that night work. He said, "Some guys still didn't want to fly at night but they were nuts. It might be nasty in winter, with pretty stinko weather, but I don't know why it should be more work unless it worried you. Then it was probably harder. I liked night runs even better when multimotor stuff came in. The air was smoother and you

With smaller airlines merging so frequently into larger companies, there were too many different aircraft models, which created problems for companies like Universal and American Airways. This Fokker Universal bears the markings, Universal Division, American Airways.

didn't have passengers chasing the stewardess up and down your aisle, upsetting the trim.

"On the mail though, you never knew what kind of airplane you'd fly until you got to the field. One had brakes above the rudder pedals, on the next they were alongside. Or it might be a Boeing if some passenger wanted to go along. That was one of the most stable airplanes in the bunch, but heavy on the wings. Almost as tiring to fly as a DH. Carry a good load though. I took one into St. Louis and Gage Mace, our operations manager, asked if it would lift 2,000 pounds. Sure, without much gas on board. Seems some bootlegger would buy it if we could carry a ton so we got sand from a lumber yard, flew it around, and he paid up. Of course he'd never stuff a ton of bottles in for sure, but that wasn't our problem. He gave each of us a bottle of rum and we'd sold off another old airplane." Airlines, even the major names, took money anywhere they could. "Most of the money we saw in those days was carried for other people though," Slonnie said. "Worst thing with a cash load was, they'd send a policeman out in the mail carrier's Ford truck. Of all the dead giveaways.... So the government would tell us we had to wear a gun to fly the mail. Next month they'd take it away again. It didn't matter a damn to me, either way. Anybody could flag me down by sticking out a red flare on some emergency field. You couldn't fly over one of those. If I had money on board, listen, I would have helped them unload it. I wasn't going to shoot it out with anybody in some boondocks pasture.

"Mostly we stuck to the main airports anyway. Fairfax in KC was nice, with one runway lit. Omaha only had a north-south blacktop runway. The diagonal was so short most of us landed north-south, whatever the winds were. St. Louis was surfaced in 1931, but any good rain could still put Dallas out of business. Newark was the first one supposed to be designed by experts. With those high-crown runways they built for drainage, if you didn't land absolutely dead center, the plane spun off a seven-foot bank." Slonnie ran into an even finer Newark feature on a trip that February—the hourly bulletin telling pilots which direction they must land, to banish accidents for all time. Nobody explained how an incoming pilot was supposed to read the bulletin board before he arrived. Newark continued to deplore its share of bent airplanes.

Johnny insisted, "I never gave accidents a great deal of thought. But one morning Slonnie didn't come home so I called the field and a voice said: 'Sloniger? He cracked up last night!' Bang goes the phone. Well, it was March and an open plane and snowing hard, but I realized it probably wasn't so bad or I would have heard. I called another pilot who told me Slonnie was fine but they didn't know how the ship was. It was on its nose in a Missouri snowbank and he was at some little hotel."

Slonnie said, "I happened to have a Pitcairn and it was down about 200 feet, ducking a terrific head wind. The snow had been so deep in KC a couple of guys walked me out to the end of the runway and got me squared away by digging their heels in like brakes. And I still hooked a landing light on takeoff, so I decided to fly right over St. Jo, where the snow was even deeper, and go straight into Omaha. My main tank was pretty dry but I figured on thirty gallons from the wing tank. Then my engine quit cold. Two A.M.

and dark, but there was a break in the row of trees right ahead. You just take what's out in front on a dead stick landing from that low. One light was dangling but I could still see the lee of this hill and stubble. Oh boy, I had this baby made. About the time my wheels touched though, I ran right smack into an eight-foot snowbank. Not a bit of damage but that was it. I'd seen farmhouse lights and followed their fence in. Knew that trick from my growing-up days on the homestead. Borrowed a big old plow horse and rode the mail maybe three miles into Tarkio. Only part that was a little rough—I hadn't ridden for years and it was such a big, fat horse, my legs got pretty sore."

Just as he fell into bed at last Johnny decided she'd feel better if she talked to him herself. She finally got the hotel but they didn't say there were no phones in the rooms. When he got dressed again and back down to the lobby and heard her voice, all he wanted to know was why the hell she had called. "Of course I'm not hurt." All he would ever tell her about flights like that was, "Oh, I got away with it okay." Slonnie learned later, "That Pitcairn had a goofy gas line. Down underneath the engine and back up to the carburetor. Condensation had frozen in the loop. The guy who picked up my ship later found a ditch wide as a room and just as deep right behind it. My tail skid touched about ten feet past the edge. If I'd landed twenty feet sooner it would have gone over on its back for sure."

Slonnie seldom considered successful forced landings luck because he always stayed ready for one. And he never figured he was paid to make headlines in that manner, although he did get into the papers again soon after his Tarkio snowbank.

Jerrold E. Sloniger Collection

Slonnie had a forced landing one night in Tarkio, Missouri, while he was flying the mail. He landed totally blind in a blizzard, missed a fence, and nosed up in a snowbank.

This time it was a record, in March 1931, when the wind blew his way. The reporter got his airplane type wrong, inevitably. Slonnie's log showed a Stearman leaving Omaha on what was usually a four-, even five-hour flight. But he picked up a terrific tail wind and did the trip in two and a half, since it boosted the plane's normal 90 MPH cruise speed to above 140. Fortunately he was still paid by the mile. Hourly pay only came with bigger equipment.

That day was hastened by one of America's most-publicized air tragedies, when Notre Dame coach Knute Rockne was among the victims of a Fokker trimotor crash on March 31, 1931. This accelerated the rush to all-metal airplanes and thus to even-larger aviation conglomerates to pay for them. United was put together that year, last of the big four, and E. L. Cord of automobile fame launched Century to fly passengers at less than railroad fares. He'd simply pay pilots less. Braniff tried to organize the independents, using faster passenger airplanes on routes parallel to mail-monopoly runs, but they were too late. Mail subsidies had bought the big lines enough time to find some passengers. American expanded again and moved the Slonigers again. It was Omaha in May '31, so Slonnie could both fly and watch over operations. "Mostly pilots still decided on any trip though," he said. "If they wanted to go, there was the ship and St. Louis was over that way."

Some claimed the biggest event of the year was AA remaining in business until C. R. Smith from their new Texas division began to move up. During the first Roosevelt campaign Smith, being a Democrat, prevailed on FDR to fly to the nominating convention in a Ford Trimotor bearing the new

AA emblem. It would show the world he was a vigorous type. Actually, Roosevelt hated airplanes but Smith courted Eleanor too, supporting all her causes, and he soon had the AA eagle on its way to top bar of the airline roost. That new insignia, staunchly and properly defended by every single AA man as the best-looking in aviation, came out of a contest soon after American Airways was put together. A British-born traffic man named Goodrich Murphy won the prize and helped give their scattered divisions some sense of cohesion. Pilots who couldn't stomach this big business climate could turn to an also-burgeoning new and militant force called the Airline Pilots Association. Slonnie said, "We founded ALPA in Universal days and I was a charter member. Kind of an advisory thing because our new top people didn't know airplanes. Gave them our flying experience. Dave Behncke came to head it though, and we never got along too well. I quit when he wanted to join the AF-of-L. It took longer for a copilot to make that left seat than for a medical student to go through internship and I never thought professional men should need a union."

Behncke fought against hourly pay at United, his own line, without minding much if copilots only drew $225 a month regardless. The lower orders could always look forward to making captain some day, in his view. That was a job paying more than the master of an ocean liner received. Top pilots were earning close to $1,000 per month, with the average salary touching seven dollars an hour. Behncke, who had elbowed aside an old friend to gain control of his union, would claim a membership of seventy percent of all working pilots by the end of 1932. He gained that,

in part, with union planks such as a whites-only clause, although no black had earned a commercial pilot's license yet. Cord provided his gut issue in February 1932, trying to cut Century salaries even further because he didn't have a mail contract. Some insisted Cord had a deal with Behncke, to cause an uproar he would use to maneuver his way from little Century to control of American Airways, achieved by October with no ALPA outcry, despite the union's moans about all those scab pilots back at Century. Slonnie was already disgusted with ALPA by then, although few pilots bothered to debate such issues when their schedules happened to cross.

Jokes were more the style with Jack Knight, savior of the night mail and now flying the Chicago run for United in a fat, three-engined Boeing design pilots called "the Blimp." Slonnie said, "The post office where I signed for my mail was down by United's hangar, so one day Knight and I were leaning against the wing of his plane in there. Of course he just wore a business suit in 'the Blimp,' but I was in full flying gear for the open mail plane, when this old duck, maybe eighty, comes up. He'd ridden that Boeing all the way from Salt Lake City and figured I was dressed like a pilot so he's telling me what a great trip it was. He was going right on through to Chicago. Knight turns and studies this strange thing and says, 'I don't know, it only has two engines, all lopsided.' We could only see one on the wing and the nose. 'Oh no,' the passenger says, 'it has three.' Knight wouldn't believe that until the old boy took him around to the other wing and proved it. Jack comes back straight-faced and tells me, 'It really does have another engine, but you'd never get me up in one

of those.' I often wondered what the poor geezer thought when Knight strolled up the aisle to the cockpit and flew that two-engined-trimotor to Chicago."

Knight would fly many more years but that same spring would be the last time Slonnie talked with Charles "Speed" Holman. "He had this little Laird stunt plane and was a very fine acrobatic pilot. Speed was doing a show in Omaha and the night before I'd been down to his hotel and told him, 'Look, I haven't had a ship on its back in years.' He told me he felt the same damn way about stunts but his line had just gotten this new run from the Twin Cities to Omaha, and part of the deal was some acrobatics for the opening. Johnny and her father and I got to the field a little late for his show the next day so I said, 'Let's just stand by the fence. Holman is taking off now and this boy can really fly.' He had a favorite deal of rolling over on his back at about 1,000 feet, diving upside-down and coming right across the field inverted, fifty or 100 feet up, to close the show. But his belt broke as he flattened out. I saw the wings wiggle and him put a hand on the upper wing, trying to shove himself back in. He was a big, strong boy but centrifugal force was too much. Why he didn't have a double belt in there, I'll never know. I always put in a shoulder strap, along with the lap belt which came with any plane. Holman hit right on that runway. Didn't burn or anything but the poor guy was gone." Johnny added, "We had finally talked Dad into watching an airplane for the very first time in his life. When Holman went in my father turned on his heel and never went near an airport the rest of his life."

In one sense Holman's death marked the

end of aviation's first age. Men who had learned to fly in the Jenny went on to give early flying far more glamour than the Wrights ever offered or wanted. Now it was time for a wider, more sober, appeal. In September 1931, Slonnie made a trip east to collect an airplane designed specifically for passenger comfort. He said, "Management sent me to New York for the first Pilgrim and even said Johnny should go along. When we got there a vice president took us to the [Ziegfield] Follies. Next day I went out to the Fairchild factory on Long Island. A Pilgrim pilot got in from the outside so their test pilot had to climb up to the door behind me to point out the buttons. There was no direct connection with the passenger cabin, just a little window. Only one engine with the nose narrowed down, so visibility was good. A stable airplane with nice landing qualities but takeoff with a full load, on a hot day, was not what you might like. Cruise maybe 115-120. Nine in back with three of them on a bench across the front of the cabin. It was a wide old ship at the waist, with a Hornet engine, the most powerful we had then. Next morning we circled the Statue of Liberty and followed NAT's route to St. Louis, because the old Pilgrim didn't really have too much range.

Johnny added, "It was all such a funny trip. First that fuss over a mere pilot in New York. Then people rushing out at every stop, all excited about this brilliant blue airplane with the lovely insignia, which was going to revolutionize the business. We'd planned to make St. Louis that same night but Slonnie tapped on the window and held up a slip of paper. I climbed up on the couch and read: 'Better go into Cleveland.' It was dark and he was getting into ice. Harold Otto, a boy in opera-

tions there, had worked for Slonnie in Kansas City, and he drove us into town." Otto was the typical early-AA ground man, first hired as a steward on Fokkers because his limited license met second-pilot regulations. The real job was making passengers comfortable without bothering them. Stewards carried a big suitcase of canned meat and fruit and bought fresh bread for each trip. In rough air the slices all came out different thicknesses. By the early thirties business was getting so good they would sometimes leave the steward behind or send him on by rail, so many like Otto moved into dispatch.

The Slonigers delivered this first of ten AA Pilgrims to St. Louis and he returned to the night mail. Slonnie didn't move to a Pilgrim run until 1932 but he would log his 10,000th hour of flying in one, between St. Louis and Chicago, in mid-May, 1933. Pilgrims remained a pleasant memory chiefly because of workable, two-way radio at last. "Before that you put a map on your lap and flew. Then we got simple radios and could talk to a few towers. About half-way Chicago faded out and St. Louis might come in. Thunderstorms were terrible and lightning felt like somebody hit you alongside the head with an ax. In rain or sleet, just take that headset off and put it on the floor. Snow was even worse than rain for static." When two-pilot airplanes became common, most captains, sitting on the left, pushed their right earphone aside to hear the copilot. "That's why we all went deafer on the left. Sure, some complained radios made it the first time a company could tell us how to fly. But I never heard them try. And I never knew a real pilot who didn't like radio. No monitoring then so you could kid a little, late at night.

There were so few, you knew every voice. If the radio cut out you just followed somebody else in, like before."

Slonnie had gotten all this tagalong practice he wanted in November 1931 and it worked then too, after a fashion. Johnny said, "An assistant to the president came through and took us out to dinner. He said they wanted Slonnie to take this Fairchild to Seattle. 'Oh? How long would be be gone?' 'Well,' he said, 'if he gets there in time, he'll be right back. But if he misses the last boat to Alaska, he'll have to fly the ship on up. And wait until spring for a boat out.' I just sat there, sort of stunned. While he was asking, he was ordering Slonnie too."

The pilot explained, "We still owned Alaskan Airlines and they needed another airplane, so somebody stuck a Wasp engine in that Fairchild. Didn't need a radio for Alaska though, so I would have to follow the old Boeing route to Cheyenne visually. Found a fellow named Bill Hoare there. He'd wanted me to leave Robertson for Boeing on my very first mail run into Chicago. I was with a dinky little outfit then and Boeing was flying brand-new mail planes, but I'd stuck. Now he was running Cheyenne where I had a deal to gas my ship. I asked Hoare to have it ready at daylight but he told me I wasn't going anyplace. They had three ships down between there and Salt Lake already. I figured if those Boeing guys wouldn't fly, I sure as hell wasn't sticking my nose in. It snowed all day but Tommy Thompson was going to try next morning, so I had my ship warmed up too. Tommy knew every turn and twist of that country so I told him, if it got too bad for me with no radio, I'd wave, and he should point at an emergency field and go on. When it

Slonnie with wife Johnny and her mother in front of a Fokker F 10 Trimotor refurbished for the Detroit Auto Show in 1931. Note Slonnie's Hollywood-pilot-style moustache.

started snowing again I flew the best formation of my life, about three feet off his wing, and he got us both into Salt Lake after dark. Introduced me to the Varney Airlines boy flying to Boise next morning. That Salt Lake airport was right down on the water and this guy never got much higher. It's a big lake from 200 feet and I'd heard of motors quitting, but he claimed it was so salty you couldn't sink. Said they always stayed low.

"I hung around Boise a couple more days. When we finally could leave and pulled up on top, mountains were sticking through those clouds like jagged pagodas. This boy I'm following kept diving down into the cloud tops and climbing back up again. I couldn't figure out why. Turned out his motor was cutting on him. Same ship I'd followed across Salt Lake. He had to dive until it caught again. But that got us to Pasco, Washington. The next boy was going around by Portland but I'd lost so much time by then I had to cut across. He said to get up around 5,000 feet and hold course until I saw a great big mountain. Just keep well to the right of that. I spotted Mount Rainier pretty soon but flew four more hours and it never seemed to get any closer. Eventually I did spot Seattle bay though, and knew where the field should be.

"I was supposed to send Johnny a telegram every stop but all the wires were down, so she got jumpy and finally contacted railroad dispatchers all along to ask if anybody had seen a plane down. They traced me to a Seattle hotel but she was so mad by then, she wouldn't come to the phone. We folded the wings and stuck that plane on the last boat. Otherwise I would have been up in Alaska, hunting walrus or something, when my son was born. Hitching back on Boeing it was still snowing, and the same trick with the motor cutting out. Dive towards the North Platte for a flat, water landing and it would pick up again. The only other passenger was a pilot too and we both figured that if this airplane ever got down, we were going to take a bus. Even a horse. But it made Omaha all right."

Nineteen thirty-one closed with thirty-five airlines flying 490 planes, figures not too far from those of 1930. Still, they were jointly closing

in on half a million passengers, up by twenty-five percent, despite a vast segment of the public which devoutly believed airplanes were fun to watch, not to ride. By 1932, American Airways alone would serve sixty cities daily and stand first in mileage flown, among U.S. lines, if you counted their Alaskan and Canadian arms. They owned nearly 100 airplanes, which flew 60,000 passengers over 7.5 million miles. That year the magazine *Aviation Business* insisted that aviation could stand on its own legs at last—assuming continued hefty mail subsidies—but admitted that a fog of mystery, ignorance, misdirected enthusiasm, and just plain lying still surrounded the nation's youngest major industry. One reach for respectability came when fourteen lines, including AA, formed an Air Transport group to police everything from safety to a common, thirty-pound baggage limit.

When Major General John F. O'Ryan, an AA vice president, flew into Chicago with Slonnie, he announced aviation's prime needs as a variable-pitch propeller and variable wing areas. Travel Air was trying steam power, why not swing wings?—although he was a bit premature. O'Ryan also admitted AA had lost $4 million in 1930 and only showed black ink for a few months of 1931. Airlines were losing money on passengers, he agreed, but all believed that would get better or they wouldn't continue. In January 1932, AA was awarded another spur from Omaha, muscling out a smaller line, and soon got Buffalo-Chicago too, unloading Alaskan on Pan American late in the year. That summer they joined TWA to form General Air Express, rival to Railroad Air Express. These two fast freight services would merge in 1935.

The Slonigers were shuffled again, back to

National Air and Space Museum, Smithsonian Institution

A Fairchild 100 Pilgrim, the airplane type in which the author took his first flight with his father.

St. Louis in April 1932, seven weeks after their son was born. Johnny said, "Jerry left Omaha in a basket set on that couch in a Pilgrim. But I wouldn't go unless Slonnie flew the ship. He finally asked the regular pilot to come sit with us and flew the first part, to Kansas City, where everybody came out to see what we had in the basket. Some people said we were crazy to take such a young baby up. Our doctor had said he didn't know of one that young flying. But why not?" He couldn't know that the first half of 1932 would be the worst six months in aviation history for fatal crashes. The new father, who habitually noted bare hours flown, as Washington demanded and because his pay depended on it, but totally ignored logbook columns for comments, now used the remarks space for virtually the only time in thirty-eight years of flying. Under April 30, 1932, it read: "Jerry's first ride." That was written on the spot, other entries were often a guess until his wife learned the rules. She said, "When we first married he'd ask what I had done with some paper match folder he'd left on the dresser. I couldn't see why he cared. It was empty, so I'd thrown it away. But he never carried a logbook, just jotted hours in any spare folder, to enter later. I learned to save every single empty paper matchbook."

Soon he had to note instrument time as well, to satisfy a new government ticket called the Scheduled Air Transport Rating or SATR, required of every airline pilot by the end of 1933. Albert F. Hegenberger of the Army had already made the first blind solo flight, and most pilots paying extravagant insurance premiums welcomed anything which might make their trade appear safer, including dials. Line pilots weren't alone. Ernest Cutrell, a government inspector who became closely identified with many blind flying advances, remembered how he just wanted to be on par with the airline men so he flew with a bag over his head all summer.

The first SATR tests Cutrell gave in May 1933, included a written exam on radio, navigation, and meteorology, then a flight test. Cutrell would put a hood up on the pilot's side and have him make a few turns each way, using compass and airspeed, then turn on the radio, and tell him to find the beam, locate himself, and come over the station. Some he tested stayed lost a couple of hours. About one in four flunked first try and some old barnstormers told Cutrell they shouldn't advance so far, so fast. Most were anxious to get the rating, of course. American Airways pilots became known as good men on the dials, fliers who feared no weather. Slonnie insisted, "Really, there is no such thing as zero-zero weather (a total lack of visibility, forward or vertically). You could always see maybe a block if you looked and I never saw a solid ceiling lower than the tops of telephone poles." Laymen loved the zero-zero term anyway. "Avery, a magazine writer and ex-pilot, was playing bridge at our house one night when I told about a nasty Chicago trip, so he wrote it as a short story called 'Chicago Run' and put in a Negro stewardess. I told him to cut that out. We didn't have girls on the Pilgrims. But his greatest line of all was: 'The weather was zero-zero—and getting worse.'"

Pilots quickly realized that their prime need for this new instrument game was a stable platform, which designers didn't always provide. Also, AA still flew a good many airplanes built before dials became important, inherited during one of their countless takeovers or purchased from a builder owned by the same conglomerate. More

engines didn't automatically make a better airplane either. Stinson's Model U trimotor was a typical near-miss, "A plane which vibrated pretty smoothly once you got those engines more or less in sync," as one AA pilot put it. The makers did claim excellent visibility, no great trick in a high-wing airplane which took even longer to get airborne than most, while boasting a glide angle both steeper and more sudden than the Ford. Commenting on a ship dubbed "Old Rubber Wings," Slonnie said, "It wasn't a bad airplane but I sure never tried to fly one with an engine out. AA had maybe twenty because Cord owned both us and Stinson by then."

Barely a score of new models of any make were introduced during 1932 and most were sold to captive airlines. With so many uneconomical airplanes around, it was small wonder passengers were charged $160 for a one-way, transcontinental ticket when a new Chevrolet only cost $445. It would be another sixteen years before airline passenger miles topped fifty percent of the railroad figure. In 1932 they stood at 1.9 percent. One strong deterrent was nineteen fatalities on domestic routes that year, a figure fortunately cut by over half in 1933. Aviation ads could only stress the forty-eight man-hours put into airplane inspection for every twenty-five flown. And there were endless press junkets, often flown by Slonnie as a kind of unofficial senior pilot for American. Peoria papers reported a typical trip. Their city had opened one of those new municipal airports the industry craved on December 10, 1932. Three days later Slonnie hauled a Pilgrim load of reporters to Chicago and back. All duly lauded lights around Peoria's new wonder, which would stay lit all night, although mail was admittedly still a small quantity in Peoria.

Lines themselves liked new airports but they were even more intrigued with new airplane ideas which might give their passengers a plus. For AA the 1933 innovation was an airplane with berths. This Curtiss Condor was not the first sleeper, but it was the plane which really provided night-flying luxury during its brief but busy career. First came movies aloft, then meals on trays, now berths a carefully calculated one inch longer than a Pullman car's. And two pilots up front. Slonnie felt, "We didn't really need a copilot to fly the Condor but I always liked to have one." Duties depended entirely on the captain's whim and most of those seniors were still considered very rugged types with experience, intuition, and mechanical savvy left over from their loner days. An old pilot's main interest was deciding beforehand what to do when the emergency hit, even discussing it with his peers while their copilots listened, without interrupting. Captains were a proud lot and should have been. No one could help them if an emergency did come up. Companies did publish guidelines: keep the cockpit door closed, avoid steep, climbing turns, never leave that left seat except for the toilet, and wear a cap, even if summer weather forces you to take the jacket off. Never discuss crashes with anybody, nor weather where passengers might overhear. And no more box lunches at company expense.

Jim Rose, later one of Slonnie's favorite copilots, recalled the trauma of landing the poorly paid, right-seat job with American. "Back in '31, anybody with 300 log hours who hadn't killed himself thought he was one hell of an aviator. So I went to see Sloniger with all the documents, plus helmet, goggles, and the joie de vivre which went with the thing. He said I might be one hell of an aviator, but they only hired from the services. My reaction was, try me against any of those army guys, double or nothing. But he told me, 'Go work real hard for a couple of years, kid.' I went back in 1933 with 1,000 hours and told Slonnie I was really one hell of a pilot now, but he said I had too much flying time. They couldn't afford to rework my thinking to AA ways. Flying had made big strides in the last couple of years and their boys even flew blind. I figured an awful lot of my flying had been pretty blind but I waited a year or so until a new guy was hiring and talked to him. AA finally took me on, for reasons best known to them."

Commercial aviation spurted forward: stressed metal skins, wing flaps, and variable-pitch props were available if not yet common. Even so, American Airways welcomed certification of that lumbering Condor as late as March 1933, and passengers still loved it in 1936. This airplane was actually covered with fabric, stretched over steel tubes, but fully fireproofed, as smokers were assured. It would carry almost any load you could close the door on, stay up for 550 miles, and land so slowly it virtually floated when fuel was low. There were even two altimeters on the panel. Disdaining purist moans about outdated canvas biplanes, that first Condor could maintain a 140 MPH schedule. The later C model did 20 MPH better. These fat matrons cost AA over $60,000 each but proved to be worth it. Since they were a little quieter than the echo-chamber Ford, lines struggled to exploit that plus. Night passengers were bedded down in the hangar around ten-thirty, while the crew tiptoed until their plane was towed onto the runway by a muffled truck, at midnight. Of course,

the raucous burps and ground-shaking vibrations of two engines run up before takeoff may well have wakened some sleepers.

This airplane's most persistent early problem was carburetor icing and even its builders admitted their Wright power plant seldom fired on both plugs in any one cylinder at a given moment. Underway, pilots blew ice out of their carb throats by backfiring one engine at a time, to the anguish of AA salespeople. That throat was up on top of the engine, out of harm's way, but a big yellow tongue of flame did tend to attract passenger attention. Once Curtiss Wright found the fix, they sent an engine man on every trip to make sure pilots used the new hot-air tubes in their carbs properly. One such shuttle technician recalled the only real danger as cold fried chicken three meals a day. Along with fine visibility and stable handling, Condor pilots treasured the first (electrically) retractable landing gear on any multiengine U.S. airplane. Until they discovered one wheel was down and locked, the other stuck in its well, which was not uncommon and far worse than no gear down at all. The builders provided an eight-foot crank, just in case. As Slonnie said, however, "They never really admitted we'd need it so there was no provision for getting it out to the engine nacelle where the wheels folded up. You just punched a hole in the cloth side, ran this rod out and twisted away like mad."

Another legend claimed this was the first transport twin which would remain airborne on one engine. Slonnie replied, "I don't even know what kind of single-engine performance the Condor might have had since my motors all ran pretty well and I certainly never shut one down to find out.

But one of our boys put a plane into the middle of some lake when he lost an engine. American sent three of us down originally to see if they should buy Condors and I went right back and said yes. But this great big guy stayed longer and sold Curtiss on lifting the control wheel over his knees. The rest of us had to look through that wheel to fly and we raised hell, but the jigs were made." Finally, there were all those struts and wires laced between the wings. Slonnie said, "The old Condor was not a very good ice-carrying ship. Wires would catch it first and start vibrating, until the struts picked it up and things kind of got on the rough side. Get the hell out of that altitude or it would jerk those struts right out from between your wings." As for the story that it had so much wing area you couldn't stall one, Slonnie commented flatly, "You could stall any airplane ever built, but the Condor was lightly loaded for sure, so it would take a pretty good weight off without too much field length. And we didn't always have much field in those days."

Most important, the public was a little happier. Ft. Worth-Cleveland only took eleven pampered hours now, although the mail went by all-metal, single-engine Lockheed Orions in seven and a half. Also, airlines could cut their fleets even further, with more seats per plane. Some 408 airplanes were in airline service at the end of 1933, almost a fifth fewer than a year earlier. Meanwhile, United was planning the Boeing 247 as the first all-metal twin and thus the first truly modern airliner. TWA riposted with its Douglas DC-1 scheme. Few realized that the Black Committee in Congress was coiled to strike first. At this juncture Slonnie was transferred once again, to Memphis, in December

1933. The land had finally repealed Prohibition, rating ten of forty-eight pages in the *New York Times*, whereas a Democratic decision shortly thereafter would inspire even more fervid head-lines, and drive strong aviation men to drink. This was an event about to skew all U.S. notions of aviation. Senator Hugo L. Black of Alabama had set up an airline investigation committee to clean out Republican scandals left by Hoover's Postmas-ter General Brown. Black milked maximum attention by late 1933, then told President Roosevelt to expect a crisis.

Urged on by the few small, independent lines which had escaped Brown's best efforts to consolidate everyone, FDR wanted to believe Senator Black and decided in February 1934, that all airline mail contracts were dirty, nay worse— Republican. He called in the head of Army aviation and asked if military pilots were capable of flying the nation's mails. That was an order to do so, of course. To airline pilots, losing their fat mail subsidies could only compare to missing the end of a very short runway on a foggy night, although the interregnum of uncertainty and condemnation which followed might be seen later as the shock which finally set their business on a fully profes-sional flight path. American Airway's pilots on that line's new Memphis-Chicago trimotor run, and that included Slonnie, had only just settled into a particularly comfortable flying routine when the hangar roof fell in on them.

February 18, 1934   Flying hours: 10,779:35

Chapter 11

Roosevelt Cancels the Mail

"You're not an airline pioneer if you weren't cancelled with the mail in '34."

If an aviation man insists that losing the civilian mail contracts in 1934 was the sole notable event in all commercial flying during the thirties—he is sure to be an old airline hand. For many it remained virtually the only non-cockpit trauma of their flying lives, right through WWII. What's more, U.S. Army Air Corps veterans felt precisely the same way—for completely opposite reasons.

It lasted only seventy-eight days, beginning during one of the worst flying winters of cockpit memory and trailing away in May 1934. But the day Franklin Roosevelt cancelled the mail contracts probably turned more airline pilots into lifelong Republicans than all the red-scare phantoms and welfare programs ever conceived. A single New Deal broadside cut the financial ground right out from under almost everybody in civil aviation. They couldn't know it would be only temporary. At the same time, this very shock also prompted airlines to buy that better equipment which their lost mail subsidies were meant to be underwriting anyway. It streamlined the nation's air-route map and cooled down many who had conglomerated aviation into a Wall Street append-

age, run by and for financiers. Equally important, those holding the Air Corps purse strings discovered how totally underdeveloped military flying skills were, once the home field dropped from sight on a sunny day.

The Slonigers were scarcely settled in Boss Crump's Memphis, a base airline families liked. The city had won national awards for services to its citizens, including the prestige of an air connection. Slonnie said, "They moved three of us down there to fly Wasp-powered Fords, which had twice the horsepower of our Whirlwind jobs. The company had bought a New Orleans-Chicago run so the New Orleans pilots would bring a trip up and we'd take it on about noon. Get to Chicago at seven that evening, lay over, and leave the next morning, to connect up in Memphis around noon again. Then two days off. Passenger traffic was picking up a little and anybody who wanted to go from Chicago to Los Angeles could connect with only an hour or so wait in Memphis.

"They had set up a lot of radio and weather came on the ticker. Nashville might say, 1,200-foot ceiling. But the hour before it had been 800 so you could spot a trend. There were no company meteorologists or flight plans and we didn't have an operations man there. Just the station manager and three pilots who did their own ops, like we had for years. Only trouble was, we

didn't have much maintenance in Memphis either, and those Fords were covered in the thinnest metal you ever saw. It would crack from the wing spar down, so you wanted a damn good mechanic to weld a Ford. Unfortunately, the best boy we had liked to sniff his acetylene. One morning I heard this terrific explosion and rushed into the hangar. He'd gotten too much and passed out, knocking over the tank. Stuff was running out like a siren. We couldn't fire him though, because nobody else could handle that tissue-paper metal. Next day our parts man came in and said, 'Look, that was a brand-new tank of gas. Do I mark it up to fixing the airplane or to entertainment?'

"We were only in Memphis a couple of months when Mr. Roosevelt took our mail away. That left us down to any passengers we could sell, to pay for gasoline and crews. I didn't really have any qualms about a job. Hell, a good pilot could always get one. They were just starting company airlines and somebody would come by every month from some oil company to ask, 'How about flying for us?' If you had a top rating with some line they'd hire you ahead of the guy out flying an OX-5 job. Oh, we thought for a while there we'd all be out looking, but American hung on. Took off a lot of schedules and you'd get a pretty senior copilot or even a junior captain in the right seat."

Roosevelt's snap decision did put 800 fliers

National Air and Space Museum, Smithsonian Institution

When American Airways transferred Slonnie to Memphis in 1934, he began flying Wasp-powered Ford Trimotors, "which had twice the horsepower of our Whirlwind jobs."

out of work immediately, apart from 6,000 in fear of their jobs on the various lines. It also came close to wiping out a quarter-billion-dollar investment, leaving 200,000 stockholders with shaky aviation paper. Even so, the decree wasn't as universally unpopular as the airline side claimed later. The President had been warned early in January that a crisis was brewing over existing airmail contracts and the Department of Justice opened its investigation on the twentieth of that month, but to airline people the most villainous date would always be February 9, 1934, when Roosevelt signed Executive Order 6591, cancelling all mail subsidies, effective the nineteenth. This hassle stemmed from Walter F. Brown's often high-handed efforts to consolidate the air network in a few stable companies. The Black Committee had been established by Congress in September 1933, to look into what Democrats called the "spoils conference"—Brown's route-awards meeting which divided a majority of all routes among the four majors. Civilian mail had always been a squabble among rugged individualists, yet their pioneering methods and more recent cooperation were moving three million pounds of mail a year by 1934. The Senate Committee of a new political party had no trouble capturing daily headlines with fraud charges. Independent carriers, smarting because they had missed the juicier routes or subsidies, claimed that Hoover's administration had favored big business. True. A Democratic Senate cried collusion, although the courts later ruled no on that point. Nonetheless, Postmaster James Farley was ordered to cancel all existing mail contracts overnight and let the Army fly the nation's letters.

This caused a military uproar unmatched

National Air and Space Museum, Smithsonian Institution

A welcome addition to the dials and gauges of a Ford Trimotor cockpit was a directional gyroscope. "Hit a bump and your compass would spin but the gyro would hold steady until everything settled down again."

National Air and Space Museum, Smithsonian Institution

Rattan seats with leather cushions suggested creature comforts, but the noise from the engines in the metal fuselage could make a passenger's ride in a Trimotor a mind-numbing experience.

until Pearl Harbor—when the Air Corps would again prove unprepared. In 1934 a 2nd Lieutenant received $125 a month, plus fifty percent more in flight pay for only four hours of air work. There was absolutely no incentive to go up after dark, never mind in bad weather. General Benjamin Foulois, commander of the Air Corps, knew all this and was eager to get better equipment and training for his men, the stepchildren when it came to appropriations. He told FDR the Army could handle mail, given time to prepare. That qualification only earned him ten days. Army familiarization flights began on February 13 and they suffered their first three fatalities on the 16th, due to bad weather and lack of night flying experience. Foulois could only plead with his crews for safety awareness, while grounding any flight faced with bad weather, as the Army began loading mailbags into unsuitable airplanes on the 19th. Their original plan covered seventy stops in three mail zones, flying 41,000 miles a day on sixty-eight trips. That would link eleven of twelve Federal Reserve Districts and keep bank transfers moving. The Air Corps only planned to fly about half the cancelled commercial routes, but those were concentrated in the East, where weather and terrain were most forbidding.

One day before that first military mail trip took off, Jack Frye and Eddie Rickenbacker of TWA set a Los Angeles-Newark record of 13:04 hours with the Douglas DC-1, prototype of what would become the world's first commercially viable transport airplane. While showing off precisely the sort of equipment airlines had waffled over buying, they were also telling the Army: match that kind of flying. Most celebrity pilots sided with airline management—some had consulting contracts. Will

Rogers was more reasonable, suggesting that military pilots were trained for different tasks and the country was going to lose a lot of fine boys by putting them on the wrong job. Fire the crooks, he urged, but don't ruin a fine industry. Lindbergh attacked FDR virulently.

Airlines, meanwhile, carried anybody they could lure aboard and made it a rule to land ahead of the mail, as the Army pleaded to be judged by its results. Their next fatality came on February 22, due to a pilot far off course in bad weather. When United lost eight in an accident on the 23rd, however, outcry was a fraction of that aroused by Air Corps deaths. The curious rationale was that airline passengers had volunteered to fly; the Army boys were ordered out. Roosevelt, badly stung by the first real wave of public disfavor since taking office, ordered the Army to cease having accidents or cease flying. Privately, he was urging Congress to pass a new civilian mail bill. Fast. Forty versions would be drafted by March 10. To bridge the gap until passage, new restrictions were laid down. Only Army pilots with two years of night experience could fly mail, unless the weather was perfect, and no man was to fly more than eight hours in twenty-four. Several military mailmen still complained that reading dials only distracted them, while a radio was mere noise, despite a regulation that they could only take off with it functioning properly. In March the Army was still canceling more flights than it was flying. TWA cut half of its personnel on February 28, while Western furloughed forty percent of both pilots and ground staff. Several airline men with reserve commissions went back into the service.

Friday, March 9, proved the most tragic

twenty-four hours of the entire operation and Roosevelt gave his generals a tongue-lashing. Service was suspended for over a week, then resumed on only nine routes, covering 25,000 miles. The Democrats blamed Foulois, whom the Republicans defended while trying to dilute a clear attempt to whitewash FDR and Farley. The Air Corps quite properly felt it was doing the best job possible with brave, eager novices. Some wanted to fly so badly they might rush off with their destination orders locked in the mail compartment, others land and be too embarassed to ask if they had found the right field. As one survivor summed up, they never lost a letter although they did lose a good many fine men. In all there were fifty-seven accidents, with twelve men killed, before the government advertised for civilian mail bids once again—called temporary to save face.

Once these were opened on April 20, 1934, both hindsight and investigating commissions could flourish. There were ample charges and rebuttals for all, ranging from a claim that the Army had been sabotaged with watered gas to reports that civilian pilots gleefully led green Air Corps boys astray. Most military mailmen insisted, however, that commercial pilots were mostly helpful. They realized the Army had no more to do with taking their jobs away than former mail pilots had to do with their bosses padding mail tonnage. By the time it was all over the Air Corps received better planes and instruments and had learned the hard way how to use both. They were supposed to have 500 log hours for that mail job but a lot of the keener ones had lied a little to get on. By the end of April the Army could return Mrs. Eleanor Roosevelt's conscripted Condor and retire the

short-range pursuit planes they had used as most unsuitable mail carriers. They were finally getting the multiengine bombers which could have done the job right, and even tried to break TWA's transcontinental record but ended by flying a slightly longer course and missing by a small margin. It was too late to rescue their operation anyway. All but one route was returned to civilian hands by mid-May.

Lowell Thomas claimed the crisis even increased passenger load totals. And large firms could quit sending mail illegally, as civilian airline parcels. The Secretary of War ordered a review board, asking Charles Lindbergh (who refused) and Orville Wright (who pleaded illness) to serve on what was clearly going to be an unpopular panel. Foulois was unfairly blamed for overestimating his men. He had known the Air Corps was not adept at flying a radio range and had never expected to carry the entire mail load or maintain airline regularity. The General would write later, "FDR didn't care if men got killed, so long as his administration didn't get a bad name." This was an old flying hand who had learned from the Wrights before WWI. He also stated he would never believe any civilian pilot tried to send an Army man to his death. Billy Mitchell, perpetually trying to sell air power to the administration, announced that putting Army equipment up against commercial airliners was like comparing a flivver to a race car.

Since the only new civilian airliner around was that single DC-1 prototype, Slonnie could comment dryly, "I don't think even the Army had many airplanes as ancient as most of ours. The ships I saw them flying were only two or three years old. As for instruments, the aids were there, beams and all. Maybe we didn't have enough dials because American Airways didn't have that kind of money, but our eight-year-old Ford did have a new directional gyro, alongside the old engine dials and compass. That was a big help, sure. Hit a bump and your compass would spin but the gyro would hold steady until everything settled down again. Of course we resented the Army pilots taking our jobs but we couldn't do anything about it, so we just accepted things and helped them loads of times. Most of us, anyway. One of our guys did boast later about a trip where the Army boy asked if he could follow him and this AA guy said 'Sure.' It was night and as soon as he got that Ford headed off on course he turned his running lights off. The mail went back and landed where he'd started. But that AA pilot was an SOB anyway.

"Army pilots simply weren't trained for it, but they were plenty cocky to start with. Kind of looked down their noses at us. Out of the way, we'll show you how to fly attitudes. They should have been learning weather sooner and could have taken over our mail and done a hell of a job, instead of losing all those boys. One of the first days I was headed down from Chicago and it was snowing when the Army man got his mail so he came over and asked how far I was going. When I said, 'Memphis,' he kind of shuffled his feet and said: 'Well, that's my run. How about the weather?' It was snowing all along the way. Flurries, then it would lighten up a little bit. He asked if I minded him following me down. I got my four or five passengers and this guy was down at the end of the runway, running up his motor, and waiting. We took off and he came right up alongside. Good formation flier. He'd hang onto my wing for a

while. Pretty soon I'd lose him and my copilot would say he was over on that side. Don't know why he kept changing. We got into kind of heavy flurries down around Bloomington and I was busy trying to hold the thing on course. When we got about a mile of visibility ahead again I couldn't find him on either side. We landed in St. Louis and the postmaster there, an old chum, asked if I'd seen the mail plane but I couldn't tell him where the hell it went after Bloomington. Next trip through I asked what ever happened to the Memphis mail. He'd landed at Evansville and they got the mail three days later.

"Couple of years after that I needed pilots for American and had loads of applications from Army boys so I talked to a couple. One kid had 100 hours of blind flying on his application. I said, 'You ought to be pretty good.' He grinned sheepishly and told me, 'Honestly, that's what I'm logged but I can't fly instruments alone. I get under the hood and the pilot outside flies around a couple of hours. I take credit for blind flying.' Had to tell him, 'Chum, I can't use you. With 100 hours of real blind you can make a low approach anyplace but you'll never get on an airline.' We couldn't hire fair-weather pilots and make our schedules."

All through the first months of 1934, when the Army was canceling over a third of all mail flights for weather reasons, Slonnie's log showed more than 155 hours, plus a two-week vacation, in those same seventy-eight days, including a Memphis-St. Louis flight on the Army's most tragic day, March 9. He said, "Our money was cut anyway of course. The ten senior AA pilots stayed on full pay but we pooled our checks to help the guys laid off. I kept about 350 a month." If AA

worked at all, Slonnie had a job, but it was so precarious and money so tight his wife didn't always know if they would last. Further uncertainty came with a stipulation that none of those former, so-called crooked outfits could file new mail bids, a sop to the original cancellation which had put the Army in such a bad light. The ban included any company which had taken part in the first Brown route conference. In practice, existing lines changed their names, dropped a few directors and got back into the business virtually where they had left it. All were overeager to recover mail subsidies so Farley got more concessions than he deserved. Particularly since these new names—American Airlines, Inc., replacing that villain American Airways, for instance—were saving Washington's face.

The airmail letter rate was reduced to six cents an ounce with the slogan, "tomorrow's mail today," and the map redrawn to add twenty-one cities and 3,300 more route miles (28,548 in all), with four new runs but fewer schedules. It had cost the country $2.21 a mile to fly the mail in military planes, versus the average civilian subsidy of fifty-four cents. It would be 1939 before the airlines recovered all their lost business. American Airlines, under new president C. R. Smith, lost a million dollars between late May and the end of 1934, flying mostly Condors, Fords, and a low-wing Stinson trimotor against lines which were just getting the new Douglas DC-2, service version of the DC-1 and the first largely successful modern airliner. AA only managed to put Condors into transcontinental service on May 5, so they couldn't hope to match those meals served at 8,000 feet, as featured in Douglas ads. They wouldn't get any of the new wonder airplanes until TWA had all it wanted—although one clause of the Black-McKellar Bill, the new airmail act of June 12, 1934, was designed to separate plane builders from operators. Douglas became the chief beneficiary of that since they had never enjoyed airline ties anyway. Lines began to buy the best planes they could get, not what another branch of the same umbrella firm built.

Civilian lines were boosted into the era of automatic pilots and wing flaps by the mail fiasco, while the Army recommended that its pilots start flying a minimum of ten hours per month. Edwin Link, the flight simulator inventor, got his real start from 1934 as well, realizing that the Air Corps badly needed blind-flight trainers.

Following Farley's April meeting with forty-five airline operators, the big lines, and American in particular, received help in rationalizing their transcontinental routes, still the glamour business. Three government bodies would now regulate an industry where holding companies were banned. The Post Office would award mail contracts, the Bureau of Commerce would install airways radio and lighting, while setting all safety standards, and the Interstate Commerce Commission would monitor fares. This troika system allowed the airlines ample maneuvering room for three decades of steady, often spectacular growth. Gage Mace, an old AA hand said, "None of us knew how precarious we really were until those mail contracts were cancelled. For a week or so it looked like the end of the world. You're not an airline pioneer if you weren't cancelled with the mail in '34."

Johnny said, "We knew we weren't going to be in Memphis any longer and nobody was sure at first how many runs would go again, so we put the furniture in storage and I went home to Nebraska until we learned what might happen. Slonnie went up to headquarters in Chicago. One night he called and told me, 'Well, we're going to live in Chicago.' He flew all sorts of runs there until they made him Chief Pilot."

June 31, 1934   Flying hours: 10,980:05

Chapter 12

Chief Pilot

"He signed Number 1—but nobody is that old."

Chief Pilot, American Airlines, Inc. That looked fine on a calling card, alongside the Chicago address of airline headquarters. Good pilots were less impressed. And Slonnie never really wanted to be a chief pilot anyway. "It came down from Washington," he explained. "Every airline would have chief pilots. Less business in '34 didn't mean a damn thing to the CAA [Civil Airline Administration], lines would just have to pay us somehow." Most companies soon realized they would need such chiefs, as flight crews expanded far beyond the first-name category. Two thousand American Airlines employees in 1934 would quadruple in a decade and close control of ongoing pilot qualifications required a system. Airline operations were striving to become a properly regulated arm of what already promised to be very big business indeed, although the decade which began in mid-1934 was at least as diverse when it came to routes and airplanes flown as any in Slonnie's career. Establishing a sane flying pattern was not as easy as realizing you needed one. Chief pilots were only one suggestion.

Slonnie said, "United had their big base in Chicago and put two chief pilots there, one westbound, one east. American only had one and couldn't even afford me. You got the same pay as a line captain and worked ten times as hard. When I got back up to a thousand a month I thought that was real money. By the same token, for a month's pay I could buy a new automobile. I was based in Chicago but had the pilots going south, plus those on the Newark run and the transcon boys. Most of those were based at the eastern end so I had to go up there to give flight checks. Sometimes you caught one in Chicago but usually they didn't have much layover time. Before we let anybody take a new airplane out any more I had to give him a check-out on it. Then the CAA put in a reg about six-month instrument checks. The chief pilot did those too. Getting the job didn't have anything to do with my seniority, although our first list appeared about that same time. AA had gotten big enough, we needed a roster to decide whether you got to fly some run you wanted. If several bid, the guy who'd been with the company longest got it. When the list appeared I was the oldest pilot in time served from any of the little lines that went into American. I'd taken a run out for Robertson the day after I was hired and that gave me the seniority number of one." Johnny felt he was always proud of that. Naturally. But there was so much to do, the only time it really came up was when they moved to another division. Then everybody realized that if Slonnie showed up, somebody might be pushed off the bottom of the list at that base.

American Airlines itself was aiming toward number one in U.S. aviation, but this hardly showed in 1934, when most people still felt it was pretty daring to board any airplane. With largely businessman traffic the objective remained better service. There wasn't much fancy equipment that summer and people weren't very knowledgeable about equipment anyway. Not yet. Good management ranked higher. Almost anybody who ever worked for AA will insist their airline came to life when Cyrus Rufus Smith moved up to president. Even Slonnie, not given to fulsome praise and particularly not of non-fliers, simply said, "C.R. was a legend. For all of us."

E. L. Cord was chief owner of American Airways at the time of the mail cancellation and Smith only one of a group fighting bitterly for control. They lost. Once the company became American Airlines, Cord petitioned Washington for more routes, commenting that one of the first things his bright, expanded airline would do was "fire those Smith boys." Cord meant C.R., a division head, and Hugh, no relation, but later a vice president. The government contact man was sorry to hear that because they were both good friends of his. According to this tale, Cord called back that very same night to say he'd been a little hasty. In fact, he was going to make C.R. president.

American Airlines President C.R. Smith hands a mail sack to pilot Bob Rentz. The airplane is a Curtiss Condor, a cloth-covered biplane fitted with sleeper berths.

As it turned out—none too soon. Slonnie recalled, "I was already chief pilot when they called about ten of us into the president's office. I was standing next to our treasurer and asked how things looked. He said we were in terrible shape. About $25,000 in the bank, which wouldn't even pay our gasoline bill in Chicago that month. Pretty soon this fellow in a fedora walked up to the desk and told us they were depositing $500,000 to our account as of that day and in thirty days they'd give us another $500,000. Mr. Cord had told him to say, 'If you sons of bitches can't run an airline on a million dollars, you might as well get the hell out of the business. Thank you, gentlemen.' The treasurer just said he would use that million up pretty quick."

Fortunately C.R.— two initials were enough to identify him anywhere in aviation— came right behind the cash. He was remembered as a man who always appeared where the action was but never blustered, as a perfectionist who understood men but not a disciplinarian, as a guy who left his supervisors to make daily decisions and always backed the men responsible for actual operations. When AA pilots withdrew from the common airline union to form their own in the fifties, it was seen as a measure of their feeling for C.R. Slonnie saw a lot of the man's personal side too. "C.R. had the corner office in Chicago so everybody had to go by his door. He'd wave you in and always had a new story. I was even crossing the hangar one time and ran into C.R. who said, 'Hey, have you heard this one?' He spotted some cleaner on a ladder and three or four mechanics. 'Hey, Jim, Fred...come over here.' We weren't so large then of course but I'll bet he knew every first name when there were thousands. A honey of a guy."

C.R.'s first task was to rationalize the largest collection of different (often indifferent) airplanes in the flying game. The Stinson A trimotor is a fair example of their mid-thirties equipment problems. Slonnie said, "Boy, was that a turkey. Blink and you'd be going in the opposite direction. Not half the airplane their high-wing had been and it was no bargain." Claims of "rigid" or "strong" were no substitute for poor stability. But the gear did retract. One pilot managed to forget that modern feature and land wheels-up—with C.R. on board.

The U.S. transport airplane fleet in 1934 was 423, averaging fewer than nine seats apiece. All lines together carried just under half-a-million passengers, at an average fare of 5.9 cents a mile, that year. Like most rivals, the Stinson A was too expensive to run, but it was built by a branch of Cord's empire, before manufacturers were separated from airlines. Luckily, AA had more modern equipment on the way. Shortly after Slonnie moved to Chicago his line advertised the sale of fifty-one airplanes, although their proposed replacement was no wonder for passenger capacity either. It was the Vultee V1-A, a fast, expensive, all-metal monoplane with one engine to pull ten passengers. It too was built by a part of Cord's realm, the Air Development Corporation. Speed was becoming a prime sales argument and this V1-A was the first transport to exceed 200 MPH in level flight. AA used fourteen of them until another government rule banned single-engine commercial planes at night or under instrument conditions. They didn't fly enough fair-weather, daylight runs to justify Vultees, although AA had a full night-operations panel and radio stack in its one-pilot version.

This Vultee boasted rapid, electrically-retracted landing gear which tucked your wheels out of sight before a V1-A cleared the airport boundary on takeoff. The engine was a 750 HP radial which would take the plane to 23,000 feet, far above the non-oxygen level. Everything about it pleased pilots except a hesitancy to get airborne on hot days, with a full load. Slonnie said, "A very stable airplane but a little short of wing. And kind of blind with that narrow vee windshield, plus all those radios we piled on the right side of our cockpits. Peoria was a long-enough field east-west but I happened to have a short, north-south takeoff one day when Bill Littlewood, our engineering pilot, was on board. We'd griped so much about poor lift the town had chopped a big swatch through some trees at the end of that short runway, in case load got critical. Nobody at headquarters would listen about poor climb, so this time I held that Vultee right down on the ground, through the alley, with treetops up above us on both sides. When we got to Springfield Littlewood figured it was a good thing somebody had cut that lane after all. 'Hell,' I told him, 'we did that with those new metal props on the Vultee.' But he changed the rating after that, taking payload off for short-field operations." Vultee flights provided many good stories, a sure sign pilots liked to fly the ship.

Slonnie and Earl Ward, Chicago Operations Manager for American Airlines, about to set the Chicago-New York speed record on August 25, 1934, with a Vultee V1-A.

Slonnie said, "We were beginning to get repeat passengers by then. One bunch was this piano player with a radio act for Sinclair Oil. Like an old-time minstrel show. I had their whole gang one night, still on a party they'd started before takeoff. No cabin attendant of course. A light on my board would come on if the outside cabin door wasn't closed tight and this flashed. With a gang you knew, the cockpit door was usually open, so I looked back and I'm missing one. The leader was sitting up front so I hollered that a seat was empty and the door light on. He checked and settled right back. Said, 'Hell that guy was never any good in the act anyway. Forget it.' I had to yell again to get the door pulled in. One of them had tried it first, on his way to the toilet."

American Airlines used Sinclair products and there were many common promotions, including a presentation watch for Slonnie's first million miles. They took it right back after the photo session but let him keep the headlines. Another ran, "Nation's leading cities less than three hours apart." This story noted that E. L. Sloniger, one of the nation's veteran pilots with more than 11,000 flying hours, and Earl Ward, Superintendent of Operations for the line, had taken a Vultee airliner from Chicago to New York in two hours, 59.2 minutes, averaging 205.8 MPH and topping 240 MPH at times. The record they broke by eleven minutes had been held by a racing airplane. Slonnie said, "I got out to the field one morning and Ward asked if I'd looked at the winds going east. It was blowing like hell. He suggested we get some officials out to certify the time and take a shot at the record. We'd just gotten the Vultee. It was a pretty routine flight except that I went up to 16,000 feet for more tail wind and we just panted. Little ice for a few minutes and clouds part of the way. Coming back, bucking that wind, it took us four and a half hours. Friends were over to dinner that night and one told Johnny that I'd set quite a record that day. He'd heard it on the radio but she hadn't known I was any further from home all day than the airport."

Another news item told a sadder tale. "Airport worker killed by plane making landing." A seventy-year-old WPA laborer, pushing a wheelbarrow down the runway, heard neither the plane nor his friends yelling and walked into the propeller of Slonnie's Stearman. Considerably friendlier than the Kansas City papers four years earlier, this report only said it was "the pilot's first serious accident in more than 20 years (sic) of flying."

It took no tragedy to fuel Slonnie's lifelong interest in better aircraft aids. Blind flight, even fully blind landings, were one such project. While most of Chicago concentrated on its World's Fair during November 1934, Slonnie was trying a new landing system, including touchdown and roll-out without ever seeing the ground. Ernest Cutrell, still flying for the government, had been working on airline blind landings nearly a year. He made some 170 fully blind ones in 1934 alone, from the enclosed cockpit of an unwieldly Ford Trimotor. Before that he tried quite a while with several different copilots but none quite dared let him go right down onto the ground. At some point that man in the right seat always got worried and took over. Cutrell finally asked a man he'd known for years to come out the next day and monitor a couple of blind landings. They made one and Cutrell slapped this man on the back and told him: "We did it." "Did what?" Ernie said, "Finally made a fully-blind landing with this Ford." The other pilot just stared. He thought Cutrell had been doing them all along.

Single-engine airplanes had achieved the feat earlier but there were special power-control problems with three engines. The procedure, as Cutrell explained it, was to intercept a glide path signal from a ground transmitter at 800 feet. Throttle your outboard engines back to 1,300 RPM, with the center one idling. Pass over the outer transmitter at exactly 100 MPH and cut the outboard engines to 1,150 RPM for 80 MPH. Descend at precisely 500 feet per minute to 150 feet, using the center engine as you passed through 200 to level it out at the 150 mark. You should contact the ground at a sink rate of less than 300 feet per minute and use the hand brake to roll out, keeping the gyro centered on rough ground until the plane stopped. During tests, all this was done with the pilot's windows covered, while his copilot monitored traffic and progress. In normal service there would scarcely be a case where visibility was nil, so the exercise exceeded real life. It also required fine flying balance.

Cutrell added that they provided both visual and aural information for the pilot, who had to keep two needles crossed right in the middle of that dial all the time. It was hard to move a large airplane like the Ford around quickly but gently enough to compensate. Throttle control was vital. You overshot with too much engine, bounced if RPMs dropped. A lot of pilots couldn't make it work. They were also solving continuous mental math problems all this time, and these came faster as the signal beam narrowed near touchdown. Then there had to be constant drift correction when those two transmitters at either end of the runway didn't line up with prevailing winds. Cutrell reported dryly—airplanes would need stronger landing gear for blind landings. Yet he was convinced it would eventually become possible to make smoother landings blind than sighted. During 1934, when airlines were shifting from individualists to outside control, various lines were asked to send their chief pilots to try this new system.

Slonnie said, "Ernie was down in Dayton in a black Ford Trimotor. Old NC 1 with orange wings and tail. I got in late the last day and did a bunch of takeoffs and landings without the hood before supper, to get an idea. Next morning the wind had changed and it would take a hell of a long time to line up the radio beacons again. I said, 'Don't bother—I'll make a couple of normal landings to get the wind drift and take a crack at it.' Cutrell, in the right seat, would take off and go around each time. I made six full-stop landings in one hour without ever seeing the ground and said,

'Listen, this is it.' When I got back to Chicago our operations manager asked what I thought and I told him it was the coming thing. I figured we all had to learn or go back to the plow. Only fly when the sun or moon were shining and the railroads would take us over. He said all the other chief pilots were leery. Claimed it wasn't feasible. He was glad I liked it."

Speaking on a radio show that same winter, American's chief pilot called blind landings: "The greatest advance in aviation since we learned to fly by instruments. Just a further development of blind flying. We'll all be putting this system into airports and I think every airline will use it." When Slonnie retired in 1958 he had made literally thousands of instrument approaches, down to the legal minimum altitude, at airports around the world, but not a single fully blind landing on a scheduled passenger run. "C.R. was interested in 1934, though. I told him the best boy in the bunch was Cutrell. And the government didn't pay much. Next thing I know, Ernie walks into my office and says he's just signed on with American. Instrument training had been on my hands too, but he had more skill and experience then—and always—than anybody I ever knew."

AA was preparing properly for the Douglas DC-2 era, putting that modern airplane on their Chicago-New York (Newark, to be accurate) run where instrument flying was an everyday matter. A pilot might climb out of his home field, cruise several hours and descend on instruments, without ever seeing sun or earth. Ice picked up on climb was still there for the final landing. Many even found Newark's black cinder surface easier to land on when it was snow-covered than shimmering on a hot summer day. Either way, making schedule—

Olive Thompson, an American Airlines stewardess, learning all about the AA patented, round navigation and flight computer design.

the pride of any line—often led to what pilots called "peeking." Every airline had its official limits, the minimum altitude to which a pilot might descend for a given field. These usually ran 300 or 400 feet, depending on surrounding hazards. If you still couldn't see ground, request an alternate destination. How far below that point a pilot might slip depended. Some were known for bravery, others for timidity. Circumstances counted too. Newark, no longer the world's busiest airport by 1934, was flat with only one tall, nearby chimney, for instance.

Chicago was ringed by intimidating storage tanks, powerhouse smokestacks, and tall buildings. Every leg of its radio range had a different quirk too. Wise pilots didn't crowd their personal minimums quite so proudly in Chicago. But what if you took the alternate and a rival line's

captain landed? Worse, each line had its separate radio frequency, giving information likely to sound like frying bacon when needed most. On one occasion, a flight approaching Newark could only talk to its operations man there by radio to Memphis and telephone back. Reason enough for the Department of Commerce to unify air traffic control in November, 1935.

Information on compass headings for each radio range leg and heights of various hazards were originally printed on two or three pages of data per airport. Slonnie got the idea of putting it all into symbols on two diagrams, as plan and elevation views. One loose-leaf page served each field and was easy to update, so everybody copied the idea. Another AA refinement was a pocket-size computer disk—a slide rule in the round—to replace their bulky, long-tailed briefcase model. Slonnie said, "Our radio guy was ex-Navy and said he could scale down their pie-tin-size model and compress our tail onto the back in a second dial. The Navy loaned us their computer face, the other side was AA copyright. Only AA pilots could buy one, for a buck-seventy-five. Not-as-good ones cost $7.50 commercially so I ended up losing about one a week. Jack Knight from United would ask how he could get one. 'You just found it on that table there, Jack.' Then I'd go to supply and tell them I couldn't find mine. Wanted to buy another one. They'd just grin. 'Captain, you sure lose a lot of those.'"

American required its pilots to fly at least two hours a month under instrument conditions but Slonnie figured no pilot on their routes did less than twenty, by choice or need. Nobody knew yet where proficiency limits lay so pilots with dial learning, on top of skill, were considered any airline's greatest assets. Each got a monthly physical check from his line in those years, although the government only required three per year. Without knowing yet what flying's age limit might be, some anticipated the day when old pilots might hold command and advise, like social captains of an ocean liner, dispensing experience while younger men did the physical flying work.

Meanwhile, every line gave six-month instrument checks. Slonnie said, "By that time we had a load of dials. I'd take each guy up and uncage them all until he was good and lost under that hood. 'Okay, take over.' He had to check direction, cage his artificial horizon, check the compass, and figure out which quadrant of the range he was in. Going away from a station volume decreased and if you got the 'A' in Morse code and didn't know whether it was the N.W. or S.E. quadrant, you

made a ninety-degree turn and flew until you hit a leg to follow in. A smart pilot could figure out where he was in three or four minutes, ease onto a leg, and hold it square. You couldn't have a heavy hand and fly instruments well, though. I put out an order that there would be a hood in every airplane. In clear weather, when the copilot could keep watch, I wanted that captain to put the hood up right after takeoff and fly blind to his destination. Right away, one old friend came in and complained: 'You mean I got to fly without seeing? I'd rather quit.' He was taking a New York trip so I decided to go as far as Detroit and show him how easy it was. Soon as we got off I had the copilot climb out while I buttoned the hood up and tuned in South Bend. Just before Detroit I started the letdown, jerked the hood off and landed. This boy said, 'Hell, that wasn't too bad, I'll try one.' He turned into one of the best instrument pilots on the line. Within six months, when we got a real sticky day, our fellows were saying, 'Boy, we're going to make money for the airline now.' Other lines would cancel and we took their passengers."

Slonnie did discover he had created a minor monster among ground people with a little flying time. "C.R. was a gentleman pilot and he stuck his head into my office one day. 'Was I busy?' He wanted to go up and fly a little under that hood he'd heard so much about. He hadn't started with seat of the pants stuff like a lot of old-timers and did okay. Told him, 'Hell C.R., next time we're short a captain, I'll send you out.' He loved that."

There were some 30,000 licensed pilots in the U.S. by then and eighty percent complained they couldn't get those plush airline jobs. An aviation columnist explained why not, in 1935:

"Twelve years wasn't a lot of experience by then, even if the Jack Knights, Hamilton Lees, and Slonigers (all with over 13,000 hours) were going to have to be replaced some day." And not just because they were a little bald or gray on top. Only a good copilot with 3,000 hours could aspire to that left seat, after ample preparation. Several lines still laid junior men off around Christmas and rehired in the spring. And no rule determined a captain's generosity in allowing his copilot the experience of takeoffs or landings. Many went months without touching the controls except at cruise, which usually meant his captain was insecure. That sort of flying didn't add much to a copilot's training.

Slonnie admitted, "I've had to ground captains too. One was even vice president of the pilots' union. ALPA never got into the picture unless some pilot appealed to them. Most just took the demotion and flew it out. That V.P. deal was a guy they had written articles about. How he was such a wonderful pilot, with all this experience. Happened I checked three or four captains at the same time. This one dived at the ground like a roller coaster, over-controlling all over the sky, until another captain begged me, 'Slonnie, can't you take it? Please!' He wanted to fight the grounding but all these other captains had seen the show. So he went to South America instead. And flew a Ford into some mountain.

"When a guy did try to buck it we usually found a way. I'd been one of the fifty who started ALPA but that was before it became a union with Dave Behncke in charge. Another boy who messed up went right down to the ALPA office and Behncke calls me. 'Would I be in his office immedi-

ately?' If he wanted to talk, he could come up to mine but I was leaving in half an hour. And we weren't taking the guy back anyway. I told Behncke I knew about three other dodgy cases the public didn't have yet and I had a lot of friends writing aviation news. One case was a boy who kept getting lost—this was another airline—so they fired him. But the ALPA made them put him back on the line. Pretty soon he got lost again and tried to push over a mountain. With a load of passengers." This provided one more slice of Slonnie's disgust with the chief pilot job. "You were either a fish or an SOB. Plus the fact, you got called at two in the morning because some guy couldn't fly his airplane. When AA decided to cut costs it was a

real break. The only captain I had to take care of was me. Rather fly the line any time."

Line flying didn't reduce his personal-appearance schedule noticeably though. Slonnie was portrayed on the Wheaties cereal package for instance, in a Champions of Speed promotion which included guest appearances on the Jack Armstrong radio show, to his son's delight. Unlike all those watches and radios he'd advertised for American Airlines but never received, Wheaties wrote regularly to ask if he'd been getting his shipment every three months and was he using Wheaties right along? On rare occasions the promotion was even connected directly with flying. Sinclair Oil used a clip of Slonnie being congratu-

(Left) Slonnie, as senior American Airlines pilot, at the controls explaining things to Jack Armstrong, "The All American Boy," for his radio show. **(Above)** Studio photograph taken specifically for Wheaties cereal boxes in connection with the Jack Armstrong promotion.

lated on 1,750,000 air miles in a movie short which they claimed was seen by four million people in 800 movie theaters.

While the world rated them in miles, pilots divided their lives into hours flown and the place to pile those up was along the scheduled routes, as Slonnie now did, taking over any AA run he wanted, thanks to seniority number one. Chicago to Newark used the best equipment AA had in 1935, the DC-2. By August they were calling themselves the largest airline in the U.S., with equal advertising space for fried chicken suppers or the only scenic route over Niagara Falls. Only 7.6% of all planes in America had been built by Douglas but those did 27.7% of the transport flying. American downgraded Condors to minor runs, without mentioning fabric covering if they could avoid it, and still had a few Stinsons and Vultees on secondary routes. All the scheduled lines together carried three-quarters of a million revenue passengers during 1935, averaging barely five per trip. At least the venerable, noisy, drafty Fords were finally retiring. Slonnie logged his last regular trip in such a tin trimotor during July 1935. "We sold six for five thousand each but there was a joker. I had to check out the head of the Columbian Air Force, who would fly them away. When I'd checked out on a Ford I flew around the field, landed, and that was it. This boy took five hours and I told the brass to get their cash before he went up alone. He insisted he and another officer would fly them to New York, so they started with two and one got there. They came back for two more and got another one to New York. At least we got rid of some more obsolete equipment."

Captains with seniority had far more joy

from the DC-2, or "Two" as all dubbed it. This looked sleek, cruised about 180 MPH—and needed sandbags in the tail for trim. Windshields leaked and any copilot who could make the heater valves cooperate was a jewel no captain would lightly part with. Yet the Two was what pilots called an honest airplane, top praise. Straight enough that Slonnie expected copilots to take alternate landings and takeoffs. "Going into Detroit once in winter, with the runways slippery, it was the copilot's landing. But that Two was a ground-looping so-and-so. It got away from him and went around the first time so fast it made you dizzy. I grabbed one throttle and finally got it stopped with power, after two circles on the merry-go-round. That was the sickest boy you ever saw. Coming up for probation and the Operations Manager was on board. He followed us into the office and asked who'd made that landing. 'I did.' He just grinned at me and shook his head no. But that was a damn good copilot. You didn't need a union most of the time."

Knowing so well that any Two was among the trickiest-landing airplanes ever built, only the greater cause of AA's future could have prompted Slonnie to go on *Flying Time*, a fifteen-minute radio program in Chicago, which modestly billed itself as the one authentic aviation show on the air, and read: "A DC-2 almost lands itself." Production of these planes reached nearly two a week by mid-1935 and number 100 was signed over to AA that July. Considered a busy plane for pilots, this $65,000 fourteen-seater at least gave their lines some hope of making a little money. "We wouldn't cancel if we could possibly help it, only if some terminal was closed down and we wouldn't have enough gas range to reach the next one open. But a

Two would outfly the Boeing 247 United used on their Chicago-Newark run so we got the trade." A Two would carry a lot of ice as well, no small virtue in the Northeast. Since this was another airplane most pilots liked, if warily, Slonnie naturally had a good ice tale too. "Walt Hunter had a brand-new copilot who didn't know ice off your props banged against that metal fuselage like you were sitting inside a big steel drum. Hunter starts fidgeting and loosening his seat belt each time some hit, like it was all over for them. When a really big chunk hit he jerked out of that seat and ran for the tail. When he peeked back to see what this green kid was doing, there he was, about half a step behind. Funny part was, our Two didn't have an autopilot and Hunter couldn't squeeze past in the gangway. But that old Two just flew along by itself, nice and level."

Slonnie himself proved quite thoroughly that the Two fully deserved its reputation for flying on one engine if it had to. He said, "I left Chicago on a night run, with just about takeoff minimums. Pulled up on top and about 6,000 feet one motor started boiling its oil. Didn't have landing minimums in Chicago so I shut it down. We didn't even have feathering props. Detroit was an instrument approach so just before we got there I fired it up again. A one-motor approach on instruments is kind of on the rough side. No rudder trim. You had to hold it straight with one foot. I'd called ahead so Detroit mechanics checked it all over and ran it up while we had some coffee. They insisted: 'All okay now.' Pulled up on top and about twenty minutes out the oil temperature needle went clear over again. So I shut it down and flew on to Buffalo. Detroit was a no-good field for night landings, with that big gas storage tank in one corner. But then Buffalo turned stinko too. Just before we got there I fired it up and made another low approach. We unloaded the passengers again and the mechanics worked a while. No more problems. Back on top and the oil temperature is off its gauge. I thought about going back but to hell with that. Ended up flying that thing almost all the way from Chicago to Newark on one engine. Had a good tail wind and damn near made schedule, too. Didn't give the copilot any landings on that trip though.

"Mostly landing gear gave us more trouble than motors in the Two. One trip we lined up for Detroit and Bill Dunne, this great big copilot I had, threw the gear switch down. Not a damn thing happened. Electric, but there was a backup lever too so he pumped away with that. Nothing doing. So take the floor panel up. It had lock screws on a spring and we didn't have a single tool on board. Put a set on every plane after that flight. He couldn't get far with a coin either. About then the stewardess came up front to tell me the passengers wanted to know why we were circling. Told her to tell them there's so much traffic we have to wait our turn. But I'd tell her a secret. We can't get the goddamn gear down. Did she have a nail file? Dunne got a couple of screws partway out and pretty soon I hear a crash. He'd gotten those big hands in there and ripped the panel clear out. Now I'd ask the ground questions and he'd push something. But nothing worked. I figured we'd have to go in on the belly, and no foam in those days. Told them I wouldn't use the runway because of all those sparks off concrete, and the wings were full of gas. No dump valves either. Just about to start down, with all the fire trucks and ambulances lined up,

when I reached over and threw that lever down one last time. Wham. The gear goes down. Dunne kind of looked at me. All okay boy, we land on the wheels.

"We only had one stewardess on then but all our gals were nurses and pretty competent. One of the maddest I ever had was a second section out of Chicago, one night when United didn't figure it was wise to fly its 247s. The weather was so bad I didn't want to put a reserve captain on and the Chief Stewardess elected to go instead of a new girl. It was a bad front but we were supposed to serve food right out of Chicago so when we got into some lighter weather stuff I gave her a buzz and said I thought we were through the front. 'Go ahead and serve.' About the time she started I thought I'd run over a cow. Told the copilot to see how our passengers were and he started to unbuckle just as we hit another one. He just said, 'To hell with the passengers,' and tightened that belt again. When I went back a little later, there was supper all over the ceiling. I can still see the menu. Cream of tomato soup, meat with au gratin potatoes, and creamed peas. The stewardess got them mopped off and took names to pay the cleaning bills and I called for more food out of Cleveland. Later that same trip, just out of Buffalo, this panel over the cockpit blew off too, so we got pretty wet. United was smarter than we were that night.

"But it wasn't near as bad as one trip into Los Angeles. That one was plain bad pilot judgment and being in a tough Two is all that saved us. AA had what we called an on-demand stop at Palm Springs but a gale was blowing through that pass like a venturi. Riding in back, holding Jerry on my lap, I thought, good God boy, don't try to land in

Palm Springs. But I couldn't say anything as a passenger. He made a stab, to satisfy a couple of passengers who planned to get off there. A bluff. I heard the gear go down and come right back up. Then we hit this bump and everything flew off the racks. The stewardess was pitched flat in the aisle. I never thought even a Two could take that kind of punishment and keep its wings on. Bill Littlewood was riding too and asked what I planned to do if that pilot had gotten us down in Palm Springs. Told him, 'Take a bus, if we made it in one piece.' He was going to be right behind me."

Johnny never thought wives were worse passengers than pilots—or laymen. "None of us would dare say anything, even though we knew a little more about flying things. It depended on the husband. Men who were very boastful, their wives were apt to think everything was always perfect. Slonnie never talked about his flying. I just knew that if anybody could get a ship in safely, he could. You can't see a man fly nearly forty years, never scratching a passenger, without believing he knows what he is doing." It was rare for Slonnie to be riding, particularly with his family, although wife and son took planes like most families rode the bus. When he wasn't along it might be hard just making a connection on this burgeoning airline. She said, "We were coming into Chicago once, riding subject to space like all company people, when I saw a must-ride ticket and knew we didn't have a chance at a seat. The clerk suggested we go via Cincinnati, so I called Chicago to let Slonnie know which plane to meet. Some kid on the Chicago switchboard told me they didn't have anybody with American named Sloniger. That seemed most peculiar. 'You had a captain of that name yesterday.'

'No, never.' I finally got his regular copilot at home and by the time we reached Chicago he had told them they did have a senior pilot named Sloniger. Slonnie never talked about copilots any more than about rough trips. Not those he liked. But if he had a poor one, he walked the floor. I never saw the side where copilots were afraid of his perfectionism. The ones he was fond of were always top young pilots and usually around our house between runs."

Good ones became even more useful after 1936, when the DC-2 replacement and probably the most famous commercial airplane of all time made its debut. That first DC-3—more properly DST—rolled out of Douglas's assembly hangar on December 17, 1935. Douglas had lengthened a DC-2 wing, widened the fuselage, and fitted bigger engines. Nothing radical but the sum of these parts proved a wonder. Impetus came from American Airlines which wanted to replace its Condor biplanes with modern, transcontinental sleepers to one-up lines flying Boeings, Lockheeds, and even the DC-2. Martin couldn't be bothered converting its bomber for only eight or ten sales, as the job appeared then. The Two had already proven hard to get, with TWA hoarding production, so AA conceived its own DST (Douglas Sleeper Transport) which quickly became the DC-3 (Douglas Commercial, 3rd model). It set U.S. aviation on its upward spiral and established new safety standards.

Lines needed that boost because 1936 did not prove a very safe year to fly. Airline fatalities tripled versus 1934, to forty-four, although it was also the year U.S. lines finally carried more than one million passengers. New airliners could carry more people and when they had an accident with full load it meant a larger death toll. American

Jerrold E Sloniger Collection

A Douglas Sleeper Transport going to the National Air Show in Los Angeles. American Airlines took the new sleeper (DST) version of the DC-3 anywhere it might get publicity. Note the slit windows for upper berths above the regular cabin windows.

opened the dismal tally with a new record loss in January for that very reason. Pilots still debate the so-called "Marshall accident" but Slonnie remained convinced the pilot had been shot. Cockpits weren't locked then. "The reason I felt that way," he said, "Jerry Marshall had a fellow on board who had lost a fortune in the market crash and just taken out another enormous insurance policy, with premiums due in a couple of weeks. Besides, his plane—the *Good Ship Lollypop,* incidentally, the one we'd used in the Shirley Temple promotion— hit a big tree dead on the nose, cutting that Two in half. The weather was wide open and Jerry'd reported in twenty minutes earlier with everything beautiful. Marshall was a good pilot. I think he would have tried to pancake it in, not aim right for the biggest tree, if he'd been alive." A pistol was found near the cockpit but all pilots carried those. Slonnie added, "That's when we put cockpit locks on. Yale key number 100 fitted the DST. And we couldn't take people up front anymore, to show them all the dials and how we did things."

American was the first line to buy DST/ DC-3 glamour, long before anybody realized this airplane would continue to be king of commercial aviation a decade later. When plane builders were separated from operators Douglas benefited most, as the only already-independent constructor and now AA, which couldn't get a front seat on the DC-2 list, gained too. They promoted the DST (sleeper versions were identified by slit windows for upper berths, above the main panes). Rolled out thirty-two years and a day after the first Wright flight, the DST wingspan alone just about matched that Kitty Hawk hop, at ninety-five feet. A revolution in the mid-thirties, the DC-3 would still be around as a

gunship in Vietnam thirty years later.

Many claimed credit for conceiving the Three, once it proved an all-time hit, but those honors really belong to C.R. Smith and his engineering pilot, Bill Littlewood. Designed as an aerial sleeper, it proved far better as a day plane with twenty-one seats. Costing some sixty-nine cents a mile to operate, equal to the Ford Trimotor, this DC-3 would carry double the tons per mile. It was that long-awaited airplane which could make money hauling passengers alone. Yet Douglas initially resisted all overtures, until C.R. promised to purchase twenty, an enormous airplane order then. The first DST flight tests began just as the 185th Two was completed. Douglas eventually built more than 10,000 of the successor, which ended the wood-prop days and survived to fly against jets. Rights were sold to Japan for $100,000 and to Fokker for $3,000 per unit in Europe. Russia simply built copies with their own name on them. Inherent stability made it a leading instrument-flight platform. Low stall speed and fine control response during slow, careful blind approaches meant that skilled pilots could land one (virtually) anywhere.

American was so anxious to get its first Threes into service, captains had to take route checks during normal passenger runs, with a check pilot riding the folding jump seat between captain and copilot—an improvement over a soap box for the third man in their very first DST. Dan Beard of AA was first to test-fly one for the line, just before Christmas, 1935, but it was April 1936, before mandatory 100-hour tests could begin with Beard, Roy Mitchell, and Sloniger flying. Slonnie appeared in the test log on April 29, when the first

plane was turned over to AA in Phoenix, to avoid California sales tax. He flew it heavily, right through May.

There were shuttle flights, photo trips, and an El Paso-Phoenix flight entirely on automatic pilot. High-blower runs—trying out the new two-stage superchargers—began in mid-May. Slonnie said, "Bob Johnson was on board for Curtiss Wright engines, like propeller people would have somebody along, or maybe air-conditioning specialists were running around the cabin with garden thermometers. The ship was usually pretty well loaded. We were supposed to fly half our trips at night and left Burbank late this one evening with beautiful weather, until we got over the mountains. To nonstop, I'd cut some corners from the marked airline route, figuring a course to hit the radio range again someplace between El Paso and Wink or Big Springs. Then we ran into a storm and the rocks get pretty tall around there so I went up to maybe 11,000. Snowing so you couldn't even see the running lights, but it wasn't sticking to the wings so we were all right. Any piston engine loses power with altitude but that Three had this new, two-stage supercharger for going up high. Johnson was sitting up front and suggested I put it on high blower for the first time. To hell with that. I'll wait to try those extra boosters over nice flat land with the stars shining, at least the first time. I didn't need a couple of blown engines right then. We kicked it back and forth and I always called him 'High-blower Johnson' after that.

"Douglas also put dump valves on, if we had to jettison fuel, so we filled one side with some nonexplosive liquid, all perfumed and colored. Went out and dumped it to see if they worked.

God, it looked like you'd taken a spray can to the underside of that wing. Littlewood extended the gadget out and down to the rear like a nozzle and it worked fine. I seem to remember we made 186 changes on that first DST after Douglas was through. No airplane up to then had been test-flown so thoroughly. Seemed like we'd never finish. For a while we had nine separate temperature gauges in the cabin, one for each cylinder of one engine because the top barrels were running hot. But they riveted a temporary baffle over that engine and we got it good and hot, low over the desert at noon, and found a cure. That original plane was old 988. The Air Force confiscated it during the war and burned it up."

NC 14988, the first DST's tail number, was finally christened *Flagship Texas* on July 11, 1936, and put to work on the airline. This was the first airplane which came with graphs, carefully worked out to show a pilot where he could gain or lose time, depending on how he followed procedure variations. Considered American's first modern airplane, it was the inevitable choice for every early flight with the brass, as well as friends and backers. Donald Douglas, Sr., flew on one DST test and drew the private Skyroom after a hot meal. But nobody on board could get its berth mechanism to work so they filled the space between two facing bench seats with suitcases and covered them with a mattress. This Skyroom compartment was actually the shakiest, noisiest spot on a DST, behind the cockpit and right in line with the engines. But since it was also the only private compartment on any airline, film stars favored AA for years. Moneyed people were finally choosing transcontinental air travel over the length of a train ride.

They left Newark at 5:10 in the evening and were due to arrive in Los Angeles just before nine the next morning, although AA didn't always manage that westbound schedule. When a New York hotel room cost $5, they paid $160 for a Skyroom seat, with drinks and a steak thrown in.

Small wonder every public relations man in the company was busy seeking promotional angles. For the tenth anniversary of St. Louis-Chicago mail—the original Robertson route, CAM 2—American made a special flight, noting it only took two hours now, half the 1926 schedule. Their senior pilot also endorsed St. Louis milk in large ads as, "The food you can take on the run." Standing in a Douglas doorway alongside a stewardess straining to hand him another bottle, Slonnie supposedly added, "I always drink a bottle or two on brief stops." A hotel-owning pal in the city suggested this new Hollywood star stop by his

Jerrold E. Sloniger Collection

(Above) Lois Long giving Slonnie another bottle of the St. Louis milk which, according to promotions, he couldn't fly without. **(Right)** Slonnie explains to stewardess Pat Mallory how Buick uses airplane-type shocks in its new car.

Barton Studios, Detroit, Michigan

Rudy Arnold, Press Photographer, Floyd Bennett Airport, Brooklyn

Slonnie flew a Douglas Sleeper Transport to meet the first flight of the Zeppelin *Hindenburg* in Lakehurst, New York, in 1936. He was made an honorary Zeppelin crew member but declined a ride because, "It bent in the middle."

tavern for more appropriate stimulants. As a guest on *Flying Time* again, he became part of the self-styled scoop of the year, an interview from DST NC 14988 over Chicago. Listeners were told to watch for the plane over Lake Michigan during the broadcast. Slonnie chatted with his pilot who praised all the room he had for flying ease and made a pitch for the safety of duplicate dials and radios.

Ed Bern, Slonnie's boss back in Kansas City Airways days and now PR maven for American, even got a DST into the Chicago Auto Show, complete with their most photogenic stewardess to demonstrate berth making. Slonnie suggested he fly it into a nearby park, saving that tow through town with wings removed. Newsreel companies agreed to attend but AA discovered they meant to throw any film away if his park landing proved uneventful. Slonnie offered 100:1 he'd make it easily with a light ship but nervous management said: "Tow." Instead they demonstrated DST range with a nonstop Chicago to New York and return flight for invited press on June 25. The plane was aloft eight hours and every report mentioned how Slonnie only used sixty-five percent power and a mere 630 of his 820 gallons of fuel. He said, "I had enough gas left to go on to Omaha but Operations said those reporters might not want to see Nebraska. Been saving gas all the way but the ground still told me to land in Chicago."

Nineteen thirty-six also brought a joint promotion with the largest air transporter of its day, the Zeppelin *Hindenburg*, which had completed flight trials about the same time as the DST. LZ 129, Germany's twelfth commercial zeppelin, was the largest in the world. Built to celebrate the 1936

Olympic year, it was designed to prove how safe ocean flights were for a large passenger list. And it brought the crowds out. One hundred thousand drove to Lakehurst, New York, in 1936 for the *Hindenburg*'s maiden arrival. AA ads boasted that America's largest airline saluted the world's largest airship, going on to offer Zeppelin passengers fast, exclusive air service, direct from Lakehurst to the rest of America, in giant Douglas airliners. Slonnie flew the DST down to meet that first *Hindenburg* arrival, where photos show it dwarfing a Douglas. The Zeppelin company made him an honorary crew member but couldn't persuade him to try their mode of air travel. "I was walking along this gangway inside the thing," he said, "and that whole zepp bent so my little sidewalk went out of sight. I did visit the cockpit. The place was wide as a room, with one crew member to go up or down and another one to go sideways. But I ducked a flight."

Whatever he might think of airship safety, he seldom thought close calls in his own, heavier-than-air flying were worth the mention. One came that August when he went West to collect the first DC-3, the day-passenger version. "We'd had some trouble with the DST icing its carbs so they switched for the Three. It was Glendale airport then, a small damn field. We were supposed to make Chicago nonstop with C.R., Littlewood, our Treasurer VP who'd gone along to sign the check, and a whole lot more brass on board. Plus a full load of gas to go clear across. Guess I was about fifty feet up, just over the LA river, when both those engines just plain quit. Took a fast look at Los Felices but that boulevard had a car every block so I decided to take the river. It was dry but they had cemented the sides and bottom for flood season. I

figured I was okay at the top but where it tapered to the bottom I didn't know if I could get the wheels on concrete without hooking a wing tip. We were way below the trees, still fiddling with the throttles and fuel settings, when suddenly both engines came on again. Like that. I never touched those throttles until we were 9,000 feet over Riverside with some room to play. The people in back kind of thought we'd had it too, I guess, but the rest of the trip was a breeze. In Chicago we found out these new, synthetic throttle valves had collapsed. I'll never know why it didn't show on tests. They were sort of upset because it meant going back to the old carbs, which iced up. So we put a couple of gallons of alcohol in a tank and piped that in. When the old motor started slowing with carb throat icing, you'd feed it a jigger."

Johnny completed the takeoff tale. "I wouldn't have known a thing except that Gage Mace called and asked what I thought of my husband's prowess. It was on the radio. When Slonnie got home I asked why he hadn't told me. He said, 'Why? Nothing happened, after all.' He just thought I might worry. He never worried in his life. At least not openly, but I think all pilots worried more than they admitted. The lines just flew them too hard before anybody knew how much a man could do."

The DC-3 did ease that problem a little. It was steady enough to be reasonable on automatic pilot and despite a rash of early crashes, from which it was absolved, the plane proved so safe that insurance companies would take air passenger trade at the same rates as travel by train, bus, or ship in 1937. Before long pilots didn't have to pay life insurance excess either. By 1938 the CAA Safety

American Airlines began calling its planes the Flagship fleet, complete with a pennant that the copilot set out on landing. The first Flagship flight was a Chicago-New York run carrying thirteen passengers.

Board would be using DC-3 specifications as a standard for any new airplane, suiting AA fine. As of June 1, 1939, they would be flying Douglas airplanes exclusively. Drawbacks included radios which seldom worked well, an aileron gap which iced up easily, and an adjustable pilot seat prone to release and slide back on landing. But a Three would carry fifty percent more people than a Two for about three percent more in costs. Maintenance was easier too. Some covered 70,000 flying hours before the airframe needed a rebuild and one of the original AA ships was still in regular service with a scheduled carrier thirty years later. This Douglas was called the most perfectly-engineered structural job ever built, meaning really that they had factored in a large ignorance component. AA eventually operated ninety-four of them, carrying more than 10.5 million passengers, and kept the

last DC-3 in their fleet until 1949, thirteen years after the first went into service and an eternity in airplane design.

Slonnie said, "The Three was simply an awfully good-flying airplane but no plane is going to take care of pilot error—that's what causes ninety percent of the trouble. It was a workhorse but, by the same token, had no real single-engine performance, never mind what the legend claims. All I could do as Chief Pilot was to make a rule. You had to stay 1,000 feet above all terrain on a ten-mile sector each side of your course. But coming through San Gregonio pass with San Jacinto peak sticking up a hell of a ways, you just couldn't get 13,000 or 14,000 on one engine. So I wouldn't sign the plane off as clean everywhere. Somebody else did and we never had any trouble."

American launched an exceptional run of

safety in 1936, not losing a single airplane right through 1940. There was more to that than the DC-3 and luck, but both helped. Another side of the Three story was the boom it fostered in passenger travel and thus in crew hiring. "That's when so many of the boys I hired for AA came on. I had to get all the senior copilots checked out and find new kids. Thirty airplanes meant 3.5 crews per ship and we didn't take many army boys, mostly private pilots. Put them with an old captain for the first few months. Some were better with new kids than others. All we gave copilots was three takeoffs and landings. Talk them down. They had to have a transport rating and 200 hours to begin with. Captains flew a straight eighty-five hours, maximum, each month with no limit on copilots. A good copilot hired then was lucky. Make captain in maybe two years and get $190 a month in the meantime. A top captain, flying the night leg on our transcontinental Mercury run, made maybe $9,000 a year."

On American's Flagships copilots had one chore other lines couldn't match. This Flagship idea arrived with the DST. They wanted special touches when one taxied up to its brass-railed boarding ramp. The answer was a three-cornered pennant with AA eagle on a dark blue background flying outside the right cockpit window. Mace recalled that C.R. came down with a flag all rolled up and a drawing, asking what Mace thought of it. He said "Lousy," but C.R. replied he liked it. Mace realized this was the boss's very own idea and said, real quick, he liked it too. Now. American even achieved public debate on how that flag could survive in so much wind—and discussions which earned the line extra mention were the purpose, after all. Nobody saw the copilot open his window and pull the flag in just before takeoff. Slonnie said, "They were silk and cost the airline seven-fifty each. It got to be a game. Leave it out and it would flap on the tin. Be half gone next stop but you didn't hear anything until you leveled off and got some speed up. Then the copilot's face would go red. Any kid who forgot one had to buy his captain a dinner. One trip Joe Hammer had an engine ice up and quit, then the other one began to ice too, and the copilot wanted to know what they did now. Hammer looked horrified and told him to hang out the flag just before they hit. 'Do you want to get us both fired?'"

Flagship pride and a proper transcontinental run were parts of a general AA effort to pull its northern and southern divisions together. Southerner C.R. made a point of mixing top people so Slonnie was sent to sort out the Southern Division next. The whole line knew that Number One was highly respected by all their pilots, as a friend explained. There was resentment down south, but Slonnie was C.R.'s best bet. Slonnie wouldn't get back to flying the line himself until the spring of 1939, and then only because of renewed friction with ALPA which boasted in 1936 that it was so important, even copilots wanted to sign up. As Chief Pilot, Slonnie was banished from the union but then, he wouldn't carry their card when they did want him to join again. Johnny said, "Of course, many pilots did resent his being sent down from the north and he didn't mix much, but not knowing AA people in Fort Worth was more my fault than his. He was gone so much we made our friends outside American, except for a few like Johnny Davidson, his assistant there. We had one

Jerrold E. Sloniger Collection

A typical Ed Bern promotion—he's pictured (middle) with Slonnie (right) and an unidentified man (left). The stuffed steer was "herded" along from the lobby of the Ft. Worth airport so Bern could get the AA logo in a publicity photo.

period when the field would call and tell me to 'Bring Mr. Sloniger's overcoat out, he was going through to the East.' A few days later they'd call again. 'Come get Mr. Sloniger's overcoat, he's going back to Los Angeles.' Those would be the only times I saw him in two or three months."

Slonnie knew, "Johnny didn't want to live in Texas and I had my Chicago deal all cleaned up and running in good shape. My pilots were doing a fine job. But Roy Mitchell could move up to Assistant Operations Manager if I took the Fort Worth end, including the transcontinental. I told them Big Mitch was worth a promotion but I didn't want Fort Worth. So they got a vice president into the picture and finally C.R. himself. For good old AA. I ran Burbank to Newark and Fort Worth to Chicago. That was twice as big as any other division in miles flown. They gave me a Stinson to do instrument checks or visit people like that guy on an emergency field out west of Phoenix. Chicago claimed his maintenance expenses were too high so I flew out for a look. It was just an old sand field in the desert. I don't think one airplane landed there in five years, but he told me if one did have to land he wanted it smooth for them. You could have shot pool on his field. I told him to let the damn grass grow and save scraper blades.

"I only flew occasional scheduled trips then. A little vacation relief if we didn't have anybody to take it. But every once in a while I did go down and play on the Link Trainer. That counted as instrument time in my log. AA bought a couple of Model C Links and put one in Fort Worth. It was a whole lot cheaper than flying an airplane, to get some practice. We tried to get everybody in once a month for an hour at least.

New copilots got extra time." American was the first line to use them, starting in January 1937, although flight schools had featured simpler models for a year and the idea went back a decade. The first fifty of Link's basement invention went to amusement parks, before the Pioneer Instrument Company finally bought one for proper aviation use. Link expected the military to welcome simulators, but both Japan and Russia believed in him before the U.S. caught up. The snag was pilot resistance, mostly from men with fifteen or more years of flying and several thousand logged hours. Veterans felt they must be pretty good already or they wouldn't be alive. Link trainers only won pilot support when old hands discovered you could even simulate fires on takeoff. That was one panic nobody wanted to try in an airplane but if you did have one, it would be too late for wrong decisions. This trainer was a completely enclosed cockpit mock-up on a pivot to give the feeling of all normal airplane movements for a pilot with no vision.

Slonnie said, "The Link was much harder to fly properly than an airplane because the early ones had no control pressures. Barely touch a Link and you'd be clear through a turn. But it had all the flying instruments and pretty soon we even got wind drift components. Get in there and have the operator set a little spider tracer on say the Fort Worth range map. It made a record of every inch you flew and sure showed if you missed even a little bit." Brother Perry recalled Slonnie showing him the Link and saying, "You know, after all these years, I had to learn how to fly all over again in this thing." But any pilot who complained that the Link was too finicky for people to fly was simply shown a perfect instrument-approach trace. Slonnie's.

Ground practice complemented another aid which eased pressures on that man in the left seat, the on-board automatic pilot. "We had our first autopilots on the DST and I had to ride twenty-five hours with each captain because you couldn't work the iron man just going around the field. I'd fly the right seat and explain how to set it up. One control for elevators, one for ailerons, and one for rudder. Hook up your directional gyro to your compass reading. When you got all that set and your ship level, just pull that lever and the iron man took over. There was a fineness control too, in case the ship jumped around a little.

"When I showed Charley Pedley [tops in log hours on American Airlines] how, he looked over at me and said, 'Don't tell Operations about this or they'll fire us all.' There wasn't any autopilot school. I learned mine during the 100-hour DST tests. It did a hell of a lot better job than the pilot because it didn't wander. Slide just one degree off the leg and it would pull you right back. Of course it would fight the plane too, if your stewardess was running up and down the aisle. Just unlock the stabilizer trim and fly that part by hand until she got everybody settled for the night. You kind of kept an eye on it too. I was watching the dials one night when my artificial horizon started to jiggle so I jerked the iron man off just as the horizon turned upside down. That would have put the plane on its back if I hadn't caught it by chance. Flying the dials properly took a lot of practice. When I first went to Fort Worth I had to ground one of the pilots with a single-digit seniority number simply because he hadn't practiced those instruments regularly. Madder than hell and wouldn't speak to me for a week. He was also the only guy who came in later and thanked me. Said he didn't know he had been flying so badly. A good man, just gotten sloppy. You couldn't do that on the dials."

American had a strong set of chief pilots as they launched into a solid year in 1937. That April they flew thirty percent more people than April 1936, with Slonnie's southern transcontinental route up a full seventy-eight percent, thanks to more comfortable airplanes. Aviation stocks were strong again and the Civil Aeronautics Board was handing around what came to be called "grandfather certificates." These protected established routes against all comers and made U.S. aviation such a closed shop the original lines would still be flying ninety percent of all traffic thirty-five years later. All this required even more copilots too. Slonnie said, "Mostly they came in and tried to tell me how good they were. I'd talk about something else. Canaries maybe. Hell, they would be on probation for a year and I'd find out by then how good they were. You passed up more than you hired. Took maybe one in a hundred. Some still weren't up to it. Cutrell was riding as passenger once when the pilot just leaned over and passed clear out. That copilot was not one of our strongest so he called the stewardess and Cutrell had to go up and put the ship on in. I checked the boy out later for reserve captain and he was awful nice but not AA material. When it was time for him to move on up, some other chief pilot put a good copilot with him. I never agreed with that deal. If the captain can't do as well as the copilot, they should trade seats.

"Later still he had a new copilot and got all mixed up for some reason. Very timid guy. There was plenty of ceiling but he poked down, saw some

Jerrold E Slonger Collection

Slonnie, a regular American Airlines spokesman, flew many of the Hollywood passengers. He especially liked Gene Autry, who was a pilot himself.

lights and hauled back on the wheel. Up into the overcast again. Did that two or three times and then stuck it right smack into the ground. Our first accident after five years of good safe flying." And the public loved to read about such air troubles. The first proven aerial suicide—a man jumped out over Bakersfield—garnered more space than a nonstop Russian transpolar flight from Moscow to California in sixty-two hours. American Airlines could only promote its Flagship Club for special people even harder and wait for bad press to die down again. Or point out that the Mercury, its southern transcontinental service, made only three stops now, with no need to change airplanes.

On that elite run captains met a good many film people, both nice (kept quiet) and nasty (made unreasonable demands), all occupying the Skyroom. On one of Slonnie's unreasonable trips, "I was flying the right seat to give a reserve captain his check. Nashville was zero-zero to start and we didn't know if it would be Memphis or Columbus to land. Got rougher than a cob. We made it into Memphis and told them to fuel it fast because there was a storm front right behind us. But the ramp was wet and the boys couldn't be bothered. That storm caught us on the ground. This cowboy star in the Skyroom knocks on the cockpit door and wants to know why we're sitting on the ground so long. Told us to get the pilot who brought us in here if we were scared to fly. We went on to Newark where the sun was shining on top but a bunch of planes were circling for low approaches. Bang on the door again. Why doesn't he land? We must be lost. The guy's wife was nice though and thanked me for such a beautiful trip. The front office usually told us before we left the coast if there was somebody

special on board. Sometimes you just thought, oh Christ. But you couldn't do better than Clark Gable or Spencer Tracy, Gene Autry or Gene Kelly. Jimmie Stewart was a pilot so he understood, and Fred Astair a hell of a nice guy."

It all piled up the flying hours. In 1937 American announced that seventy-nine of its 250 pilots were million-milers and almost all of them family men. The top man had 15,000 hours, versus 13,000 for Slonnie. Nearly half were college grads, twenty-eight military-trained. But they still used Number One to fly those specials. Celebrating the tenth anniversary of Lindbergh's Atlantic flight, RCA's *Magic Key* program gathered men who had known or helped the hero. Following a couple of classic numbers from the stage of Chicago's Civic Opera they would bring in New York and Paris, plus Slonnie, to speak while supposedly clipping the fleecy clouds above Chicago. After a fulsome introduction the announcer was to say, "Contacting the pilot Sloniger flying above us. We ask him, are you ready to come in, Sloniger?" Slonnie would answer half a dozen questions about Lindbergh, flying between St. Louis and Chicago and so forth. The call went out on May 16: "Come in, Sloniger." He said, "I wasn't even flying the ship and they had somebody there to read my lines in case I keeled over. Plane was full of RCA people. I had a headset on and answered the questions but kept telling them aside that I wasn't getting out. And the ground kept calling, 'Come in, Sloniger.' Somebody had changed frequencies and we were talking to AA operations instead of station WBBM. Going back their radio guy asked me, 'Listen, does a wing ever come off a DC-3?' Told him none had yet and he said, 'Well, I hope one comes off today. I sure

Metropolitan News Photos, Municipal Airport, Chicago

For the tenth anniversary of Lindbergh's transatlantic flight, Slonnie was supposed to be broadcast in flight during the RCA *Magic Key Hour*, but he never got on the air, since a technician on the airplane had plugged into the wrong radio frequency.

hate to go back to that station.'"

In the summer of 1938 four AA pilots received ten-year pins with a diamond from C.R., including Slonnie, whose log time would pass the 14,000-hour mark before the year was over. He had been flying twenty years by then, although ten was considered pretty special when *Time* published its list of old-time pilots. Despite all its experienced captains and every known public relations ploy, the single event which did the most to put passengers on airliners to stay was a natural disaster. Several lines had flown mercy missions in January 1937, taking medicine to flood victims in Kentucky, but when a hurricane swamped Boston in September 1938, those same lines established an enduring name for service which people remembered. Up to then American Airlines had averaged 200 Boston-New York passengers a day. After the storm, most days topped 1,000, plus thirty tons of mail and thirty more of supplies.

Slonnie said, "That storm hit hardest north of New York but it smashed things all up and down the coast, clear up to Boston and inland to Hartford, where they had water on the second floor. That called for every spare airplane we owned. In those days each line had its exclusive runs and Boston was ours, but we just didn't have enough airplanes or pilots. Not even enough dispatchers. Every station sent their extras and AA handled dispatch for everybody, but we still had to borrow planes and pilots from all the others. At least the weather helped. We only had one rough night for about five days. We could go over the top in about an hour and a half, whereas trains wound all over and took five and a half hours. All the Western Union and phone lines were down too so people mobbed us, wanting to fly in and see how families were. It got so heavy we didn't even sell tickets. Roll a ship up to the ramp and count off the first twenty-one people behind the rope. You could get trampled, standing in their way.

"Normally we had maybe eleven Boston-New York flights a day. On that deal it would be flight eleven, section eight. Went like streetcars. Coming back to Newark, Washington Bridge was

the call-in point. One trip I estimated Newark airport in so many minutes and then heard a mechanic telling the tower that motors and radio on another ship were fine. He identified it as 'Flight twelve, New York to Boston. Pilot Sloniger.' Boy, I was turning around fast. Still inbound and they had me on the ramp going out. Captains had to stick to eighty-five hours but we had a lot of reserve captains so I could fly the right seat too and call it a check ride." Slonnie's log showed nearly sixty hours in twelve days, including 10:30 for six trips on a single day. "If a guy went over eighty-five hours in any month, before the war anyway, ALPA would howl. You could only send him out if he'd be back by 84:59. It was okay if he went over eighty-five a little bit because of a head wind on the last leg home, just so the paper schedule worked. The company liked to use them the full eighty-five of course but we had to watch it. Same with an overload. We couldn't even take twenty-two people on the Boston deal or the CAA would have our ticket, even though you didn't need much gas. During that job they wanted me to take a load of fresh money to Hartford. It was the insurance center and they were paying cash advances until claims could be worked out. The ship had been loaded until you couldn't slip another dollar bill in. I had to tell them to take some weight off or I just couldn't go.

"The whole deal set us up in passenger traffic. Of course, all the other lines who'd helped wanted in too. AA fought like hell to keep the exclusive but we couldn't hold them all out. When you got more than one line on the same route it could be pretty rough. Like United on Newark-Chicago. They left about ten minutes ahead of us

with the old 247, when we still flew Twos. We had to go the long way around, with landings at Buffalo and Detroit, while they only landed in Cleveland, but we'd hit the end of Lake Michigan about the same time. The UAL boy would see me and stick the nose down for extra speed, but that was costing him altitude. One trip we got to the reporting point, with me well out in front, so I picked up my mike to report over Gary. Before I could speak, here's United flight so and so over Gary, estimating Chicago in ten minutes. The tower tells me I'm number two to land. I told that tower United was fifteen minutes behind me and got into an argument but I landed first."

Airlines took any available edge. As the self-proclaimed World's Fair line out of New York in 1939, American plugged the Epicurean level of 300,000 meals served aloft each year, claiming a passenger would almost never eat exactly the same meal twice in any twelve months. After one of four juices or eight soups, entrees ranged from lamb chop or Virginia ham to duck, chicken, or turkey, even chop suey and chow mein. You could expect one of fifteen vegetables or a dozen salads with equal variations in the (mostly frozen) desserts. Pilots doubtless appreciated such a range of food most, since they ate far more meals aloft than any passenger, but their prime concern remained safety. U.S. lines jointly received the Collier Trophy in 1939 for their safety record. Yet Slonnie admitted, "I always bought that extra insurance any time I flew another airline. Defied them to kill me when I could bet a quarter against $25,000. We were up in Seattle once, checking out Boeing's first four-motor airliner, which was a turkey. Four of us had ridden up on another line and were checking in afterwards to go back to LA when this boy came through the terminal with captain's stripes on his sleeve. I asked if he was taking our flight and the counter girl said 'Yes,' very proud. I started buying extra insurance and one of other other chief pilots asked if I knew the guy. 'Yeah, and he never could fly worth a damn.' You got to sense who could and who couldn't, but that wasn't the only criteria.

"When Wrong-Way Corrigan got back from his Atlantic deal with the old Curtiss Robin, they had him down in St. Louis for some promotion. Robins had been built there. Ed Bern was in town and told me, 'You know, he's going to fly for American now.' I asked, 'Since when was the publicity department hiring pilots?' Bern had told Corrigan he could have a job on my division. 'That's what you think, Ed. Suppose some passenger sees that name on those tags we put up by the cockpit door? Starts asking if this is the wrong way to Chicago?' The kid made one hell of a good flight, but he wasn't going to fly for us. Sometimes it worked the other way around, keeping a good pilot in spite of his ideas. We had one boy who would come in from every trip with a squawk sheet on the airplane a mile long. Say things like, 'This ship shouldn't be in the air.' Chicago said we had to get rid of Henry Meyers. I agreed about his attitude but then, I didn't like a lot of attitudes. He was a damn good pilot and that's what we needed most. Dressed him down instead. If that airplane ever got into trouble and the CAA found his squawk sheet, we'd all be out of business. Anybody else would say, 'Left engine a little rough.' Or maybe, 'Brakes aren't holding very well.' You wrote them up because nobody wants to pass on a bad airplane. But it wasn't up to the pilot to take one out of the air."

Slonnie with one of his favorite copilots, Bill Cooper, in a DC-3 cockpit.

Slonnie was tangling more and more often with the pilots' union over men he grounded. One was an old hand, following an instrument check into Fort Worth. "Ranges are similar there. The only catch was that Fort Worth's was north of the field and Dallas had its range on the south side. I looked out when he put the gear and flaps down and we were right over the middle of Dallas, coming in from the north like it was Fort Worth range. Nothing but houses out in front. So I took him off flying. They raised hell. Didn't want me as chief pilot any more and I never wanted the job anyway. There was a boy who did want it and I went back on the line, flying Dallas-Burbank. We could still live in Fort Worth. That Mercury going west was the best run in the whole of AA. It was on the Mercury that this stewardess was flying with me when they put in a deal where you signed off a trip by putting down your seniority number instead of

your name. When I wrote '1' she told somebody, 'He signed Number 1—but nobody is that old!'

"Copilots couldn't bid by number of course and usually couldn't get away with staying next to one captain very long. Except that Bill Cooper was a super salesman and wanted to fly with me." The wants of this chunky copilot would have been immaterial to AA but Slonnie was equally happy to keep him. Cooper joined American as number 382 and could expect to break into the prestigious, two-digit territory by the time he retired in the sixties. Meanwhile, he had a good seat for evaluating captains and since he had piled up more flying hours than most copilots before he was hired, he had the basis too.

"You flew with a lot of captains," Cooper said, "but when I was assigned to Sloniger we got along great. That was a lot of man there and I sure appreciated his experience. He just seemed to always make the right moves. But I had been flying around Southern California before he went on that run and knew all the streetlights leading into LA and that tickled the hell out of Slonnie. In those days, if you could find the airport, you'd go in. The beacon for Los Angeles was on a Griffith Park mountain and sometimes we went in so low we were looking up at it. I still remember my second trip with Slonnie. He reached into his flight bag and took out a rubber butcher's apron, with that smile of his. So I got one too. It rained harder inside a DC-3 than outside. Sometimes we'd scrape half an inch of ice off the inside of the windshield. Slonnie would be flying blind and tell me, 'I got that range trucked right under the inside arm here.' Meaning, straight down the middle of that airplane. 'Let's go in.' He gave me a landing in Tucson and another in Burbank on an early flight and I guess I did all right, so he saw I got a couple every trip. Some captains just had you twiddling your thumbs between stops. Originally we had to load baggage too. Shuttle trips were hell, with fifteen or twenty mail sacks. Smell like a goat on the summer run. I used to take the uniform off and fly in shorts. That was before I flew with Slonnie and we had to go back and talk to the passengers."

Slonnie always insisted, "Best feature of the westbound Mercury, the passengers were all sound asleep when I got it in Dallas, so you didn't bother with them until Tucson, which was about daylight, and they put food on. Between there and Burbank you went back and gave them the old baloney." Tucson often provided the landing to remember for Mercury crews. Cooper recalled one. "There was about six inches of water on the field and the radio went out on our first pass so we had

to go around at the last minute. I retracted the gear fast, without Slonnie yelling. Next shot he said, 'Let me know when we are over the edge of that field.' He's on the dials so I watched and said, 'NOW.' He slammed it down hard. That was the only way. Later he told me, 'Son, I'm damn glad you pulled that gear so fast. We'd have hit the hangar otherwise.' Jack Benny was on and said his next contract was going to have a clause that he never had to stop in Tucson."

The comedian should have been on another landing Slonnie made there with Jim Rose flying copilot. "He was the boy I'd turned down in Chicago," Slonnie said, "because he didn't have two years of college. Somebody else hired him and put him with me as copilot. He told me later, he figured he'd had it with AA right there.

"Maybe his language was a little rough but Jim was a damn good pilot. When he called for Tucson weather this one trip they gave us a 45 MPH crosswind. And Tucson only had one runway. Phoenix, a little further up the road, had light winds and a better field so he asked if he should get a clearance there. He claims I just told him, 'The Mercury lands in Tucson.' The way Jim told it, he figured, God, I'm only a poor copilot but this guy's crazy. We went on in and I'm practically crosswise to the runway with one wing way down on the wind side and crabbing along. Knew I'd pull a tire off unless I got it straight just before we touched. Coming down at this awful angle, I was pretty busy juggling the airplane but I'll always remember Rose saying, 'Dis is it, dis is de end.' Got straightened out at the last second and pointing down the runway, jumping on one brake because that wind was working hard on my fin. Plus lots of right motor,

giving it the gun to hold the plane straight until we slowed down. It wasn't too bad, really, but Rose told the story for years and always claimed that landing was IT!" Rose also remembered wondering if he was really cut out for airline flying after that one, if Slonnie expected every copilot to do the same before they moved to the left seat.

This flying standard was what Cooper had in mind when he said, "Some copilots didn't want to ride with Slonnie. He was too quiet and they were a little afraid of his skills. Outside the cockpit he was different entirely. Jack Knight asked Slonnie one time why he put on a clean shirt just to fly home and Slonnie cracked, 'With those gray ones United wears you need logbooks to know when to change.' But I loved getting my captain's check from Slonnie. He wanted everything done the right way because it was the only way. He'd say, 'We have standards so do it by those, day in and day out.' We all took a lot of pride in American Airlines but it took men like Slonnie to establish our record. He was never away from that ship for ten seconds, his concentration never slipped. Always thinking of what might happen next. I remember most, how his hands always reminded me of a man who should play the piano. Had a very expressive way of talking with his fingers. Never once ruffled."

Of course even Slonnie might have been shaken at least slightly with a wild animal loose in his cockpit. The DST had a compartment across the aisle from its Skyroom and animals traveled there, enjoying cabin heat. Slonnie said, "Vic Miller was coming into Dallas when he looked around and saw this lion cub strolling up the aisle. He made a grab for it and the lion naturally spit right back. So he called Dallas and told them he had a lion loose in the cockpit. 'Get a new box ready.' When I got to the field to take his run on west they asked me, 'How big is a lion?' They had about ten different boxes, from something you could have put a couple of grown lions in down to little bigger than a cigarette carton. When I went aboard, Miller's copilot, who was part Indian, was holding this cub on his lap, scratching its ears and tickling its tummy and having a great party. But Miller was having no part of any more lions on his ship."

If livestock wasn't savaging some captain it was sure to be blocking his runway —in Tucson of course. "The field was fenced but that broke down all the time and a bunch of cattle would stray on. The tower called once to say there were steers on the runway and everybody was going out in cars to herd them off. Finally, they called again and said they thought all the steers were off but I should be very careful landing. Ray Fortner was about thirty minutes out, still on the tower frequency so he comes on: 'Make my hamburger rare, Sloniger.'" The steer hazard didn't make their statistics, although the CAA had been reorganized with a Civil Aeronautics Board (CAB) added to investigate accidents or trouble spots. After Charley Pedley's crash it became evident, however, that only the airlines were properly policed in the forties. All the experience or hours in your log— Pedley was tops for AA—couldn't avert fate or a careless Army pilot.

Slonnie said, "Pedley flew the Mercury a day ahead of me so we'd have lunch when I got in and he was due out of Burbank. This time his copilot was ex-army and had run into some service chum at a party who was ferrying a plane east the

same day. They set up a rendezvous over Riverside. We don't think Charley knew a thing about it. He went over Riverside just fine and was headed through the pass when this army boy in a recon plane caught up. But he overshot, so he went around and ended up under Pedley's tail. Of course he was blind above so he just hauled the stick back to find them and ran right up on that Douglas's rear. Cut the whole works off. There wasn't a damn thing Pedley could do with no elevators or rudder. He'd had it. Told the radio about it all the way down, fighting that ship and saying goodbye to his kid just before it hit. The army boy landed okay, with red marks on his plane just the color of AA's international orange trim, so we wanted to charge him with manslaughter. But civilian courts couldn't touch him as long as he stayed in the service and his army commander said he was a nice boy. He got off free. Said that airliner moved into him. I flew an awful lot of Douglas airplanes but never saw one that could back up."

Conversation among aviation legends—Jimmy Doolittle, with pencil, Phil Love (left), Jimmy Mattern of Lockheed, and Slonnie (right).

Freak crashes probably received less publicity by then since the public was slowly coming to believe in flight safety, although airlines still had to sell some tickets on the time plan as late as March 1941, with no down payment if they knew you. American Airlines carried its four-millionth passenger that year, shortly before war began. Thereafter people begged for seats. "The government set all seat priorities and paid our regular fares but instead of flying ten or twelve we took twenty-one every single trip, with another twenty-one pleading to get on." The Slonigers had moved to California but Slonnie still flew the Mercury, from the other end. "I could see big airplanes coming where you would have to be at one end of the U.S. or the other. We were going to be flying them clear across." Knowing the services would have that fancy equipment first, he also tried to enlist in every single branch but transport pilots who weren't in some reserve squadron had been declared essential and frozen in airline jobs.

Even there they might brush against the war, as Slonnie did only a day after Pearl Harbor. He said, "We were flying to the coast on [December] the 8th and suddenly they told us to shut down all transmitters and land in Palm Springs. So I took my headphones off and let the copilot listen. We couldn't send anyway. Suddenly Harold Level says he is getting funny talk. I grabbed my headset and hell, it sounded like Japanese. We took a direction fix and they discovered this nice little Japanese gardener up in San Jacinto—Jerry had gone to school with his kid—who their Navy had planted there years before." Fearing imminent invasion from Japan, a different face was painted on California. "The first time I took a new copilot into Burbank, once we started going clear through again, they had gotten fancy studio scenery artists out and painted a town all over that airfield. Sprayed it with fake house roofs and roads and backyards with swimming pools. I came in low, calling for my gear and flaps, and this kid just looked at me. This nutty captain was going to land on the housetops. You just had to know which roof was the start of your runway."

Douglas was building planes called C-47s now, olive drab DC-3s in mass lots to supplement airliners reclaimed from the civilian carriers. Young pilots were called up and aging was thinning airline ranks. By late 1942 Slonnie was the fourth-oldest employee of American Airlines in terms of service at age forty-six and senior among four pilots receiving their fifteen-year pins. Each was credited with more than three million miles in the air, so they often got the VIP passengers. Eleanor Roosevelt was typical. "Of course she rode priority-one so I went back to say hello as usual. I always

called her 'Too-too' after that. The flight was too wonderful, the food too tasty, the weather too beautiful. I thanked her for being on board and escaped to the cockpit. Not long afterwards she was on the trip behind me. I was cleared right into Burbank but they were told to land in Glendale. Sounded funny when you could see clear to the coast so her pilot asked why and was told: 'Land in Glendale!' There was a laundry-crew strike in Burbank. She wouldn't cross a picket line, not even to get off an airplane, so all those other passengers had to ride a bus in."

In the middle of that year, about the time Greyhound filed with the CAB for postwar helicopter routes of some 49,000 miles to cater to small loads, Slonnie landed in Los Angeles and found himself involved with the largest load-carrying airplane ever contemplated in America, Howard Hughes's flying boat. "I got into Burbank and found a message that Ed Bern was in town and had to see me right away. By the time I got cleaned up a great big station wagon pulled up and a good-looking gal in a Hughes Aircraft uniform asked for me." The one-time KC Airways and AA promotor had been sales manager for Hughes Aircraft since late 1942 and General Manager of West Coast enterprises since June 1943, with direct responsibility for the controversial cargo plane. He also had firm ideas about who should fly it. This wonder airplane went back to a 1941 decision by the Joint Congressional Aircraft Committee which urged more plywood in aircraft construction. Henry J. Kaiser, the Victory ship man, set out to build 5,000 flying boats of fantastic size but soon backed out of the KH-1 project when it proved too much for even his expansive style. By then, however, he had

brought Howard Hughes in, a man who had flown big boats in the early days and dreamed of a vast one.

Hughes threw himself into the airplane project by day, completing final scenes of his movie, *The Outlaw*, at night. When Slonnie met Bern in the penthouse of a fancy downtown hotel, the plane was still a concept, soon to be renamed H-4, then Hercules, following an employee contest. The public nickname of *Spruce Goose* never amused Mr. Hughes. Since the millionaire remained a phantom to even his closest associates, Slonnie's brush with him when Hughes walked through the penthouse was rare indeed. "He needed a haircut and hadn't had those clothes pressed since the day he bought them. He did say hello, with a look that really meant he would rather throw me out of some window." As this strange man once said, "I suppose I am not like other men. I am not as interested in people as I should be I guess." However, this lanky, exasperatingly successful, lone wolf was also a pilot who had won both the Collier and Harmon trophies for aviation achievements, as well as a medal from Congress and a greater weight of Broadway ticker tape after his record, around-the-world flight than even Lindbergh received. Slonnie said, "He'd done a hell of a lot of flying. In fact, he flew for American once as a copilot, under some alias, to learn instrument work for that world trip. I knew he was going to be number one on any Hughes project. But I went to lunch with Bern and their lawyer. They would give me $25,000 to fly a little recon job first, and $100,000 for the boat. I told them they were wasting a lunch. Hughes was never going to let anybody else fly any airplane he made."

Johnny was more emphatic. "I just didn't see any sense in his doing Hughes's dirty work. I

National Air and Space Museum, Smithsonian Institution

Howard Hughes's gigantic wooden flying boat, the Hercules, was nicknamed the *Spruce Goose* by the American public, much to the millionaire's chagrin.

didn't know what the test involved and neither did he, at first. But I figured test flying was ridiculous at his age, with his time in aviation. Hughes had to prove it would fly somehow to protect himself from Congress."

Slonnie said, "When I first saw that eight-engine boat in their enormous hangar [a rare concession for anybody in- or outside the firm], I told them it looked like a Douglas and got hushed up fast. Seems Hughes had gone by Douglas and asked some top boy what he was getting, then upped it by half. Still, I knew that boat would get off the water, which was all I had to do for the hundred grand. Provided he let anybody else near the cockpit. But Johnny said I was worth more than that to her so we dropped it." During Senate testimony in 1947, Bern, who had resigned from the project after a few hectic months, citing the chaotic situation (no access to Hughes, the only man who dared make a decision), felt the boat was viable but the payroll had been so padded with Hollywood names ducking the draft they had scant chance of getting anything done. Plant politics prevented his firing one engineer, for instance, although Hughes dropped that same man sixty days after Bern quit over the issue. Once Hughes lifted it a few feet off the water the Senate quit bothering about whether it had been a giant waste of taxpayer money.

In February 1944, various government agencies recommended the boat contract be cancelled. Two months later Hughes shared a Lockheed Constellation with Jack Frye, president of TWA, which Hughes also controlled. Frye was repeating his grandstanding DC-1 flight of 1934 by setting a sub-seven-hour LA-Washington record. A

day later Secretary of Commerce Jones was duly
impressed by Hughes's PR abilities and authorized
completion funds for the big boat after all. Chief
problem all along was the enormous leap beyond
contemporary airplane dimensions, never mind the
all-plywood specification. Wing area was a 350
percent increase over the largest plane flying then
and even the Boeing 747 Jumbo of today is a
smaller airplane. Hughes's workers called it the
Jesus Christ. People seeing it for the first time
simply stared.

　　　　Long before the *Spruce Goose* flew, or at
least hopped, in 1947, Slonnie decided he was
going to get into those new, four-engine airplanes.
The only chance at one of those in 1944 was the
worldwide Air Transport Command, or ATC. In his
case, it would be the Atlantic division. He left the
Mercury for the only quasi-military job allowed to
accept a pilot frozen on so-called vital airline duty
and AA, typically, got in one last promotional job
as he headed east to join the ATC. He said, "That
Spinach Special was a deal where some big chain in
Dayton wanted a load of fresh spinach picked in
the Imperial Valley and put on sale in Ohio the
next morning. They got to American and we rigged
up a ship with coolers and put a guy on board who
ran up and down during the entire flight with a
mist gun to keep it fresh. I took it into Dallas and
another boy went up to Dayton. I deadheaded into
New York and joined the ATC." A month later
American Airlines opened regular, transcontinental cargo flights, using the DC-3, but Slonnie was
already juggling four sets of engine controls on the
Atlantic shuttle.

September 1944   Flying hours: 19,198

Chapter 13

Air Transport Command

"When Sloniger misses an approach, the weather is damn lousy."

Older airline captains began to take considerable interest in the Air Transport Command towards the end of WWII. Their ATC—never to be confused with a shuttle bearing the same acronym but flown by military pilots—was where the aviation action was by 1944. Domestic lines might carry four million passengers that year, but the ATC was flying 300-plus trips a month to Europe, well over half of them in Douglas airplanes, especially the brand-new, four-engine C-54, née DC-4.

Slonnie explained, "Before the ATC I had tried to get into the Air Force and they offered colonel but the airline insisted it was too short of pilots to let me go. I tried the Marines. Gave my experience and this officer told his clerk, 'Lock that door.'

"'Look,' he said, 'we need you but the best we can do is major.' It takes God to make major in the Marines right off so I went for the physical. Just about the time I got stripped some sergeant rushes in and asks if there is a Sloniger in the room. 'Get out of here quick.' Somebody had wired headquarters they had a hot one and got the answer, 'That guy Sloniger is absolutely off limits.' So I decided it

would have to be the ATC. American tried to talk me out of that too. But they flew Fours on the Atlantic. We would be using them pretty soon on the line so I took the job. It didn't pay all that well, despite what some army boys thought. More than the Mercury but I worked a hell of a lot harder too.

"We had twelve hours training on the ship. Takeoffs, letdowns, the usual stuff, and went through the same celestial navigation school as the navigators. The Four was a hell of a good airplane. Easy to learn. Then we had ditching practice. Out in Flushing Bay [New York], and colder than hell. Raining too. We got out on this barge and put on trunks. Threw rafts overboard, inflated them, and jumped in. Put up a sail and set up the little radio. George McCabe was streaming wet from this freezing drizzle and asked me, 'You know what I got in this bag? A bottle of brandy.' I told him to get that out, right now, or we weren't going to survive this survival course."

The ATC was something new in U.S. aviation history—using vastly experienced men to fly anywhere, anytime. It's often forgotten that nobody had flown across the North Atlantic in the months from December to March before the war. The Air Force had been ferrying airplanes to England for some time, and losing a good many en route, but the idea of putting airline pilots into military uniforms to do the job was dropped when

somebody realized domestic schedules were vital too. Besides, ALPA boss Behncke didn't get the stars he expected for his shoulders and devoted the rest of his war to seeing that union men flew to strict civilian rules. The compromise was ATC, civilians in semi-military uniforms. This proved better for the pilots themselves because Gen. Harold "Hap" Arnold had the sense to name C.R. Smith as his number two to run this worldwide network on an airline basis.

Most ATC pilots were older than combat fliers, with ample practice at getting through, regardless of weather. Eager youngsters from the airlines had gone directly into the service, the less adventurous clung to civilian routes. Captains came from every domestic airline, including 116 AA men who flew the ATC with seniority numbers ranging from 13 to 472, until Slonnie arrived. By 1944 there was an ATC takeoff or landing every thirteen minutes at the New York end. A year later they would be flying a quarter-million people in July alone. Wounded were the chief justification for this curious airline. They could be home forty-eight hours after stretcher bearers picked them off a battlefield. More than 11,000 were air-evacuated in the month Slonnie joined the ATC and almost all were touchingly grateful, literally getting better from the moment of takeoff from Europe.

The eastern end meant Scotland or Paris

and one AA captain recalled that you would meet everybody in aviation somewhere on the ATC. Slonnie said, "The military sent us wherever the loads were. Stevensville in Newfoundland, maybe, or Goose Bay, Labrador, then jump to the Azores and Scotland, or maybe via Bermuda to Casablanca. AA had nine trips a day and one always went to Bluie West 1, an airfield on Greenland. In Iceland it was Keflavik. See a man on the street in Flushing with fur-lined parka and boots, you knew he was ATC." Within this general team there was fierce competition for a smooth crew. "I only had to fire one bunch. Told New York to give me a whole new crew, even if they were the youngest we had. I was through with that bunch of whiners. Crews were easy for me, mostly. Harold Level called when I got east for instance. 'Could I get him on my crew?' 'Who are you flying with now?' He said, 'O'Connor.' Easy. I'd known Chuck O'Conner for years. Told him, 'Listen, you have a copilot named Level. That kid only had 200 hours when I first got him.' Chuck said, 'Slonnie, I love you, but you are not going to get Level.' I didn't dare say Harold had asked. Just said, 'Look, I trained him.' O'Connor said, 'Well you did a hell of a good job and I won't give him up.'

"Boy Harper was another one. There were nearly 120 AA crews on the Atlantic and only maybe eighteen top-rated flight engineers. Harper was one of those. He was so good they put him on testing but he was with Johnny Davidson when a ship caught fire, so Harper said he'd quit if he couldn't go back on the run. Flight engineers transferred gas mostly, to keep the ship level. We had eight tanks on those early Fours. But it was good to have a man like Harper along any time. If

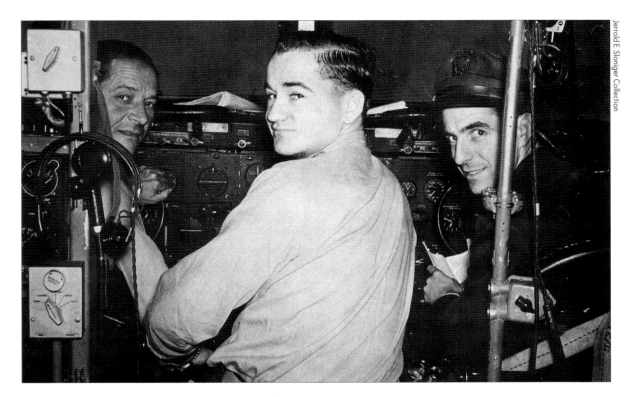

A DC-4 cockpit with Boy Harper (middle). Slonnie (left) called him the best flight engineer on the Atlantic. The copilot (right) is unknown.

Jerrold E Sloniger Collection

Jerrold E Sloniger Collection

Air Transport Command (ATC) was run with civilian pilots
from various airlines, flying the latest DC-4s to and from
various theaters of war. They carried high-priority cargo,
VIPs, and often wounded back to the U.S.

you got a rough motor, call him up front. We didn't have many dials but he would listen a minute and know whether it was okay to go on. They would pass the word among themselves too. 'Tell your captain to watch number three engine.' I really hung on to Harper. Same with navigators. A really good boy, and I had a couple of damn fine ones, could take a three-star fix, plot it, and have a position for you in a few minutes. I'd gone through the same class so late at night I'd have him hit the sack and shoot a couple myself, when it was calm. Little on the slow side but I liked to keep in practice.

"Had one navigator go nuts on me too, heading for the Azores. We were between layers of overcast so all he could get was a faint sun shot. He came up and told me, 'We have to change our flight plan, we're making about 250 MPH.' Told him to bring the weather map. 'Look at those barograph lines, three inches apart. That means no wind. Now take another speed shot and you're going to tell me 150 for the second hour to balance that 250. This airplane does 200 honest.' He comes back and tells me we've already overshot the Azores. But how could I be east of them at 200 an hour? Just common reasoning. It was getting dark though and we had a very dinky radio station there, one AA had pulled out of Guadalupe Pass by El Paso, as a matter of fact. The radio compass wouldn't even pick it up. But he's sure we are past the Azores, heading out to sea and running out of gas. He started pounding on the copilot and I had a kind of dull kid that trip who began to believe this captain was going to put us all into the water. Two hours of gas left and that sure wouldn't make Morocco. I left that navigator sitting on the Azores—after landing there pretty

The Azores airfield on the edge of a cliff.

Jerrold E Sloniger Collection

much when I expected to.

"Another thing, besides wind, which could really put you that far off course—I had one copilot, good boy, who was also a fine photographer. He threw a light meter up on the shelf above the instrument panel one flight and I said, 'Chum, don't do that. Let me show you something.' Put that meter near a compass and the needle starts spinning like a top. Don't know where I'd heard it but you sort of watched for those little things. Radio was mostly voice. Talk to other ships when they got close enough. But it was no good at any distance so we all had to learn the dot-dash stuff too. Voice would skip all over hell, like it had back home. One trip I got New York via Australia. Sometimes it would get you some more weather though, or we'd send our barometric pressure to help them update the maps for the next guy out.

"The Air Force had one captain in Stevensville, Newfoundland, who was the sharpest meteorologist I've ever known. Got AA to hire him after the war. He'd tell you what kind of weather you were going to get and by God, that's just what you had." Pilots were generally more mistrustful of their forecasts. Slonnie had a favorite tale on that. "I had a month off the Atlantic and was riding the jump seat into Nashville so I ducked into operations. Fuzzy Robinson was taking the ship on to Cleveland and the dispatcher shoved his clearance across the counter at him with a pencil. I was reading it upside down and there was no-good weather. It was stinko. Robinson looked it over two or three times and shoved the clearance back. Said, 'I hain't impressed.'" It became a family catchphrase.

Characters were found all along these

runs, even—or particularly—in Labrador. Slonnie said, "I knew Fish Hassel from barnstorming days. He was a pretty good pilot but always going up into the North for some reason or other. When he got into the Air Force they stuck him into Goose Bay, which gets pretty damn cold, and it suited Hassel 100 percent. He sure built a good base there. Before it was just a gravel strip bulldozed through the trees and a few wooden huts, but by the time I flew in it was big, with real billets. Little Swiss-chalet houses with snow piled right up to the roof. Captains got a room to themselves. I woke up one night, forty below outside, and heard pigeons cooing. Drop off and pretty soon, more pigeons. At breakfast I asked if my crew had heard those damn pigeons. They thought this captain was off his rocker. Turned out there was a USO troop around and their magician had the room next to mine.

"It was wild country but they put in one of the smoothest runways anywhere. Must have spent billions to make a perfect airport, with runways over a mile long, on a high, flat plateau between two rivers. Nothing but the Atlantic east of there but the approaches were pretty good except for little hills on three sides. The main runway ran east-west though and wind was westerly ninety-five percent of the time. Just come in over the range, about two miles from the field, and let down. You were clear of everything. Until one night when we called for weather and they gave us unlimited ceiling. Which it was, except they were looking straight up through blowing snow to see those stars. Started letting down and hit this blowing stuff. Just like flying into a blizzard and I missed the lead-in lights. Let down a little more but I couldn't tell how far along the runway I was when I finally got

its lights. If I ran off the west end I'd get a moose or something. So we went around again and let down a little sooner to be sure I had a whole runway out in front. Made it with no trouble and went into operations where another airline boy asks me, 'What's the visibility?' 'About 200 feet off the ground it's a hundred miles, but ten feet up it's nil. And you have to land on the ground.' This operations sergeant insisted, 'No, it's a mile.' That other captain came back with one of the nicest compliments I ever received. He said, 'Look, when Sloniger misses an approach, the weather is damn lousy.'

"Sometimes you landed on a foot of snow but they would roll that like pavement. And the Four had an air brake, a compressed-air bottle good for one shot, until we got metering valves too, a lot later. Army boy came in one time. No brakes so he went around and made a beautiful approach the seond time. But the minute he got his nosewheel down he pulled the air bottle. A Four came in at maybe 120 and it was a heavy airplane for its day. Stopped him for sure. He ended up with three-quarters of the runway left and no tires. Cost a thousand for a new tire, too. Snow didn't bother us much. Been landing in snowstorms all our lives. And we had prop deicers on the Four. Throw a chunk of ice off one prop blade, you put it out of balance, so we'd shove some alcohol on it. Never saw so much ice a Four wouldn't carry it. Took off from Goose once and lost a motor about fifty feet off the ground, where the end of the runway was a forest. Fully loaded, but we just went around again, like it had all four working, and landed. They were overloading us more than allowed back home. Except for gas. Always tried to short you on gas to get something else on. We were allowed an hour extra. Run into head winds or heavy ice on a long leg and you could come out kinda short.

"Fortunately those engines were pretty reliable most times and all our boys got through. Planes the Army lost were something else. Pilot trouble, mostly. Almost every trip some base commander would call you in and say he'd sent twelve bombers off and hadn't heard a word. 'Where was I planning to fly?' Ten or twelve thousand, usually, but I could stay down on the deck to look for them. 'Oh, don't bother,' he'd say. Hell, there were eight guys on every one of those planes. Lot of them just got lost for good. Simply hadn't been trained to fly weather.

"We had five in our crews and copilots were usually pretty senior, except one trip when I had a boy just checked out, and it was one of my roughest trips on the ATC. Three of us were maybe fifteen or twenty minutes apart that night, going into La Guardia. Terrific rainstorm, no visibility at all. First guy over the station, I heard him call he was going on to Washington because of turbulence. He had cargo but I had a load of litter patients and had to get into New York or go back to Presque Isle, Maine, where they had hospital space. Couldn't use Washington. Roughest storm you ever saw. They held me over Hartford a while, circling, then gave me a clearance to go in for a peek. They were giving 300 feet, which was the minimum, and the wind blowing a gale. But they had just put ILS on runway four, a new blind landing system we weren't supposed to use yet, except for practice. I turned that on too. This copilot was about as much use as a red silk kimono, so I had my old-time navigator and the radio operator come up front and watch for

the lead-in lights. I didn't dare look away from those instruments. We got down to 300 and couldn't see a thing but I decided to shave another hundred off and if we didn't see anything at 200, it was Presque Isle. They both hollered just about the time we got to 200 so I went another fifty on instruments and the ILS and we got in okay. It wasn't a very long runway but I didn't need much once it was on the ground. Just about then the tower calls to ask what ceiling I had. I grabbed that mike before the kid could touch it and said, 'Three hundred.' Tell the truth and I was illegal. Taxied up to the hangar and this kid says, 'If this is the kind of flying it takes to make an airline pilot, I'm quitting tomorrow.' Well, he just beat me to firing him.

"Next morning I got to the field and this personnel carrier was unloading a bunch in ATC uniforms, but from some other airline. Their navigator pipes up loud, how they were the first ship the night before and went on to Washington. He says, 'It was too rough to play with but some smart son of a bitch in the number two ship landed anyway. He sure isn't going to live long.' I got pretty mad. 'Do you know how to fly an airplane chum?' 'No.' 'Well, I'm the SOB who got in here last night and I've lived an awful long time at flying.' Their captain pulled him aside. Maybe he was almost right about that landing through."

Despite their best flying, American did lose a plane at Stevensville when the weather was far less appalling. Slonnie said, "The guy was thirty minutes ahead of me. You came down over a bay there and the runway started right off the water. Let down over a marker on this island and go on in. I never could explain what happened. He just flew into a mountain. We took whatever was out there

and kept flying, mostly. One trip through Stevensville I met an Army boy who had been taking flying lessons when I was on the Mercury. Asked when he was going out and he said he didn't know, weather wasn't too good over the Atlantic. I went to Scotland, laid over, came back, and here's the same guy, waiting in Newfoundland. That was the Army on flying weather.

"Had my first try at GCA, where they talk you down from the ground, up there too. I hit the coast and they told me Stevens' was kind of on the stinko side. I could have a Ground Controlled Approach though. I didn't even know what that was. Told me to come over the station at 3,000 feet and get onto GCA. Then go out and let down to 1,500 on such and such a heading, make an 180° right turn, and come back. And to repeat everything they said until the last one, when they told me to quit repeating. It sure was ground control. We had to land over hills there and I got to wondering about their radar guys but they kept very good track of me all the way. Also, I had the navigator and radio operator up front, looking for lights. About the time GCA advised I was 100 yards from the end of the runway and fifty feet up, they spotted them. On my landing roll the GCA boys asked what I thought of it and I gave them a glowing vote of appreciation. A landing couldn't have been made in those conditions without it. That was my only GCA experience until the Korean lift when we'd use it in Tokyo any time the weather was down."

Not even GCA could help an airplane into Bluie West 1, however. "Couldn't even go in there after nightfall because you had to follow a winding fjord with no lights anywhere. It was the worst field we had. BW1 didn't have much runway and you had to land uphill, take off downhill, regardless of wind. If there was a storm you got real wind coming off those hills too. Little on the rough side. Just finding the right fjord was tricky enough. They had a radio range on a rock off the coast so you headed in on that and picked up the fjord mouth. Sometimes go through at 300 feet with walls a thousand above you so a Four couldn't even climb out. Some places it branched but you didn't want to take the wrong one. Just before the field there was a great big wide, inviting branch. Take that and you were sunk. A dead end. I did all the BW1 approaches personally. That was the only really bad spot.

"Azores to Bermuda was maybe the longest, dullest flight in the world and going into Iceland seemed worse because the people didn't much like us there. Had to convince their government to push their German pals out first. Besides, weather was always low. Heavy rain in summer and pretty strong winds in winter. We landed at the Keflavik base where the Army sent all its bad boys. Food was lousy besides. You could take a bus into Reykjavik, where they had a couple of nice hotels, but it wasn't very friendly. What Keflavik needed was a Hotel de Gink. I never knew where that name came from but they had them all over. Transient billets. Bunk bed with shower down the hall was two bits in a barracks whereas a twin-bed room at some de Gink was only a buck a night and worth it. They were heated properly and meals were better than the mess. Only time I fooled with a mess hall was when they had lobster. Supper was fifty cents and all you could eat. Go for a third lobster if you wanted."

Prestwick, original eastern terminus on the ATC, had rooms and dining in a castle near the

(Above) The fjord leading to Bluie West I, an airfield in Greenland, during a rare clear-weather flight. **(Right)** Boy Harper and Slonnie in Keflavik, Iceland, another ATC gas stop and layover.

field, south of Glasgow, but food wasn't a strong point at one of the busiest airports in the world, so Slonnie found himself operating his vittles run. "Ed Bern had bought an estate on Long Island and got into the chicken business. I told him, 'Look, I'm going to get one of those folding crates for twelve dozen eggs. They get one shell egg, as they call them, a month in England.' He told me to get it and he'd provide all the free eggs I could carry. I'd take them to the guy who ran the castle mess, for all his friends. Then Johnny's manicurist said her brother in Goose Bay would just love some fresh milk. Couple of weeks later I had a Goose trip, about four in the morning, but there was a big dairy truck outside La Guardia. He had an extra crate so I had it put up front with the crew luggage. The Army unloaded us so I asked the kid in Goose if he knew Sergeant so-and-so. 'Sure, right over there.' 'Tell him I want to see him.' Told him, 'My wife knows your sister and she said you'd like some fresh milk. There's twenty-four quarts of it.' He just stared.

"Or maybe you'd take oranges from Morocco to Scotland. During '45 we often went from Casablanca to Prestwick, swinging out wide at first because of German fighters. Stayed well off the coast, then cut back over Land's End and up the Irish Sea. One trip though, up comes some Irish ack-ack. I got on the radio in a hurry but they claimed it was only practice. Didn't know I was coming. Not much communication but we knew they weren't really very much on the British side either. We only came that close to getting shot one other time and that was by our own side. Trip before, it had been a nice shiny day between the Azores and Bermuda and I happened to look out. Yelled at the navigator to get me a position and put

(Above) The accommodations in Prestwick, Scotland, where a control tower was added to the castle-like building as the eastern ATC terminus. (Right) Aircrew lived in Hotel Suisse in Casablanca when German fighter activity was heavy on the coast of France.

that on the radio. There was a sub, just starting to submerge, down there. At Bermuda the head man asked what color it was. 'Gray.' He said, 'Well that's German sub colors but are you sure it wasn't a whale?' 'Look, it had a coning tower and mast.' Turns out there was an extra-big convoy coming through and it was waiting for them. Coming back, cutting up to Stevens', the sun was low and I had taped a newspaper over my windshield. Suddenly the copilot said, 'Look at that!' Here are a couple of U.S. destroyers from this enormous convoy rushing like hell to get under me for a shot. I jerked that Four up on one wing and took off. When they saw me turn they gave up. Just a dumb old passenger ship, but you were absolutely not supposed to fly over convoys."

Johnny remained convinced such trips aged him early, no matter how easy he claimed the flying was. She said, "They did fly long hours, often doing three months work in two, and Slonnie was older than most." He only said, "The older you get, the slower your reactions. Maybe you got a little tired, a rough trip, and made just a little mistake. But pilots only got to make one of those, as a rule. All the young boys lacked was experience. Every six months we took a CAA physical, plus one from the company. If you were warm you passed the CAA. It hadn't changed much since the mail in '27, but the company checkup was very thorough. When AA got too big to send us all to Mayo's, they gave us the works in New York. On the Atlantic, it was a medical before every trip. They were too busy to doctor us in Europe so they even checked for colds. I was due for my yearly and Tom Gentry, our own AA doctor, followed me out afterwards. He said, 'Tell you what. We are going to have to do

ATC flights were grueling periods of keeping watch, hoping you would find some speck in the ocean on schedule. Slonnie was nearing the age of fifty when this photograph was taken.

something for your appetite. You're down on weight.' Everybody was sitting there with thermometers in their mouths. He said, 'You'll have to take a drink before every meal. Highball, glass of sherry, or something.' All those thermometers came out in unison. 'How the hell much does that prescription cost, Slonnie?' I just told them, 'When I take a shot at top of climb, that's medicinal now.'"

But the ATC was winding down. Slonnie spent Bastille Day, 1945, in Paris, trying to find places he had visited as a young Lieutenant at the end of another war, twenty-eight years earlier. In just over a year on the ATC Slonnie had added 880 hours to his log, roughly normal for a year by ALPA dictates, except that it included one month of 118 hours, half-again what any flight surgeon felt was safe or desirable. He had also reached a plateau all professional pilots aspire to. About halfway

between New York and Newfoundland, on September 5, Slonnie racked up his 20,000th hour in the air. He landed the last of his eighty-eight Atlantic trips in New York, took a ten-day break, and was back on the commercial run out of Burbank, just as the first surplus C-54 arrived for American Airlines tests. "At first it was still used on an ATC contract. Ferrying soldiers home from the West Coast. I'd take them to Tulsa. About four months of that, because we didn't have so many Four pilots. Then the regular line.

"I chose Burbank because the middle of any run was no place to be with big airplanes. American used Burbank first, then moved to LA International, but that was close to the coast and the fog would roll in so you'd be sent over to Burbank anyway." Johnny said, "We were living in the San Fernando Valley and only had one car so I

At the end of the war Paris was a nice destination.

would drive clear to Long Beach and discover he was landing in Burbank. Finally I asked one dispatcher if Slonnie was really going to International like they said. Because if I drove fifty miles through traffic and they'd put him into Burbank, they'd better start running. By the time I got to Long Beach it was really closed in but I could hear this airplane going around and around. Finally I had the gate guard ask if that was Slonnie. 'Oh yes, he'll be down in a little while.' They were holding him because I said how mad I'd be if he went to Burbank. When he did get in and came out to the car he was burning. 'Since when have you been running American Airlines?' He thought it was

funny later."

Slonnie said, "We finally got our first civilian Fours in 1946, although the first ten had really been going down a line at Douglas in 1941, before they painted the AA eagle over with khaki. Then we bought fifty surplus military planes, too. Took the cabin tanks out and put three in each wing. On the Burbank-Dallas run we could carry maybe fifty-four passengers nonstop. Ample gas for that." Passengers simply demanded four engines as the country flew into its second aviation boom. Almost all lines used surplus C-54s, priced at around $90,000 each, since Douglas couldn't build new DC-4s fast enough.

A widely-sought promotional plum was the first nonstop, transcontinental schedule, meaning more power would be needed. Water-alcohol injection was already common for extra takeoff urge and a 3,000 HP prototype engine existed, but the limit for piston engines proved to be propellers, which could no longer turn fast enough and remain efficient. Lines flying the DC-4 found this limitation particularly galling because TWA, with a corporate lock on Lockheed, put the only available Constellations into regular cross-country service in March 1946, the same month AA launched a like schedule with the Douglas. The "Connie," as pilots called it when not using stronger language, since it was not a pleasant airplane to fly, simply moved faster than the best DC-4. Slonnie said, "We beat the hell out of those engines, trying to stay with the Connies. And damn near did it. We only had one airplane when we started the transcontinental run so I'd take it to Dallas, another crew to New York. By the time it got back to Dallas those engines were a little shaky.

Nothing to do but stick new plugs in. We had a 240 MPH schedule and the old Four was honest at about 200. Wide open, maybe 240."

Low surplus-airplane prices and the boom in air travel also led to new ventures called "nonscheds" about this time, giving established lines very unwelcome competition. A first CAB attempt to curb the worst-run of them came in May 1946, just about the time the last of 10,691 DC-3s was delivered to a Brazilian airline. American was hiring pilots right and left—men they would have to lay off again in 1949 and 1950. Then ALPA struck TWA, outraging a public who couldn't see how those making $10,000 a year could need more. Philip Murray of the Congress of Industrial Organizations (CIO) called it "a row between capitalists" but it let the nonscheds prosper.

Slonnie was about to move in that direction too, but in a very special way. Thinking about easing out of steady flying, he made a decision in June 1946, which no other captain could believe. He resigned the most coveted seniority number in all aviation to set up operations and hire pilots for a brand-new air carrier— 1926 all over again. It was his first change after two decades with AA, but with more than a million flying licenses issued since he first joined Robertson, he felt retirement would be facing most pilots in their fifties anyway. His new line carried a sailing ship name famous throughout the Pacific. Slonnie would only leave American Airlines for a firm of equal repute: Matson Navigation.

June 1946   Flying hours: 20,632:44

Chapter 14

Matson Air

"AA was the finest airline in the world. But we could beat it."

Matson Navigation Company sailed relatively smoothly out of the war years. All those ships lost, loaned, or chartered to the government had brought ample reparations. San Francisco gossip insisted the firm's cellar vaults were laden to the gunnels with raw cash in 1946. The waterfront claimed all Matson had to do was paint its famous liners white again and follow the moon to Honolulu with old-time charm.

Slonnie said, "Management there was mostly ship-oriented, naturally. Very much so. Except for the president and old Roth, who had married a Matson daughter and was chairman. But their vice president for traffic was a big Swede who had come up from sailing ships and wouldn't even get on an airplane. Nor would the secretary. When he had to get to New York in a hurry he insisted Matson take out fifty thousand extra insurance for one flight. With the traffic side absolutely against aviation it meant we never got the help we should have from that great ground organization. Hell, Matson was all over the world." Only their cannier brass seemed to realize that the Pacific was no longer their private pond. By 1946 more than 7,400 miles of overocean air routes had been charted and

passengers flying them topped the steamship ticket sales figures for the first time ever. That fact alone forced Matson to try the air business. Slonnie joined with every reason to expect his rosiest aviation dreams of an ideal airline might become reality there. In personal terms the move was basic enough. He resigned number one at American because Matson's offer seemed so good. Johnny said, "They asked him to choose his own pilots and set up the whole flying part. That sounded terrific. Also, he was a little upset at the way American was going. So big, it wasn't the line it had been. So he decided to start all over again and set up the perfect little operation."

Afterwards he refused to rehash busted dreams, saying only, "I saw a real chance at Matson. American was the finest airline in the world. But we could beat it. I was called Director of Flight. Don't know who thought that one up. It meant hiring pilots, checking them out, organizing operations, and flying the first trips to Hawaii myself. Same sort of job as a chief pilot, for $14,000 a year." Herb Jones, the captain who stayed longest, saw a wider achievement. He felt that a lot of people didn't appreciate Slonnie's full abilities. Besides the flying. Finance just couldn't understand airline speeds but Slonnie could whip up estimates in his head. Tell him San Francisco-Fiji and he'd come within a few cents of the final figure right off.

Slonnie as Director of Flight for Matson Navigation Company's new airline, wearing the four sleeve stripes of a ship's captain.

They'd hem and haw for days and come out the same place. He once told Herb he practiced mental math by taking numbers off of boxcars going by his commuter train. Add a while, then subtract. Jones thought Slonnie just ran best at high revs and got a kick out of direct battles with the top brass. But mostly, he was caught in the middle with nobody to pin down.

Slonnie always assumed, probably too simply, that everybody must share his own dedication. He said, "We made a hell of a lot of money by the end, despite overhauling Navy planes at a loss in a deal somebody else bought. Made it back on passengers. Pan American had a good mail subsidy and still lost money, flying right alongside us, when all we got was the seat fare. Any line needed about $1.65 a mile then, so they put fifty-four seats on a DC-4 and filled maybe half. We only carried thirty-six and gave them the difference between a kitchen stool and a lounge chair. Easy to make seventy percent of capacity and break even. The planes were cheap enough."

Airliners would never be offered at such a small fraction of their value again. That lured some 2,370 self-styled airlines into the sky in 1946 alone. Taken all together they barely owned 5,500 airplanes. Shoals of ex-servicemen clubbed their mustering-out pay and bought a surplus C-54. The real cost was crews. Pilot salaries had gone up nearly sixty percent since the war while copilots received eighty-five percent more than they had in 1941. Avgas only cost a third more, however. One Matson pilot remembered that the first hassle over hiring came when Slonnie told the ship people what he would be paying a captain. The company blew its stack. Said they had sea captains working

there twenty years and only getting five or six hundred a month. Took a couple of days to sell them airline salaries. Slonnie's crew standards did nothing to cut costs either, but he wanted to be sure everybody knew Matson was different.

A navigator who made this select roster agreed that any nonsched then would be very precarious, sort of glorified barnstorming again. But they all figured when the rest went under Matson would always be in business, with all that cash backup. Actually Matson turned out to have less longevity than marginal starters like Transocean. For one thing, a fare war broke out. Passenger-mile figures had boomed by a factor of ten over 1938, yet established airlines with fat in their overheads still insisted nobody could fly people across the country, much less over the oceans, for nonsched fares. Admittedly, some of the new operations got pretty marginal trying, making nonsched a dirty word to old lines—who had begun in precisely the same hard-nosed way twenty-odd years earlier. By the forties, airlines with recognized names flew regular runs printed in formal schedules, with government protection from competition on many of their best routes. The nonscheds were basically charter operations which could print ads offering to fly a planeload anywhere but were forbidden, in the United States, to print, or even fly, a regular schedule. Most of the smaller hustlers were forced out in fairly short order but that nonsched tar brush would have daubed even gold-leaf Matson if they hadn't countered with quality, meaning elite service and crews.

Slonnie said, "Most pilots knew me and after I left AA I had calls on top of calls. From TWA and United boys as well as AA. Gee, I only

needed four crews for two airplanes to start. Told every damn one of them, 'Look, it's a gamble. We all know what the airlines are going to say about a surface carrier in their business.' When Ernie Gann called, for instance, I told him to deadhead out and look the show over first. Maybe he wouldn't like it. But he said, 'No, if it's good enough for you…what do you pay?' I could guarantee him $800 a month, fly or not. If you fly as much as I hope, you can make some real money." Gann, soon as well-known to the public for his best-selling novels as he was to pilots for flying skills, later quoted an old AA captain as saying, "Only a fool would leave American because all oceans belonged to Pan American by order of God and the President." That proved prophetic.

Herb Jones remembered that when Slonnie quit, American really got worried. Then Johnny Davidson went to Santa Fe, another surface carrier. The kingpins were leaving, so lots like Jones began to think about it too. Sure, they lost their seniority, but Matson had that 52 million bucks. Younger men signed on direct from the flying services. Navy pilots talked about airline jobs a lot but most figured they'd never make captain. They might fly left seat for the Navy but Matson required 10,000 hours to even talk about a captain's job and that was an awful lot to young military pilots. One with 4,000 hours and an Air Transport Rating went in every day, hoping to get on as second pilot. When Slonnie hired him as a first officer he almost passed out right there. Matson sought some plus factor like that ATR. Ron Jones was lucky to have 3,000 hours of DC-4 time alone so Slonnie hired him too. His first job—one of the board members had bought a Twin Beech and

Slonnie told him to bring it up from Dallas. Ron hadn't flown one of those for years but Slonnie said, "Hell, I hired you as a pilot. Go get that Beech."

Strictly speaking, Slonnie wasn't Matson's original pilot. A man boasting loudly of both sea duty and ample flying time had signed on before Slonnie arrived. "Jim Ferris was already there and thought he should be chief pilot. Then we needed an extra captain on a trip. Never gave him much thought before that but I went along as check pilot anyway, since I didn't know him. Let him fly the left seat. It was going to be an instrument takeoff, down over the water and up through an overcast. Top was maybe 6,000 feet. He tells me, 'Listen, I've heard so much about you, I'd like to see how you do this.' 'Who's checking who around here? Let's see how you do it, Ferris.' He was a great talker though and the ship was all loaded, so finally I took it off and he flew over on top, all wide open to Honolulu. But I got to thinking."

When Ron Jones flew with Ferris he was told, "Whenever we fly, Ron, I want you to do the whole thing. You're going to be a senior captain some day." Jones also recalled Ferris congratulating him on not missing a single radio marker cone all the way to Seattle. Ron thought that was how it was always supposed to be. Slonnie began to add such tales together and decided to give the man an instrument check. "I assumed Matson wouldn't have hired him, even as test pilot, if he couldn't fly blind. You got a lot of fog and plenty of night work, just circling Oakland Airport. Then he couldn't find the field on instruments when it was right underneath him. So I grounded Ferris. He went crying into the office that it wasn't a fair chance so we tried again and got just as lost with a CAA man on

board to make it fair. That's when they told him to turn in his instrument ticket until he got that blind flying brushed up. And discovered he'd never held the rating in his life. Nobody ever thought to ask."

Matson did things properly, using three pilots per trip even though, "We could have gotten CAA permission as a nonsched to fly just two," as Slonnie explained. "But that wasn't going Matson-class. My first officers all had quite a bit of Four time, plus the ATR, so they were easily captain material on any other line. Just didn't have as many hours as that guy in the left seat. Standards were the same I'd put up at American. I wanted college men who could talk to the passengers without saying 'dem' and 'dos.' We found a chief stewardess and let her hire all the cabin people, girls and stewards both. The men were put on board to carve that great big roast of beef. Matson didn't have all its white ships running yet and wanted to keep some of the sea people busy." A navigator remembered the stewards as guys who always stood at the ship gangway with their hands out when passengers got off and wanted to do the same on the airline.

Several of Slonnie's own people even had two ratings, both pilot and engineer for example. One stewardess was a licensed radio operator from the service. Often pilots did a little navigating too. Herb Jones took a star fix every trip and Slonnie knew all about celestial. But navigators had no other duties. "Just being right," as one put it. "It's a big ocean." The law required one position report every hour, plus weather. But the copilot was looking out for that. Then navigators had to calculate wind from a drift meter and smoke bomb. They weren't getting bored for twelve hours and more. As one pointed out, any pencil line would be

a quarter-mile across on that chart. A plot could be thirty miles wide if they got sloppy. Even captains generally got a fix less than five miles across. The first couple of Matson airplanes were put together by a sailing master, so they had huge navigation tables, which were a luxury. Those were turned into crew bunks later and navigators were back to the usual little foldout table.

In theory, Slonnie's crews worked to the same standards and perogatives as all airline men but his answer to ALPA affiliation was, "Oh, but no. Unless it was a hangover from their old line. With maybe twenty-four crew you could keep personal track of how they flew." With so much talent on hand Slonnie only flew once or twice a month himself. "When some pilot wasn't feeling too good, or when I wanted to keep in touch with Honolulu ground people." When he was on board, the gold braid could sink a four-engine airplane. "That came from up top. Our captains would wear four stripes like sea captains, so copilots had three, third pilot, navigator, and radio man two. We put a tiny wing above our four to show we weren't cleared to sail the *Matsonia*. They never quite got me to wear commodore's stripes but sure tried hard for our very first trip to the [Hawaiian] Islands." That inaugural was met by the obligatory hula girls, guitars, and a giant paper lei for the airplane's nose. Christened *Sky Matsonia*, their first airplane made the cover of the Matson house journal, which devoted its center spread to this new Air Transport Division. Ship people learned DC-4 wings would span the first nine floors of the Matson Building and the plane had more power than their 7,000 ton freighters. A company picnic, reported in that same issue, showed seas of hula shirts and Slonnie, the only man wearing a necktie.

Aviation wasn't really all that strange to the Hawaiian Islands, where a lady had been the first paying air passenger clear back in 1913. There were no nonstop flights from the mainland until 1927, when an Army plane beat the Dole winner across, but Rogers of the Navy flew most of the way in 1925, before a forced landing at sea forced him to taxi and sail his float plane the last miles. The direct air route is shorter than New York to Los Angeles, except that it offers absolutely no rock to land on if your equipment has second thoughts. By 1928 Honolulu was already no more than a gas stop on Kingsford-Smith's U.S. to Australia flight and the Army made mass ferry crossings a full dozen years before the *Sky Matsonia*. PanAm had flown passengers to a timetable as of 1936. Now Matson offered to take your heavy luggage by boat while you flew for extra days of sun.

Slonnie's pride was meeting schedule. "I allowed my pilots five minutes either way and they made it. That first proving trip we had a terrific tail wind and only company people on board so I stalled an hour in Oakland and still pulled the throttles way back to come around Diamond Head on the dot. We had to make one run before July 1st to be eligible for a certificate but the cabin wasn't furnished yet so we stuck in some quicky chairs and took our operations and publicity managers, plus a couple of others." The goal of every nonsched was to establish a presence on one or more routes, prove their worth, and be accepted as a new, scheduled airline. Meanwhile, they flew irregularly but as often as the lack of a formal certificate allowed. Matson fitted in more trips by using various departure points along the West Coast, although

The maiden flight from San Francisco to Honolulu for the new Matson airline. From left to right: Sidney Walton/VP, Ferris/navigator, Forsey/copilot, Ted Schmitt/Operations Manager, Frazer Bailey/President, Slonnie; and kneeling: Larry Snow/flight engineer and Fred Hughes/radio operator.

their home base remained Oakland. A veteran aviation-watcher there recalled watching Matson load all that gorgeous food into a galley in the tail, so much weight they had to stuff 500 pounds of lead in the nosewheel well for balance. It was unheard of, being rich enough to put lead on an airplane. Slonnie explained, "DeGorig had been a chef for royalty so Matson had to have him. Then he insists on sterling tableware, even service plates."

Herb Jones added, "Picture a maitre d' with his silver tray of roast beef. Cut the slice of your choice. The crew was served anything, at any time. I often thought they ran the line for our benefit." On show flights Matson might offer two dinner sittings, with captain or first officer presiding over relish tray, blue point oysters, crab and a Riesling, fowl with a Cabernet, and Baked Alaska in DC-4 shape. The chief stewardess saw another side. Once she ordered steak and kidney pie from the Royal Hawaiian hotel, which catered for the airline at the island end, and got plenty of complaints from the pilots. Breakfast was eggs to order, at least for the crew. There was a lot of waste at first. And foolish things like a ten-pound roast to carve on a card table, hoping they wouldn't hit a bump. The stewardesses always had a lot of fresh things to mix, like hearts of palm salad. Another regular treat was a huge coconut cake, cut fresh.

Slonnie said, "Our seats alone cost twice what most lines paid and the walls were mahogany with an inlaid 'M.' We could only charge the fixed CAA fare but our planes went first class for the same money. Outside they had a big pair of gold leaf wings with an 'M' in the middle. Basically these were Fours, but we stuck in more tanks and good motors, plus some advanced radio and Loren

Matson Lines boasted one of the most luxurious DC-4s on any run.

gear." In immediate postwar form, the chief fault of a DC-4 was an oft-converted fuel system. With sixteen basic engine controls and twice as many ancillary knobs or switches, plus thirty-two engine dials and a dozen tanks, every civilianized Four was an open invitation to fuel blockages. "We wanted the latest, Dash-13, engines and that meant B wing panels to get away from cabin tanks. American had used -13s to try and stay with Constellations and Matson had to have the best motor too. Only problem was fuel transfer. I came in from our first trip with one prop feathered. Tried to cross-feed and got all loaded up with air so I made my schedule on three. Pulled back to idle for five minutes, it would run like a million dollars for a few more, but that prop turning slowly was a drag on one wing.

"Pratt & Whitney claimed it was the pilots. They didn't know how to handle this new engine. I hit the goddamn ceiling. 'Look, I took the first -13 out for AA, trained by P&W people. One of your boys sat right there. To be honest, AA is pounding theirs to death and I'm not going to do that with Matson motors. Okay, maybe I don't know how to run a Pratt, but I know everything your school said so let's not talk about new pilots. Let's talk about an engine that will run clear across that ocean.' [Ernie] Gann happened to have most of the bad times but we all kept hourly engine logs and he was using exactly the same RPM and manifold pressure as the rest of us. As a rule, ninety-five percent of your trouble in aviation is pilot error. I've always said that. But Gann knew those motors. So we took a P&W engineer up and headed west. About two hours out all four motors began to skip and backfire and just plain quit. And their guy couldn't restart them. I told Ernie maybe we'd better turn around. That water was warm enough but it might take the Coast Guard hours to find us. He'd learned the answer by then though, how to restart them, so he let that engine man sweat good. It was the end of pilots don't know how. And we finally solved the gas feed problems."

Meanwhile, Slonnie had the funds available to keep a spare plane ready at all times. "Another trip, leaving LA, we were pulling takeoff power ten minutes out and it started sounding like a bunch of giant firecrackers. I called back that I was returning. Warm up the spare ship. We still made original schedule, just pushing a little. I'd always rather have 100 hours on a piston engine than ten right out of the box. Get past fifty and they will continue to run okay."

Even so, it only took one engine out during some special charter to revive those nonsched accusations. This happened to Herb Jones and wasn't fuel trouble. He said, "We were taking the baseball Giants to Hawaii and some of them must have thought Matson meant a boat trip. Rebelled right at the airport. Happens my steward-ess weighed about 100 pounds and was attractive as hell, but she'd made maybe thirty Pacific air crossings as a nurse so I sent her out front to show those guys up for the babies they were. Then we lost an engine going over. Fortunately it was night and the same guys who claimed they were terrified slept right through. We got girls and leis out to meet them and smoothed it all over. A P&W guy I knew out there said he recognized the trouble, but he'd get fired for telling me officially. Our engines

were only guaranteed with one brand of oil. That was all running straight to the hottest point, by the valve seats, and starving the guides, so they blocked up. He told me to put Valvoline in one engine. Well, I had to call Slonnie on that one. He said, 'Put the Valvoline in.' He'd worry about the guarantee. That took guts at $25,000 an engine."

Slonnie added, "Of course Herb knew everybody, so when he told me what this engine boy said, I told him to pour pineapple juice in the damn thing if it would get him home. We had a contract with Standard and the CAA had ap-proved them so I expected an argument with the chairman. But Roth wouldn't have known an airplane if he found it floating in his soup. What-ever I wanted was okay." Their baseball special returned with new oil in one engine. Jones said, "I had the reporters coming back and feathered one engine just past the point of no return, then had to reduce power to maybe 400 on another. And the third began to snort over Catalina Island. By Burbank I had one good engine left, the one with new oil. That didn't sit very well with the press. Slonnie said, 'Take that old oil out of every Matson engine. Now. To hell with the guarantee.' But our regular company changed their oil characteristics right about then and we never had any more trouble on that score."

Matson brass did realize the DC-4 could only be their bridge to new airplanes. Slonnie said, "First we kind of debated the Martin Mars flying boat. Fast as a Four and twice as roomy. Everybody could have a bunk. It would have cost like hell to operate but takeoff from San Francisco Bay was no problem and Hawaii had plenty of water to land on. We at least considered every fancy airplane

built. The first month Roth was going out to see the new DC-6 and said, 'Skipper, will you ride to the field with me?' 'Look,' he said, 'we have to get into the aviation business.' They had lots of money and patience and they were going in. I told him they'd make more money from flying in ten years than on all the white ships afloat. Douglas's chief pilot had brought this Six up for me to fly. Later I went back and sat with Roth. He thought it was a pretty fine airplane. 'Right, Skipper? Let's buy some.' We could have those in a year so I ordered six. Next, an old Lockheed chum brought the Constellation up. Told me, look how you can balance a cigarette on the console. So the board decided to order some Connies too. Then the president called me in. Would I go up to Seattle and see the Boeing Stratocruiser? He'd heard that airplane had them all beat. Sure, but they hadn't even started on it yet. Well, we got a big sales talk and Matson put down some more deposits. But it turned out to be a two-deck turkey. I was holding out for the Six. Fast and didn't have a lot of funny characteristics. The Connie wasn't as easy to fly. Developed into a good airplane later but the first one was half a turkey."

Boeing wouldn't complete its first double-decker until July 1947, barely a month before the last DC-4 was pushed out Douglas's door, so Matson never flew anything but converted ships, using the best ones from their own overhaul base, a handy sideline. "One day though," Slonnie said, "that shop charged our own airline with four or five men on service for a ship which was out on a run. Operations wanted to skip it. We were making money anyway. But I walked into the president's office. Here's a bill for fifty hours on an airplane

Overhaul was set up to maintain Matson Lines airplanes properly and soon proved to be a good money-maker for the company, providing maintenance and overhaul service for other airlines.

The crew Slonnie chose himself: Ed Drake/copilot, with three stripes and captain-rated; Bob Hayes; Stan Smith; and Larry Vaclavick. There is no record of which man was radio operator, navigator, or flight engineer.

dispatch will confirm was in Honolulu. We canned the guy in charge and with a new boss they did a damn fine job. When United had fire trouble on their first Sixes and had to ground them they hired two of our spare airplanes, plus another Four from Transocean as a backup, even though I promised our pair was enough to go over and back every day. Then American called about some maintenance and I suggested we lease them a ship while we did a major on theirs. Good painter could put the AA eagle on in half a day. Bill Littlewood thought that was one hell of a good deal but AA didn't want us to have any kind of work in the end. We could do a major in thirty days where it took Martin two months to get an AA ship out."

Meanwhile, Matson was still pioneering its own runs in hopes of becoming a regular line. Seattle and Portland were naturals for an airline with deep-sea ties. Tons of northwest fruit were

only waiting for Matson's CAA permission to turn the longest overwater hop in the world into a regular run just like their one-off charters. But that would challenge the airline which considered the Pacific its fief. Matson and Pan American had signed a cooperative agreement as early as 1935—people by PanAm, luggage by boat—and the older airline wanted to keep it that way. Through friends if necessary. When President Harry Truman issued what was called his Latin American decision in 1946, overruling the CAB to let rival lines fly south alongside PanAm, Matson thought it a good omen. A month later Truman opened the Pacific as well—but to United, which didn't even want to fly to Hawaii at that time. The obvious but unstated reason: United wasn't a surface carrier trying to expand into air travel. The portents became gloomier.

Politics apart, Slonnie's crews could outfly

any line in sight. He recalled, "One of the few times we had two Matson ships close together, I was about an hour behind [Herb] Jones and heard PanAm in between us radioing about bad ice. I flipped on the mike and asked Herb how much ice he was getting up there. He told me if he scraped it all off one wing he could make a pretty good highball. PanAm turned back and wanted me to do the same. But hell, my own guy was clear so we went on in." Jones told the same story, except that he credited the punch line to Slonnie. Herb felt his chief was being gracious as usual, saying the joke was his. Slonnie continued, "We often left LA thirty minutes behind PanAm but with those -13 engines we always caught them about Maui intersection, to go on in ahead. One trip we caught up right by a big cumulus cloud. I went around the north side with no trouble but he elected to take the shortcut through. About this time we saw black smoke coming out of his motors. He's patted those babies on the back to race me. Well, any time you hit a cumulus you get a rap going in and a bigger one when you come out. Just as we lined up to land I heard his call: 'Please have an ambulance on the field. Ran into severe turbulence.' At a debriefing they asked if I'd hit any bumps. 'No, because I went around them.'

"They were always trying the old trick of calling in first to land when they were behind you. Honolulu only had three gates and two were around the side. One trip I came past Diamond Head and heard this boy we'd overtaken ten minutes back estimating number one. I gave my real position and got the okay. 'Matson for gate one.' He tried to claim one was reserved for PanAm. Of course, they weren't getting the hotel service Matson enjoyed in the islands either. Another trip we got to the Moana about 7 A.M. and here's a PanAm crew sleeping in lobby chairs. Their captain wants to know how come we could sign right into rooms. Told him to have PanAm buy the hotel from Matson and I'd be the guy sitting up. Our survey trip they even put my bosses in a double room and me in a suite. Manager claimed Matson captains always had a suite. Later they wanted to put my captains up at the Royal Hawaiian, which we also owned, but we stayed with our crews. Just once they were short of Moana rooms and gave me the King Kamehameha suite at the Royal. I could stand that for one night.

"One thing for sure, PanAm was scared to death of us. When United got our contract a PanAm captain told me they were tickled to death. I said, 'Chum, you can't sit on your cozy cans and compete with UAL. Those boys fly hard.'" Long afterwards a Matson crewman still recalled the sense of shock when that first United crew stepped into the Moana. "Oh boy, there went the ball game." Only gross political misjudgment could have pushed Matson out of the Pacific skies. In 1944 the Senate actually favored air route competition. Eastern lost its Miami monopoly and AA had to accept even more competition on its Boston-New York gravy run. But a steamship company in the air was something else. When American Overseas Line sold its new air routes to PanAm after scarcely two years of Atlantic flights the CAB ruled that this sale was not in the public interest. Truman agreed. Then the President reversed himself to demand approval of the monopoly. The CAB chairman resigned, claiming such a sudden White House turnaround was due to political

pressure unparalleled in U.S. history. No less than eleven airlines applied for permanent Pacific routes, where PanAm and Matson were the only ones actually flying. United bid without wanting any of them, in response to Washington urging, and Northwest bid without equipment. They couldn't open Seattle-Honolulu service until the spring of 1948.

Slonnie recalled, "We went to those hearings as the only ones not asking for a mail subsidy. When PanAm wanted $4.15 a mile from the government, on top of fares, just to add Seattle or Portland to its schedule, I suggested we'd take the same money, fly you over for free, and give you 65 bucks when you landed. Matson made money flying without a printed schedule to pull them in and if they'd let us go daily we'd have made lots more. Of course we lifted about a ton more on takeoff with -13 engines but P&W would sell those to anyone who'd pay for the best. Also, we had trained crews already working. The rest had to hire back navigators and radio men they'd fired after the war. But I could tell by the third day of hearings we weren't going to get it. Wound up with the CAB describing Matson as the only line which was fit, willing, and able to fly to Honolulu as of tomorrow. But United and Northwest got our contracts. Matson people were just not very good at politics. They thought presidential candidate Thomas Dewey was bound to get in and put on the biggest bandwagon you ever saw for him. One of the first things Truman said after he won was that he saw no reason for surface carriers in the air. We were sunk."

They continued to fly for a while but everybody knew they weren't going to build a super

new airline after all. Charters, with no hope of graduating to regular runs, was not the Matson way, so the only tasks left in the wind-down were odd jobs like a trip to Paris. Slonnie said, "The story behind that—San Francisco was a great dressmaking city. The president of their trade outfit had about six martinis one night with Adolph Schuman, who was Lily Ann clothes, and suggested taking a fashion show to New York. 'Hell with that, we'll take it clear to Paris. That's where fashions come from.' Schuman told me all this himself. They had a telephone plugged in at the table and started calling around. We want five grand from you, ten from you. Then they couldn't back down and began checking airlines. I heard about it when they asked Matson to chip in for good old SF. I suggested we take them over at cost instead. About half what other airlines bid. We flew maybe eight fashion models, plus writers for the magazines, designers, and wives. They even got some movie star and her mother in. Filled two airplanes. Nonstop to New York, some publicity, and on across. With ten more miles of tail wind we could have nonstopped to Paris but I gassed in Shannon to be safe. Even so, Matson ducked all this great publicity beforehand. One vice president was all worried: 'Suppose those ships don't get there?' Listen, if they thought I was going to get on an airplane and not get out in Paris they were crazy."

Ironically, Matson very nearly got the kind of notice that executive feared, as a navigator tells it. "This was a sort of swan song for the line and I was on Slonnie's ship. First we blew a tire in SF and had to go back to Oakland to have it changed. We were late and by then it was a terrible, rainy night. I had a free ride across the States and was watching

Flying with Matson Lines was a full complement of models on a trip to France for the "San Francisco Fashion Première in Paris." Two planeloads made the trip, including invited members of the press.

the takeoff, just calling off distances from a radar altimeter to keep busy. We got into a stall situation, climbing out over Mount Diablo. Not just once but twice. That airplane was bucking so hard the radio man had to shove his cabinets back into place and we were running out of air space very, very rapidly. We finally cleared that peak by no more than 100 feet. What Slonnie was really up against—the radio range was supposed to take us alongside that mountain but there was some kind of freak wander in the beam that night so we went right over the highest point. He was plain fighting for any altitude he could get. He came back about an hour later and told me, 'I guess you know, you came about as close to buying it there as you ever will.' He'd kept that great big plane right at the edge of stall intention-ally, figuring it was better to mush in at ninety than hit at 120. Damn few pilots could have even done that. Or would have had the guts to try."

Crews had a party in Paris, although San Francisco was thirty years too early with fashions for France. Slonnie said, "They had invited all the finest designers in Paris to our show so afterwards a Russian gal we had along took me to a private French showing in return. Called me her 'beezniss partner.' Their poor models all looked starved to death after our gals and their shoes squeaked." San Franciscans saw a repeat showing of these fashions at the Opera House but Matson never extracted much benefit. They were in a winding down mood anyway, letting flying people go. Word went out they were cutting back and crew members held meetings, trying to figure out how they might take over the airplanes and keep going, when they didn't have fifty bucks between them. There were always lines starting up around Oakland then but

Jerrold E. Sloniger Collection

A film star models a wedding gown as the culmination of the San Francisco to Paris fashion runs. The trip was one of the last true Matson Lines flights, which were first-class in every way.

this one had been different. Some airplanes were leased, others sold. The Seattle operation was typical. Matson leased planes to a fly-by-night Alaska operation with two of its own pilots flying the right seat to see the new owners didn't bust up an airplane before it was paid for. "Matson charged a hell of a price for pilot services and one day the head guy couldn't pay even that. Okay. Back to SF with the airplanes. Couple of weeks later he'd disappeared with his secretary."

A three-airplane deal with Australian

National was far more solid. "The catch was," as Slonnie said, "the Aussies didn't have anything but pounds and we didn't want half a million dollars worth of those. Air Colombo had green dollars though, so we delivered the planes to them in Ceylon, on paper, and they passed them on. Actually we ferried east because you had more ground help going around the world that way. First trip, with a 100 MPH tail wind, I made NY-London in ten hours with seventeen worth of gas on board. Just Herb Jones and me, plus a combo radio man-navigator. Pete Gibbs from ANA took over that first one in London. We took the next plane down to Athens. All routine stuff. Oh, a little storm on the Atlantic tore all the radio aerials off, but nothing much." Jones corrected this. "Those all-night trips were an ordeal, really. I got some bad food one run so Slonnie sat there all night alone, with a sort of radio man. And he was more concerned about my health than his own ability to keep going."

Their nadir came with the loan of men and planes to a Puerto Rican project. It was a charter deal for Trans Caribbean, who needed Fours. Not too bad until Gann quit and the third captain's father got sick. Then Ron Jones flew all the trips alone, by taking illegal turns with two crews. Not even time for a haircut. Les Walker, flying with Gann, had vivid memories of the aviation fringes then. "God, they were trying to break every rule in the book. Herd people in like cattle. One trip I worked the load out was five too many and I wouldn't sign the clearance. Their guy said: 'We have to take them, we sold the tickets.' About that time lightning hit the stewardess so we put her in a bunk and I told Gann we had a

problem. This agent said they always flew five extra. I was just a troublemaker. Ernie blew his stack. Picked the guy up by his shirtfront and asked him, 'How would you like to swim without a life vest?' The guy says 'Easy, see, you can hold me up.' Gann dropped him and sat down in the shade. Told them we wouldn't move that ship until they got five bodies out. Next trip some Trans Carib pilot wants to fly it. Tells us he's the chief pilot of their line. Gann took the right seat with me standing between them. It was a long, wavy runway and he bounced off the first hump yelling, 'Gear up.' I slapped my hand down to block the lever but Gann's was already there. He growls, 'Nobody's moving that gear lever.' Their guy does the same trick three more times before we have enough speed to really climb out and retract the gear.

"When Ernie went back for a snack he told me to sit on the right and never take my eyes off this guy. Then I heard a yell. 'Bone sandwich!' Gann had two pieces of bread with something that looked like lizard. He told me, that was it. He was quitting. He'd been in aviation a long time but this was going backwards. He'd recommend me for captain. All I could say was, 'Let's not be hasty about this. It's the only job I've got.' Right after that Matson closed down anyway."

Herb Jones said, "Those were dark days and I don't know how Slonnie kept up his courage. To see it all dissolve before his eyes." Around Oakland Airport, another airline was gone. Little more. A few insiders realized what Matson had done but so many lines talked about so many grandiose deals, no outcome was surprising. Most people lumped Matson with the other nonscheds, according to a man who did realize the difference.

That ranked them with the outcasts *Aviation
Yearbook* studiously ignored, although these same
nonscheduled air carriers had flown the past nine
months without a fatality, right alongside long-
established lines which racked up 1.8 deaths per
100 million miles and were lavishly praised for the
low figure. Even the Oakland regulars were aware
that Matson's boat people resented the airline,
although they would deny it later. People who
wanted to fly, even one way, were put off by
Matson's own ticket offices.

By 1949 Orville Wright had died and the
U.S. was thinking satellites. That April Slonnie
received a standard Office of the President letter
from Matson. "We are truly sorry that circumstances beyond the control of any of us have forced
the liquidation of the Air Transport Division." The
pilot could only add, "It was the finest airline that
ever operated and I'm not the one saying that. I
heard it a dozen times. From everybody. I think
Matson was one of my greatest claims to fame."

May 1949   Flying hours: 22,116

Chapter 15

Closing the Log

"Just pioneers all over again."

Slonnie flew a good majority of the airplanes built during the first three decades of his career, taking them to all corners of the world. By getting into commercial aviation when it was even younger than he was, and airplanes were hard put to lift even one man, Slonnie also managed to do all his flying prior to 1949 as the pilot in charge—whether as a solo stunt, test, or mail flier, as an airline captain in the left seat, a chief pilot, or even Director of Flight.

But when Matson quit the air transport business, sacrosanct airline seniority numbers caught up with him as well. He had resigned number one to join Matson, expecting to ease out of regular flying and into operations there. When the steamship line folded its wings he could either seek a position on the management side or—in theory—join some airline as its most junior copilot. His new seniority number would have had four digits. Actually, no line in its right corporate mind hired copilots in their fifties. There were only some 100 active transport licenses still held by men over age fifty in 1949 and many believed fifty-five might be the age to retire them. Copilots only justified their escalating training costs by staying with the line long enough to graduate and fly that left seat,

hardly likely for a man starting at age fifty-two. Not to mention cockpit command problems when your copilot was already a quiet legend, one of barely half a hundred airline pilots in all America with more than 20,000 hours in his logbook. The only real option left in aviation was another nonsched where you flew whatever seat was empty and seniority numbers weren't recorded. On the other hand, this longtime pilot really preferred operations to flying if he could find a ground slot.

The first such job came with a go-anywhere nonsched named Transocean and his title was Assistant Vice President of Operations. He said, "One night Orvis Nelson called and asked what I was doing. 'Nothing, come on over.' But he said, 'No.' He meant, 'Could I see him in the morning? They needed help.' I figured, why not? But I never did any flying for them." Transocean was really just one man. Nelson had been an airline pilot himself but was even more of an aviation promoter. Launched in early 1946, his line would become the world's largest contract carrier by 1953, out of 2,000-odd companies with similar dreams. Their ranks were only thinned when the CAB ended blanket exemptions for the nonsched way of doing things. Washington really meant to cancel them all in 1949 but TO survived.

Slonnie said, "Nelson did a hell of a lot around the Pacific. Took laborers out to build a

harbor, brought them back on leave, supplied their fresh food. He'd fly anything he could get on board. Not enough passengers? Stick some lettuce on for Wake Island. Or fifty hams to Guam. But I left after a fiasco down to Paraguay. We'd picked up a load of Russians from Asia, going down to start a settlement in South America. Well, Ed Bern hit town and told me, Panagra—which he was running then—would pick that load up from us in Panama. The Canal Zone is as far as we would go. Panagra owned the radio beams below there and they'd turn them off. I said, 'They wouldn't dare,' and he just said, 'Hell he wouldn't.' So I decided to go down the east coast. Nelson figured that was the long way around but a DC-4 with Dash-7 engines and no pressurization wasn't even legal at 17,000 feet and if you didn't get higher than that, going in from the west, you were going to hit a rock. Nelson left town and the rest at TO were yes-men. They checked on the printer and came back with Nelson's answer: we go down the west side. Panagra did turn those beams off too. We had a hell of a good pilot on board, fortunately. Took off from Lima and kept flying until he found a 'sucker hole,' as we used to call them. Dove down through that and got onto some pasture maybe fifty miles from the real emergency field. Hauled the passengers there by bus and brought back enough gas to hop the ship over too. Got away with it."

Les Walker, once a first officer for Matson, had joined TO too. On his first flight they got just over the Farallons, barely out of sight of San Francisco, and the autopilot went out. The captain said they might as well hand-fly it as go back because TO wouldn't fix it anyway. He knew the outfit. They were over gross weight besides. Slonnie soon discovered he could only make strong suggestions, not final decisions. "We had a ship in Hong Kong, for instance, and got a cable: 'Offered $10,000 for an hour's flight up to so-and-so and back.' Traffic came in, tickled to death, and I told them, 'That spot is red. They can take away your airplane, impound your crew, and you'll have to pay those guys every damn minute for maybe fifty years.' Traffic said, 'Jesus, Slonnie, ten grand for two hours flying.' I could only repeat, honest rate was $500 an hour and if it was my airplane I still wouldn't touch it. They wired the pilot: 'Okay to make flight with captain's approval.' Just passing the buck. He came on home instead and I got out. There was no place at Transocean for my kind of experience."

Les Forden of TO operations told another China tale, proving there was a real need for old hands though. "Typically, the deal broke on a Sunday. We always had ships out somewhere and you took a beating when you parked them. The teletype came on—a load from Oakland to Taiwan. But which airport? We figured there must be more than one or they wouldn't ask, but the dispatcher on duty couldn't even find one listed. This was the kind of case where they had told us to depend on Slonnie. He came over from home and got right on the phone. He could call the big people for help and they'd do it because it was Slonnie. Had Taipei

sorted out in an hour or so."

Johnny had her own memory. "He also got in a hassle over a pilot Slonnie wanted to ground. Orvis said no, so he quit. Later Slonnie was flying through Honolulu for another outfit and friends were going to be there too, so I thought I'd meet them all. Transocean had the cheapest fare and one DC-6 to Hawaii by then. We were late getting out and when I looked up, here was this same lousy pilot's name as captain. I was sick all the way. I'd never been airsick in twenty years. Just plain scared. Coming back I told Slonnie, 'Anybody but that pilot.' I'd swim instead. But the man taking my run was good and we had a nice trip. He turned the ship over to that other one in Oakland and they lost them all. I only missed it by one trip."

Aviation generally was in shaky transition. Big airlines retired their last Threes, sold their older Fours, and eyed jets. President Harry Truman favored any line which would ignore turkey tales and buy the two-deck Stratocruiser, since Boeing had been a notable campaign contributor. During 1950 and most of 1951 Slonnie was entirely out of aviation, his longest spell away from airplanes since 1917. Johnny said, "A good friend was in realty and talked Slonnie into trying that. He read a book, passed the test, and told me there wasn't an honest person in real estate. I almost asked, 'What about me?' I was in it then, too. Slonnie only rode around a while, never really used the license. But when they first called from California Eastern he said 'No.' He didn't want to fly any more. Then he was made Vice President or something of this line in New York. I didn't even go East because he wasn't sure it would jell. And it didn't."

The company this time was Overseas

National. Slonnie said, "It was another ex-Navy pilot who didn't fly anymore but if you had been in the service you got a deal on surplus airplanes. He bought four, then had trouble getting them loose from Oklahoma City, so he took four crews down and cranked the damn things up and flew them out at midnight. I thought he had his neck out a mile but he got away with it. He offered me a job so I went to New York but I was only there about four months and didn't like it. One trip we had a full load ready but this smart gal who'd been in the business a while had warned me: never pull away from that gate until I had the money in my own hand. Crew there, ship all gassed, but I didn't have all the money. One travel agency hadn't brought in its share so I wouldn't turn a prop. I'd been flying before those boys were born. No mañana for me. One guy jumped in a taxi and found some cash. I counted it and told my pilot to start turning number two engine over. A bunch of scavengers, just hurting aviation, and I told them that. Other trouble was, you couldn't hire steady pilots because you couldn't pay a salary and maybe fly the guy once a month. I had one crew. Get another charter I'd go out and hire another. There were boys by the dozen who couldn't make an airline or were too old for copilot. Loads had plenty of Four time. Some pretty good, some just flotsam. Finally I told ON I'd been with airlines which ran like businesses and went back to San Francisco. Later I heard they were making a million and had a bunch of jets." Overseas National would become the biggest of all nonscheds within ten years.

"Then a Cal Eastern guy called again and said, 'How about lunch the next day.' Found out later he was thinking of putting me in as operations

Jerrold E. Sloniger Collection

California Eastern was one of the better nonscheds, where Slonnie closed out his career during and after the Korean War. Planes were surplus DC-4s.

manager but when we got through talking and I was walking down the hall the current operations manager yells through his door: 'Slonnie, come in here.' Could I take a trip to Tokyo for him? He was awfully short of pilots. The Korean thing was on. He would pay me by the trip or the mile or the hour. Any way I wanted it. Just one trip, so I said okay. They found a uniform which kind of fit, but the brightest blue you ever saw. I took one trip to Tokyo and back home. About eight days later Operations calls: 'Captain, you know you're due out tomorrow morning?' Told them I didn't work for Cal Eastern. They should ask their operations manager. Operations said he's the one who told them to call. They had to have a pilot. Hell, I wasn't doing anything else. Then they said, couldn't I stay until they got some more guys? They never got enough but it was a nice run so I said I'd fly it six months or so." Johnny added, "He was check pilot later too and Cal Eastern had a bunch of fellows he liked. Good pilots, doing a good job, so he just stayed on. Ended up, he flew over three years for them."

California Eastern first became an airline immediately after the war but went bankrupt. Sam Solomon, one of the older hands in aviation management, took it over with a transcontinental coach-fare idea. That word "Eastern" in the name originally meant New York. When North Korea attacked South Korea in 1950 Cal Eastern became one of the first contract carriers on the Pacific, flying four leased airplanes. They soon owned ten outright, flown by crews constantly being laid off and rehired, although at the peak of the Korean lift, flying was pretty steady. Cal Eastern only lost ground again when that so-called police action ended and Japan Air Lines grabbed a Pacific route the Americans had coveted, despite senators who blamed the CAB for giving too little thought to free enterprise. Slonnie was gone by the time Cal Eastern closed its offices, located in a late-twenties building at Oakland Airport originally built as one of the first on-field airport hotels in America.

During his tenure the routes were almost all Pacific runs. He said, "Always via Hawaii and mostly through Wake Island to Tokyo. Sometimes we'd be switched at Wake and go down to Guam or over to Saigon. Usual schedule was twelve hours to Honolulu, twelve more to Wake, and ten into Tokyo, with twenty-four-hour layovers at each place and maybe an extra day in Japan. I might even get back in six days total. We flew to rules like the ATC, no more than 300 hours in three months, so you usually got ten days off after every trip. Damn near a vacation. I did that a few months and they moved me to check pilot, which was better for an old man. Paid the maximum a pilot could earn plus $200 a month. Did that about eighteen more months, until they decided they didn't need a separate man. I went back on regular flying."

Les Forden felt Slonnie settled happily enough for check pilot. Flying a run if he was needed. He wasn't dreaming of being in management so much by then. The old pilot was more effective at devising improved cockpit procedures. Cal Eastern pilots had been taking as much as thirty-six hours flight time to Tokyo, just sitting there at 2,250 RPM. They were paid by the hour. The slower a trip, the more money they made. Slonnie got them started flying pressure patterns with pay by the mile. Cut six or eight hours off airplane time every trip. The company saved

Oakland was far more a working airport than a scheduled airline terminal, with many freight-hauling and charter airplanes on site. For Slonnie, it was "barnstorming all over again."

money but the pilots made more for flying fewer hours—just by using their skills.

In theory their cockpit people were only hired to fly but when a pilot got stuck in some foreign place he effectively became the company. Operations had to use snap judgment about accepting collect telephone calls. Guess whether it was a real problem or some captain just wanting to bitch. At least once a passenger let the captain use his credit card to buy gas. Pilots were given maybe $1,000 cash if it wasn't a routine Tokyo flight and they were supposed to have a gas card too, but not every field would accept Cal Eastern's. Sometimes pilots even had to pay cash for repairs or parts in out-of-the-way places. Experience led many of them to manage their own ground service on occasion. Slonnie said, "It was around Christmas and I found about six inches of snow on the wings of my Four in Tokyo. The mechanic said Operations didn't care but I told him to get that snow cleared or the airplane was going to sit right there until it melted off next spring. Snow on a wing is the most dangerous thing in the world. You get maybe halfway down the runway, just about flying speed, and if that snow comes off only one side, you've had it. Like chopping half your wing off. Told him, 'See that United ship over there?' Its captain was smart. About ten guys with brooms up on the wings. We waited until they were through with the brooms and got the Cal Eastern plane clean too."

Yet Forden insisted most of their crews were impressively dedicated people. The Air Transport Association put out gobs of publicity. How this nonsched lot were a bunch of misfits and castoffs but actually, he said, "They were just

pioneers all over again." Slonnie added, "Some of the flight crews were pretty damn good, a few were beaten-up guys. But that's the side of aviation I never liked to talk about. You could sort of pick a crew and have your own. The kids I got were good at their jobs and if they would rather fly with me, fine." Forden explained that Slonnie was older than most of their captains by twenty years and a guy might wonder if that man in his late fifties could still fly. The name didn't mean so much around Cal Eastern at first. He needed courage and personality to get along with younger pilots and gain their respect, especially when he had to fly the right seat on a trip. Pilots have been called the most jealous bunch of prima donnas in the world, ready to pounce on anybody they didn't think could fly. Pretty soon, however, when a man was due to be upgraded to captain the word was, "Put him with Slonnie. If he's any good he'll pass and if he isn't we'll know for sure."

Ray Fisher, in charge of operations, agreed that pilots were pretty jealous but most were pretty honest too, admiring any guy who was outstanding. The young fellows might have been more capable in the sense of sharp flying by then but they hadn't been through the mill Slonnie had. "Sitting up there, driving the airplane, isn't so complicated," Fisher explained, "it's what you do when you're in trouble." Like one cargo flight. It departed for Tokyo and the first Cal Eastern heard about trouble was around 2:30 A.M. when their dispatcher called Fisher and said the pilot reported losing number four engine—the outside right one. He was returning. About forty-five minutes later another call came. They had lost another engine. Fisher hurried to the airport and found they were preparing to

ditch. That went fine and the plane floated nine hours, in fact. The crew was rescued by a freighter. Their chairman was about to make that pilot a big hero for ditching so successfully but Slonnie didn't think it rang true. He had flown Fours a lot of hours with two engines out, even on the same side.

At the CAB hearing this captain said number four lost oil pressure so he had to feather that prop and then lost number three—the inside right one. A peculiar thing was that the copilot was hiding until his wife finally prevailed on him to report in. Under cross-examination he said the first engine which gave trouble was number one—outside left—not four. But the pilot had been asleep in back. He woke up suddenly, rushed to the cockpit, and feathered number four in error. Asked why he didn't tell the captain of his mistake, the copilot said he was a man you didn't correct. That was hard for the hearing committee to understand but it was a true cockpit situation. As for number three, that did fail, but just before going into the water they brought four back in. That was how the captain could ditch so well. Slonnie had said right away that this guy had been a ditching instructor for Transocean. He'd frequently said it was a shame they couldn't prove the rules by physically ditching an airplane. He was just mentally ready to try so he did.

Overall airline safety improved in the early to middle fifties and fatalities fell to 0.4 per 100 million miles on domestic runs, although the overocean rate was double that. The oft-smeared nonscheds suffered only one fatal crash in 1952, while flying some 24 million revenue miles over two oceans in equipment which was clearly aging. Their Korean lift effort was proclaimed the finest of all time, topping even the Berlin airlift. While the Korean war lasted no line could fail to profit, but hostilities were winding down and an end to contracts in 1954 hit nonscheds hard. Pilots scrambled for jobs, a difficult prospect for anybody fifty-eight years old. Some layovers were long enough to rest and recover, other runs were too much like Slonnie's last flight: sixty hours in the air out of 106, Oakland to Omaha to Puerto Rico, back to Oakland.

As he came to the end of a thirty-eight year cockpit career, U.S. airlines, which had boasted a handful of open-cockpit mail planes when Slonnie entered commercial aviation, now flew 24,336,000 passenger miles per year while their last pre-jet airliner, the Douglas DC-7, had just been announced. Maximum airspeeds had risen from the barely 100 MPH of a WW I fighter to over 1,000 and one Navy Neptune proved an airplane could fly more than 11,000 miles without landing. The CAA would enjoy its largest budget ever for 1956 and—finally—modernize the U.S. airways system. The number of American airports had spurted from 1,364 to 6,839 between 1927 and 1956, while annual aircraft production increased by a factor of six during Slonnie's flying career. The DC-4, which accounted for most of his last logbook hours, had been America's key airliner right after the war but now made up only half the fleet, less than a decade later.

Slonnie told his wife he was through immediately after landing from that marathon trip. A couple of days later he made it official in Ray Fisher's Cal Eastern office. Fisher said, "He came in and without a moment's hesitation told me: 'I have decided to hang up my wings. I always told myself

that when I could not do as good a job of flying as I demand of others, I would stop. On this last trip I made the instrument approach into Chicago. It was a lousy job.' I could tell from his expression there was no talking him out of it. But I told him to think it over anyway. There was no urgency. Slonnie just said, 'No, this is it.' I'd had absolutely no indication of anything and never did get any definite description of his last trip. He must have wavered just a little and Chicago was the busiest airport in the world then, with terrible visibility most of the time. The other two captains on that trip were twenty years younger and came back exhausted. One of the other men told me—it was a hell of a lot better approach than he would ever do!"

Forden summed it up. "Slonnie quit while he was ahead. A man who keeps flying beyond his time becomes an object of pity but nobody ever pitied Slonnie. Never!"

He closed his last logbook just short of the 25,000-hour mark. Men who set records or earned flying headlines for some super feat might well be among the best pilots in the world but they were seldom the high-hour men who had maintained top standards for decade after decade. Once heroes performed some notable flying job they had to spend too much time on the ground, promoting or defending their results. They might not have been headline seekers originally but few of them found time to log more than ten or twelve thousand hours. High-time pilots, those over 20,000 hours, had skipped the limelight by choice or chance and just plain flown for a lifetime. Slonnie was one of their breed, a pilot's pilot. He preferred it that way.

January 1955   Flying hours: 24,375

Chapter 16

Pilot's Pilot

"You can't take Number One away from any man."

Flying Slonnie's way was a totally demanding game, one so fascinating it was all the job he'd ever wanted. When a pilot of such single-mindedness retires himself from the cockpit, for pretty much the same reasons which had made him so good there, he's left with a private pride and many memories, but little else to hold his interest.

When Slonnie stopped flying it almost seemed as if the luck he'd flaunted back in 1919, by declaring for the first of many times, "No airplane is ever going to kill me," had been exhausted. There were certainly plans at first, from operations jobs to an application (accepted) for the post of U.S. Air Attaché in Kabul. But his luck remained out and Afghanistan missed a great deal of accumulated flying wisdom when the 1956 Suez crisis canceled all overseas appointments. Always an outstandingly healthy man, the retired pilot would soon be plagued by heart and lungs contesting the honor of doing him in. He refused to bow easily, so it took three heart attacks plus lung cancer thirteen more years to claim him. In most of that time, as Johnny recalled, "He did nothing. Just went crazy. Oh, he gardened, grew orchids, talked to people. But his age was against a new job. When that

Afghan thing folded he was beside himself. There were lots of sad times then, but lots of good ones too. It was never easy for Slonnie but he didn't complain once. Not too long after he retired, there was the party too. Ray Fisher had that idea."

Johnny said, "Fisher called right after Slonnie had been in to quit and said Cal Eastern was very proud of him and even if they weren't a big airline, they wanted to do something. Give a dinner and have people there from all of Slonnie's career. He wasn't saying anything until it was all worked out, so I didn't mention it either. A couple of weeks later, Slonnie had gone to bed early. Said he wasn't feeling too well but I think he was just kind of blue, really. Fisher called and pretty soon Slonnie came into the kitchen with his eyes sticking out a mile. He asked me, 'Do you know what Ray Fisher wanted? They want to give a party for me. Now, why do you suppose they would do a thing like that?' I told him I just couldn't imagine. He could ask as many as he wanted. Did I think they really meant that? We made a list and maybe there were people we should have put on it, but he was reluctant to give them so many names. Then they asked many more and people were just wonderful. Over a hundred came from all over and the rest wrote or wired."

There would be many other gatherings of flying friends, of course, although a few less each

time. Most were men who agreed easily with an *Associated Press* article written some two years after Slonnie retired: "When old time airmen like Charles Lindbergh or Gen. Jimmie Doolittle get together, one of their stories of aviation's colorful past is bound to mention a pilot named Slonnie. His name may not be familiar to a jet age public which thinks in terms of the speed of sound. But to the fliers who best remember the days when an airplane was little more than a bucket of bolts the name of E. L. Sloniger means pilot's pilot."

The men Slonnie had hired and trained as young copilots were senior captains with American Airlines by then. And always ready to ask him up front when he rode one of their airplanes. Flying by computer never seemed to erase the standards he'd lived by and passed on in hand-flown days. Slonnie said, "Red Allen asked me up for the takeoff from New York one trip and there were more lights on that Boeing 707 board than I'd ever seen. We took off for San Francisco, just chatting, but when I looked out we were heading right up the Hudson. I asked if San Francisco was north of New York now but Red told me, that dial over there says we go around by South Dakota to make the trip on time. He put us into SF right on the button too. Allen told the stewardess to ask Captain Sloniger if he would like to come up and watch the landing. What can you say? I'd seen a million of those, but I got into the jump seat again and he just slid that thing on. I told Red we were going to count that one a real good landing and he said, 'That's the way you taught me, Slonnie.'" An old pilot's eyes would fill then, without any shame. If Slonnie was proud of never scratching a passenger, he was prouder still of men who had started their own careers in the right seat beside him and still flew what he called properly because there was no other way. It was enough in his final years to know his kind of pilot understood.

He said, "I ran into Ray Fortner at some OX-5 dinner. He had moved up to one on the American Airlines list after I left and the two in between us retired. He'd always been number four which was just as high, really. Only that his company happened to start flying just a little bit later than I did for Robertson. Well, after dinner everybody was introduced and he was called out as: 'Fortner, Number One with American Airlines.' Old Ray stood up and said, 'Listen, I'm not really One and I never will be. This boy sitting across the table from me is and always was. You can't take Number One away from any man.'"

A great many of the tales woven around him, along the bars where pilots met, were far too lurid for Slonnie to admit or even remember. "They told a lot of funny stories about me that just never happened. I only laughed." But Fortner's tribute was one the retired pilot might even share with his family. Then he'd kind of duck his head, giving that shy, easy grin.

Slonnie died, age seventy-three, in 1969— and in bed as he had firmly intended to do throughout nearly four decades of an active, often adventurous, aviation career.

INDEX